TRENCHES 2 FREEDOM

TRENCHES 2 FREEDOM

A JOURNEY FILLED WITH REALIZATIONS

JUJHAR SINGH KHUN KHUN

A MAGIC MIND SQUAD PRODUCTION

Trenches 2 Freedom: A Journey Filled with Realizations

https://trenches2freedom.com

https://magicmindsquad.com

Copyright © 2021 by Magic Mind Squad Productions Inc.

All rights reserved.

Editor: Dr Simon J. Tilbury https://www.themightyword.co.uk

ISBN: 9–781777–351106

Original cover design: D. Neddi

Digital cover design: Allegra Printing Abbotsford, BC

Printed by

Printorium Bookworks

905 Fort Street

Victoria, BC V8V 3K3

info@printoriumbookworks.com

Trenches 2 Freedom

As fellow human beings we all walk this incredible journey of life, together; at times unaware of the footprints we leave behind. *Trenches 2 Freedom* is an invitation to elevate our thinking through positive inspiration. Using personal stories and self-realizations, author Jujhar Singh Khun Khun encourages everyday people to open their mind and to make a difference in the community around them.

The experience of losing loved ones weighing heavy on the heart, with each loss a new lesson and a deeper understanding emerges, showing us the frailty of life, its balance and its treasures. Guiding us through his journey from the 'trenches' all the way to freedom, Khun Khun offers a beautiful perspective on the Sikh way of life. Through the lens of values acquired through his experiences – some extreme and highly challenging – the author discusses society, politics, and culture in a humorous yet impactful way.

Jujhar Singh Khun Khun

Born and raised in a city once heralded as the gang capital of Canada – Abbotsford, British Columbia – Jujhar Singh Khun Khun survived multiple attempts on his life (including a suicide attempt following the tragic death of his fiancé) before his eventual arrest and incarceration. Once a household name connected with tensions of escalating violence in the lower mainland, Jujhar is currently serving an 18-year sentence in a federal institution in Canada.

His love of writing, reading and questioning the status quo started at a young age, but came to full realization after incarceration. He quickly devoured knowledge from historians, educators and philosophers, and found himself reconnecting with a religion he had been running from for a large part of his adult life – Sikhism. Reflecting on the choices he had made from a low level of awareness, Jujhar began writing *Trenches 2 Freedom* as a way to share his newly–acquired awareness.

Jujhar credits a higher power and energy present within Gurbani (the Sikh scriptures – literally "the speech of wisdom") as the reason he has managed to stay alive. At present, Jujhar is actively engaged with like-minded beings, with the intention of being part of a creative, inspiring collective bringing positive uplift to the community as a whole.

INTRODUCING...
A NEW SOLDIER OF THE HEART

Jujhar Singh Khun Khun is on a mission. In fact, he's on several, and his mercurial debut weaves them together to produce a compelling, uncategorizable read.

Written while serving an 18-year sentence in a Canadian prison, Jujhar explains how his early years growing up in a devout Sikh family became an adolescence marred by disillusionment, dislocation and trouble at school. His troubles made him vulnerable to the lure of petty criminality and gang culture. Though his family were loving they were ill-equipped to reverse his descent, and before long Jujhar found himself pursued by the police for violent offences.

A gang-related shooting put him in a coma. Waking to find himself incarcerated and at his lowest ebb, Jujhar began the long road toward emotional, physical and spiritual recovery. Prison had one valuable thing to offer – solitude. An intense period of study and self-discovery led to a string of insights, and to the rediscovery of his Sikh faith, alongside which Jujhar, in this book, places truths from many other traditions and thinkers, new and old.

The result is a work that is as personal as it is universal, in which empathy and compassionate action become the cornerstones of a new utopia, toward which everyone should strive and within which all will benefit.

Jujhar Singh puts every ounce of his energy into inspiring the reader – in his maverick, funny, 'speak-write' style – to turn away from self-interest and violence, to fight the good fight. No matter what the past held or what the old world made of us, we can all start out on the path. Wounded seekers we may be, but we seek, and we heal, together.

DR SIMON J. TILBURY

Trenches 2 Freedom is written with the hope that it is the beginning of many conversations.

This book is a Magic Mind Squad production. The first of many. And so, without further ado, let this journey begin.

12 May 2020 – happy Mother's Day, Mum.

Jujhar Singh.

A learner learning.

CONTENTS

Preface   xiii

Timeline   1
1. The story in short part 1   13
2. Do not conform, says Zolaal   20
3. Why are we here?   25
4. How simple it is   33
5. Identity   39
6. Realizing the importance of questions   45
7. Questions definitely worth asking   50
8. Where are you headed?   66
9. Mas Preguntas (more questions)   73
10. Responses to a curious person   83
11. What I gave up   88
12. Uncool and capital K Kool   96
13. The remedy   103
14. What do you want to be?   107
15. Walk your own path   117
16. Remembering what being brave means   126
17. The story in short part 2   136
18. Life in prison   152
19. Effects of female influences (EOFI)   160
    Bubu
20. EOFI   168
    Giggles
21. EOFI   177
    Sis — this too shall pass
22. EOFI   181
    Unexpected warmth from nurse
23. EOFI   186
    Bubu and Kylie 'the trend setter' Jenner
24. Sukhvir's Care   190
25. A lesson in judgment   196
26. Sharing/giving   203
27. Being   207
28. Realization of home   224
29. Sex   236
    (yup, we're going there)

30. Trust your heart: include   249

31. The story in short part 3   262

32. Unawareness   277
DIA (dumbass in action)

33. Now I realize   286

34. Maybe   299

35. Guess what?   320

36. And now we're like basically there   329
#letsmakeadifference

Words from the author   338

Acknowledgments   341

Unsaid words   350

O Boy (a poem)   355

PREFACE

IK-Onkar – One Universal Creator God.
Satnam – The Name Is Truth.
Kartapurakh – Creative Being Personified.
Nirbhao – No Fear.
Nirvair – No Enmity.
Akal Moorath – The Immortal.
Ajuni – Beyond Birth.
Saibhang – Self-Existent.
Gursparsaad – By Guru's Grace.
Jap – Chant.
Aadh Such, Jugadh Such – True in the beginning, True before
ages began.
Hai Bhi Such, Nanak hosi bhi such – True at present, says
Nanak, True God shall ever be.

—Guru Nanak
"Mool Mantar"

On 15 January 2013, I was shot multiple times from the back at point-blank range, shot two more times when I was on the ground, and then left for dead. Well, I played dead. Imagine playing dead through an intended final finishing shot you feel to the core of your bones. Oh yes, definitely not nice, but... primary concern was survival. I held my breath till the crunch, crunch of the shooters running away faded into the dark, cold, crisp night. Then, I located the keys to the SUV not far from where I'd been left for dead, ran to the SUV, hopped into the driver's seat, and, topping speeds of 180 km/h, pulled up to the ER entrance of Surrey Memorial Hospital, located in Surrey, British Columbia (BC).

I woke up 28 days later in a body that had been rearranged and a life dismantled. My life would keep on coming apart at the seams after this, and my inner world would be torn from its hinges.

18 bullets, to an 18-year sentence, to the loss of loved ones, to heartache and pain; but the suffering and torment held within them the seeds of a new way of being, seeds of realizations that would teach me how to let go, learn and grow in ways I would not have thought possible before my world came crashing down.

The Universe continues to reveal what needs to be seen.

In this book, I talk a lot about how things can be seen in terms of "energy" and "vibrations" – these ideas might seem strange to some at first, and I will do my best to explain what I mean as we go along. A lot of what I say draws upon "the law of attraction". This idea has been on this Earth for a long time, and is alluded to in many different cultures and languages, but in recent years, interest in it has exploded. Discovering the law of attraction was an important part of what led me toward positive change, and to the writing of this book. In very simple terms, this law states that what you give out is what you get back. I wish I'd taken the time to really understand what that meant earlier. I wish I'd taken the time to listen to what my father and mother were telling me from the get-go.

My underlying theme centers upon making a difference, not only individually but as a whole. The earliest drafts of this book had no chapters; in my "attention deficit disordered" head it all made sense, it all "flowed", as it did for certain friends as well. But, my lawyer sent me back to the drawing board, rejecting the manuscript for lack of organization and... coherence. I would need to divide the book into chapters, and this process began in December 2018 and January 2019, while locked down for 2 weeks, 24 hours-a-day, awaiting completion of an extensive search of the entire community compound of the Mountain Institution medium security prison. In late March 2019, I was emergency transferred to the Kent Institution (maximum security), where I would stay for 3 weeks while waiting for a hearing process to determine whether or not I would be deemed manageable in a medium security setting, still. The trip there was just a role in a bigger play the Universe orchestrated to put me exactly where I needed to be, when I needed to be there.

This happens a lot.

While I was there I was able to concentrate on the book and the organizing of chapters without interruptions. It was like a mini-vacation, and a perfect reset. A much needed one.

The warden supported my placement back into Mountain's medium security community and I was back in 3 weeks. Upon returning, I would learn that the only thing missing from my effects were the floppy discs that contained the book. All 3 discs were nowhere to be found. I did have a printed copy of the latest saved version of the book, so I took it as a sign and started typing from scratch. I had much to type up already as I had just spent the better part of three weeks hand-writing new content and planning the structure. I had to retype a little over 90,000 words, but – as everything happens for a reason – the discs going missing was the best thing that could have happened for the project. The law of attraction, in full effect, was on display before mine and my loved ones' eyes.

The inspiration to start writing and expressing thoughts came in waves. One of the biggest inspirations was after watching a video in August 2017, which was left behind by the late Gurmit S. Dhak, a video that was intended to make a difference in the lives of kids, and perhaps younger men and women. I wasn't young in age, but I was young in thought – perhaps that is where the age factor really matters – and that young mind of mine was certainly affected. His words made a real difference in my life.

They were a game changer.

Having someone I looked up to say the things he said, in the manner that he did, made me look deeper at myself, where I was, and where I needed to be. It left me feeling alienated on a path that no longer made sense.

It was never the intention, in this book, to share a chronological auto-biographical account with the world, nor for this to be a sort of self-help book. What I wanted to do was share thoughts and opinions on topics, realizations that have come to affect my journey for the better, and a few memories. And so that is what I have done. I share my perspective on things, happenings, and history that I have realized are meaningful to me. I was told not to worry about what others might say, and just to publish the book – I am so glad we didn't. Through a humbling referral, we – the Magic Mind Squad, that is – were put in touch with an editor from the United Kingdom – and what a pleasure it has been. The writing was not ready for publishing, and many revisions have taken place since October 2019. Never anticipated launching an informational webpage months in advance of a book launch, but it was part of the learning experience.

Who are the Magic Mind Squad? Well, we are a squad of friends who have come together to share a vision. A squad full of dreamers, believers who harbour a never-give-up attitude till we're called home by the Creator. The slogan for Magic Mind Squad Inc. is… *envisioning dreams, manifesting visions*.

Another intention behind the book is to bridge the gaps my dysfunctional behaviour opened up – those divides in the community I grew up in, caused by the immature behaviour my friends and I displayed. The biggest divide I created is in my family and those connected to it. It has put distance between me and my mum; we are not just separated by a fence with barbed wire and guards armed with assault rifles patrolling the perimeter – a wall has gone up between our hearts. A wall of misunderstanding, hardship and much lingering pain. It is my greatest wish that, one day – and I do believe this – those wounds will heal. For the both of us. In the meantime, I have a sentence left to serve, which each new sunrise brings closer to completion. And that in itself, is... humbling.

In April of 2018, while at Okanagan Correctional Center (OCC), a couple of weeks before being sentenced to 18 years, I laid eyes on my father and a family member for the first time in 5 years, through a dividing glass, and I couldn't bring myself to look at my father. Where it showed I had been recovering well physically, looking better and stronger than I have looked in years, my father showed the visible effects of the past 5 years written all around his eyes and over his hands. He is a hardworking man who strives to earn a living through utilizing the skills he has as a labourer and technician in multiple fields of trade. The wear and tear that comes with the gig was in front of me, in plain sight. I had to accept that I had played the most significant role in the wear and tear he showed, the experiences he had endured, and the extra years of aging visible around his eyes. On this visit I disclosed that I would be getting sentenced to 18 years, and I also disclosed that I was writing a book that would share my perspective on things that had come to mean something to me, along with shedding a little light on Sikh history, and that it was well underway. I had wanted to release the book as soon as possible, so I could shoulder the financial responsibility of the household and take away the physical hardship my father bears the burden and blessing of.

Words can barely express my gratitude for the support and confidence of my friends and loved ones. Loved ones, is a term I use throughout the book, and that is because I cannot afford to share anything more than that.

Why? Because—

This is the world I have created for myself. The air of mystery isn't done to create a mystery, but to be mindful of the fact that I have made certain choices in life, and those choices came (and continue to come) with a price.

In May of 2018, while at the Regional Reception and Assessment Center (RRAC) – a couple of weeks after sentencing – words spoken to me by a friend triggered me to take on a new angle. With his words, another bell had rung off in my head, fueling new motivation and a wave of inspiration for the book. This wave formed the beginning part of this book, because it meant that much to me to get certain words out. I even directed a portion of the writing towards a young man of Abbotsford BC, in hopes that he would read what I truly had to say about certain things, and that it would affect his path for the better. I was told he looked up to me, and that at certain times he had been compared to Geni (me). There was an urgency to get the book out and the words into his hands. I wanted the words to hit him in the heart, because that was where I was aiming. Deep down I knew that they would resonate, and really mean something to him.

But.

He never got to experience the jolt within the words that were directed towards him. He never got to read them. I did, however, get to see his face flashed across the screen. Man down. Shots fired. Too little and too late as the saying goes. My eyes filled with water.

It hurt.

That young man left behind a sister, parents... a family. And no one can ever give him back to them. Once a physical body has expired and is no longer able to house the light of life within, there is no woman/man or mortal-made formula that can breathe life back into it.

Perhaps a High Energy Being, with the consciousness level of an Avatar could've when the body was still salvageable, but – I do believe performing such acts dubbed as 'miracles' are forbidden by those who have come to possess the ability to potently connect with the energy such power flows from.

Baba Attal, son of Guru Hargobind Sahib, had revived a boy who had been presumed dead after being bitten by a snake. Those without the understanding of the higher laws dubbed the spectacle a miracle, while Guru Hargobind Sahib simply said to his son that, "Two swords cannot be sheathed in one scabbard". The various manifestations of nature are sometimes taken as miracles by the uninitiated. The path that Guru Hargobind was continuing as the 6th Nanak was not one that condoned the use of spiritual powers, the main reason being, that it would keep many from believing in the Unseen, Formless, One God.

May the parents and sister of that young man of Abbotsford BC find peace. May what they went through be the reason others in the hood snap out of it. May it be something that brings families together. May it be what mends misunderstandings, heals wounds and helps set aside petty differences.

In June 2018, while still at RRAC, I shared a piece of what I had written with a soul I met in passing, who not only helped reinforce my confidence to continue writing, but reignited an inspiration to follow through on a promise made in late 2007. Sukhvir – my fiancé – sustained injuries a little after midnight on the 8th of October, 2007 - major trauma to the head – in what was dubbed a freak accident by many. Despite the efforts of an emergency surgery, she passed on the same day. I realized that, if I wanted to succeed in bringing these words to the world, it couldn't be for me and my gain alone. I had taken a lot in my life, by force and default, and I realized then more than ever, that it was time to reverse that energy flow. It was decided then that 50 per cent of the profits be used to make a difference in the lives of our one family – humanity.

That intention is alive today.

Sukhvir wanted to help others. We (loved ones and friends) wanted to manifest that desire by creating Sukhvir's Care, in her name and to give form to a dream we have all put much thought and energy towards. We, the Magic Mind Squad, have much planning and attracting to do to manifest that vision. We have complete faith that it will materialize when it is meant to. Who knows? – maybe one of you reading these words here will play a key role in the creating of Sukhvir's Care. More about this project later.

The words in *Trenches 2 Freedom* describe aspects of my personal journey and share my perspective and opinions. From the dysfunctional thinking that creates gorges of distance between friendships and potential friendships, to the suffering experienced in the hood and within families; from the disconnect that prevents us from tapping into our true nature, to the instability that is putting at risk this Earth we spend our moments upon: the poison is all the same – ego.

TIMELINE

NOVEMBER-DECEMBER 2012 – DETAINED IN USA

— Detained for illegal entry into the USA, held at Immigration and Custom Enforcement Detention Center – Tacoma WA, USA.
— Waiting for hearing to be voluntarily released back into Canada (an option for Canadian Citizens).
— Two friends pass on (gunned down).

MID DECEMBER 2012 – TRANSPORTED TO PEACE ARCH BORDER CROSSING

— Received by CFSEU (Combined Forces Special Enforcement Unit) officers. Agenda: to make progress in homicide investigation.

15 JANUARY 2013 – SHOT IN THE BACK (SURREY BC, CANADA)

— Shot in the back multiple times at point-blank range, just after 12 a.m.. Shot twice more while on the ground. Played dead.

15 JANUARY-13 FEBRUARY 2013 – ROYAL COLUMBIA HOSPITAL ICU (BC, CANADA) – COMA

— 28-day coma.
— Body heavily infected. Stay in serious condition for long period.
— The vibrations from recited Gurbani, love of my parents, Bubu, prayers of many, and the surgeons, specialists and nurses stabilize the body.

13-17 FEBRUARY 2013 – ICU

— I wake up.
— Parents visit. Can't really talk or move arms.
— Find out Bubu and Dad have been in contact – gulp.
— Learn I have a colostomy (poo-bag) attached to my stomach.
— 14 February (Valentine's Day) – Bubu denied entry by lead investigator.
— 15 February – Bubu gains entry to room. I want to prove I'm alright. Tell them I'm ready to walk – umm… a good first start.
— Begin making plans to take a flight where I can focus on recovery.

17-22 FEBRUARY 2013 – MAJOR TRAUMA WARD

— 21 February, last time I see Mum. Haven't seen her since. Won't see Dad till April 2018.

22 FEBRUARY 2013 – CHARGES LAID

— Charged with first-degree murder and multiple counts of attempted murder.
— Hospital room turned into temporary jail cell. In the custody of North Fraser Pretrial Center (NFPC) but under CFSEU Emergency Response Team (ERT) care.

— Waiting for health to improve and skin graft surgery to provide temporary skin over open abdomen.

— Improperly discharged, without lead doctor's approval.

22 MARCH 2013 – TRANSFERRED TO NORTH FRASER PRETRIAL CENTER (NFPC)

— Female CFSEU officer and her partner come by before transportation. Show kindness.

— A Large CFSEU transport team. Support units called in from local detachment to secure area before reception at NFPC.

— Can't urinate on my own. Using catheters.

APRIL-DECEMBER 2013 – SURREY PRETRIAL SERVICES CENTER (SPSC)

— Close friend passes on 15 May.

— Cousin gunned down 23 June.

— Begin to unravel (internally) and self-destruct. Cut my hair a few days after cousin's passing, only to realize that I had cut it on my mum's birthday.

— August – denied venue change. Trial will be held in Kelowna BC, Canada. Courthouse to be modified to accommodate high security profile. Multi-million-dollar budget approved.

— Kelowna Sheriff's building will go through interior renovations and modifications to be turned into a remand center. Heavily armed sheriff convoys and CFSEU tactical teams work together on movement and transport strategy. They rely on local police units to help further secure area.

— The fighting with Bubu has begun. I am self-destructing fast.

2 DECEMBER 2013 – TRANSPORTED TO PEACE ARCH HOSPITAL (WHITE ROCK BC, CANADA)

— Hospitalized after spike in temperature (ripped a stitch after attempted pull-ups). Blood tests and X-rays. Allergic reaction to antibiotics.
— Acute attention required, medical team at Royal Columbia Hospital consulted, decision made for immediate transfer in ambulance.

3RD-MID DECEMBER 2013 – ROYAL COLUMBIA HOSPITAL

— Back in same room I saw Mum, previous February.

14 FEBRUARY 2014 –NFPC HEALTH-CARE UNIT

— Require extra medical attention.
— Start doing push-ups more. Begin testing legs with squats (not ready yet).
— Meet Giggles.
— Begin friendship with someone who becomes like a sis through this journey, someone I call Sis by choice.
— Begin urinating regularly for first time since February 2013.

APRIL-DECEMBER 2014 – SPSC

— Self-destructing continues, pulling relationships apart.
— Begin training. Concentrate on body-weight workouts. Fair Share Sco (a friend) begins pushing me in training.
— Giggles begins visiting more. Started playing Kirtan (over the phone) every now and then.
— Decide to regrow hair on 30 August 2014 – never cut it again.
— Diagnosis of possible Crohn's disease brings about a change of atti-

tude. Mindset for positive attitude and thirst for new knowledge
attainted.
— New learning begins: the "spiritual quest".

2015 – SPSC

— Time of learning. Introduction to meditation. Awareness of healing.
— Driven to read and keep reading. Realizations begin to surface.
— Bubu begins to pull away.

2016 – SPSC

— New wounds in spring – friend, who felt like a little cousin, gunned
down.
— Meet new friend, Reppid. This ushers in a wave of...
understanding.
— Period of letting go and deep acceptance. Understanding the detri-
mental effects of attachment and ignorance.
— Diagnosed with ADHD. Test trial of medications. Adderall a perfect
fit.
— Being able to focus (with the ADHD medication) opens the door to
an intensely committed period of self-learning – with a real thirst.
— Intense healing experience shared with friend (Reppid).
— Bubu leaves to start new life.

2017 – SPSC

— Sublime oneness state experienced during meditation on 1 January
2017. Experienced for almost 4 hours.
— Body healed.
— Reppid is acquitted & I am granted the go-ahead for reversal of
colostomy surgery on the same day. Waited four years. Intensely
happy.

— Happiness cut short. New wounds yet again. Two young lives become a statistic on the street.

— Time of intense meditation and a disciplined 4 a.m. Gurbani recitation practise.

MARCH-APRIL 2017 – ROYAL COLUMBIA HOSPITAL

— Pre-surgery: isolated for 2 weeks. Extra monitoring of phone-calls while security measures put in place. Much planning and coordination on part of SPSC administration, CFSEU ERT, hospital security and administration – down to vetting and strict screening of staff.

— Transferred to hospital on 28th. Surgery will happen on "30th b-date". Hear "Happy birthday!" a lot that day.

— Surgery a success.

3 APRIL 2017 – DISCHARGED BACK TO SPSC

— Before transfer, report not feeling well.

— Upon arriving at SPSC, say not feeling well again. Nurses stay close. Temperature spikes. Transferred back to hospital emergency wing for examination.

— Temperature continues to spike.

4 APRIL 2017 – ADMITTED TO HOSPITAL ER

— Infection between fascia and skin. On-call doctor performs emergency procedure.

— Infection has spread. Admitted indefinitely.

4-31 APRIL 2017 – ROYAL COLUMBIA HOSPITAL

— Trauma ward (third time same room).

— Infection not contained.

— Put under for draining procedure.

— Wake up in ICU. Same room I woke up in 13 February 2013. Opportunity for deep reflection. Realized the broken promises, the destruction, from a clearer vantage point. Begin writing.

— Antibiotics administered. Infection not slowing down.

— Blood work sent to Center for Disease Control (CDC), no antibiotics are working.

— Genius surgeon (Dr Konkin) stops antibiotics. Temperature spikes. And then, the body begins to level out. In rare cases, the surgeon explains, the body makes friends of uncommon bacteria (dangerous in most cases) because the body needs it (so much bacteria having been killed off by antibiotics).

31 APRIL- 15 MAY 2017 – SPSC

— Spend time in isolation. Continue to write. Continue to reflect.

— 1 May – Jordan (delay of trial) Application begins in Kelowna BC. Attendance via video link.

15 MAY 2017 – TRANSFERRED TO KELOWNA BC, CANADA

— Left SPSC with large Sheriff and CFSEU convoy transport. Received at private entrance of Abbotsford International Airport. Loaded onto a plane.

MAY 2017-MAY 2018 – THE TRIAL – KELOWNA AND OLIVER, BC, CANADA

— Delay application denied.

— Antsy Judge begins first-degree murder trial, before written decision is provided.

— While in court, housed at Kelowna Remand Center.

— Court days: Monday-Thursday. Days off: housed at Okanagan Correctional Center (OCC).

— 6 months isolation period at OCC before being integrated into the prison population.

— Graduate with an A score in Spanish 11 and Spanish 12.

— Meditation, recitation of Gurbani continues.

— Epiphany, after reading Eckhart Tolle's *The Power of Now*. Triggers new wave of writing.

— Friend Rokhi sends me Eckhart Tolle's *A New Earth*. Something happens inside me. Awareness is jolted.

— For the first time, Sukhmani Sahib (peace of mind) begins to make sense. Other insights follow.

1 MAY 2018 – GUILTY PLEA AND SENTENCING

— One year after trial begins, guilty plea is entered for conspiracy to commit murder.

— Sentenced to 18 years. 8 years credited. 10 years remain.

14 MAY 2018 – TRANSFERRED TO REGIONAL RECEPTION ASSESSMENT CENTER (RRAC), ABBOTSFORD BC.

— CFSEU team leads the way from OCC to airport near Oliver, BC.
— Returned to home city, with a chance given by God to make something of this life.
— Large CFSEU team leads the way for Sherriff's convoy to RRAC from Abbotsford International Airport, ushering in next phase of journey.
— Admitted for assessment.

MAY-JULY 2018 – RRAC

— Face-to-face visit with Giggles – through glass – first time in 4 years. She asks me 3 questions that send me back to the drawing board (and the desk) with pen in hand.
— Lovely (a friend) sparks inspiration to direct the writing towards the streets.
— Writing starts to become clearer. Sitting in Abbotsford BC, home city, in the heart of Farmville, where I grew up, has a lot to do with it.
— Employed in kitchen.
— 16 July – informed of final long-term placement – medium-security Mountain Institution.

22 JULY 2018 – EMERGENCY TRANSFERRED OUT OF RRAC

— Emergency transferred out of RRAC by ERT team – from cell-to-cell for segregation at Matsqui Institution, Abbotsford BC.

— Allegations of making remarks of a threatening nature and, thus, putting in jeopardy the safety and security of the institution. Allegations that my behaviour will destabilize the institution.

22 JULY-2 AUGUST 2018 – MATSQUI SEGREGATION

— Waiting for rebuttal process to commence. Write my own rebuttal.
— Enjoy time of isolation. Blessing in disguise. Quiet. Hot sunny days. Good for health, mind, and writing.
— Rebuttal accepted. Authorized to continue to Mountain Institution.

2 AUGUST 2018-21 MARCH 2019 – MOUNTAIN INSTITUTION

— Breathtaking, peaceful setting of Mountain Institution. Spend as much time as I can outdoors.
— Allowed access to computer. Get to typing.
— Meet Zolaal – aka Zelda – whose poem *Scent of Freedom* screams to be included somehow in the book I am writing, and that he is meant to be in my experience.

21 MARCH 2019 – EMERGENCY TRANSFERRED TO KENT INSTITUTION

— Emergency transferred to Kent Institution, next door to Mountain Institution.

21 MARCH 2019 – 12 APRIL 2019 – KENT INSTITUTION

— Awaiting rebuttal process/hearing.
— Quiet time to organize book.
— Rebuttal accepted.
— Returned to Mountain Institution.

12 APRIL 2019 – MOUNTAIN INSTITUTION

— Discs of book missing. Retype over 90,000 words from a paper
copy.
— Book ready for loved ones. Sent for reviews.
— *Think and Grow Rich* by Napoleon Hill lands in my hands. The idea
for not only the Master Mind, but the Magic Mind Squad forms.
— Searching for an editor. Through Skyler West, put in touch with
editor from the United Kingdom.

8 OCTOBER 2019 – WEBPAGE AND SOCIAL MEDIA PAGE LAUNCH

— Launch informational webpage, thinking book would be ready for 1
January 2020. It wasn't.
— Brainstorming marketing strategies with Magic Mind Squad.
— Assembling of Magic Mind Squad continues.
— Editor is on board.

JANUARY-MAY 2020 – EDITING AND REVISION

— Receive first batch of comments, critical feedback and suggested
amendments. Can't think straight. Panic mode. Level out after a week
and begin the editing.
— Editor cautions "imbalance" as he progresses – significant rewriting
anticipated. Real panic starts here. Didn't want to talk to anyone or
look at anyone – creative period. The book needs… detailed attention.
— Shared state of project with Angel. Angel helps apply edits to the
first 6 chapters (over the phone). I hum and haw, concerned that the
book release is being delayed. She puts it to me straight. Snap out of
it. What is the rush Jujhar? Get to it! Her words help me step to it.

JUNE-SEPTEMBER 2020 – FINAL EDITS AND REVISIONS – PREPARATIONS FOR PUBLICATION

— Editor takes new content through a developmental editing stage.
— Magic Mind Squad is official.
— Squad grows.
— Heart of Marketing Squad assembled.
— ARC copies hit the streets.
— Proofreading by editor and official arc reader begins.
— Book launch preparations commence.

CHAPTER 1

THE STORY IN SHORT PART 1

Who are we to correct or supersede God's laws?
The Creator is not subject to error.

Nahi hot kachhu dou bara
karnaihar na bhulanhara.

—Guru Granth Sahib
Gaudi Bawan-Akhri Mahala 5

Waheguru Ji Ka Khalsa, Waheguru Ji Fateh.[1] That's the way Sikhs greet each other, and it's my way of saying hello to you, here at the beginning of this book.

My name is Jujhar Singh.

My name was chosen by my mother (Bhuloh). It was her wish to name her son after one of the sons of Guru Gobind Singh Ji, the 10th Divine Guru and Master of the Sikh Faith.[2] The custom of choosing a name for a newborn is done at a Gurdwara, the Sikh place of worship.[3] A prayer and supplication is first made, in the presence of Guru Granth Sahib Ji, and then Guru Granth Sahib ji is opened and the first letter of the first recited word of the Hukumnama (the teaching) is taken as the first letter of the newborn's name.

It was a J.

My mother's prayers had been answered twofold. She was blessed with a son, and further blessed to name him Jujhar Singh – after Guru Gobind Singh Ji's second eldest son. She hoped her son would live up to the ideals of that name; that desired, manifested and chosen name.

She was young, blessed with natural beauty, married to a devoted, loving, caring and hard-working husband. She had dreams, ambitions, and hopes for not only a successful future, but a proud family story. She had the pen in her hand, and the opportunity to write it as she went. She loved painting and colouring white canvasses with bright colours. She enjoyed drawing flowers and birds, but more than that, she enjoyed writing out Gurbani in fancy script, and putting colourful borders around it. Gurbani means "the Guru's words" or "the speech of wisdom", found within Guru Granth Sahib. These teachings, which are written out or spoken (as they are transcribed) in the present moment, contain awakening jolts beyond imagination. As one progresses spiritually, the study of the teachings begins to reveal higher and higher awareness, moving one towards the Fountainhead (God). When Bhuloh was painting and drawing, she was expressing her spirit, singing it literally and figuratively.

She loved to sing.

Still does actually, and her voice is one that draws you in. To say that she has a talent for it... would be correct. Religion comes first for her, always has. She is a disciple of Guru Granth Sahib Ji, and an enlisted member of Guru Gobind Singh Ji's colourful Khalsa, the community of the initiated. For her, the merits and code followed by members of the Khalsa come before everything.

They even come before her son.

She is married to the Faith first, husband second and this life experience third. She had expectations that her son would carry the torch of religion and culture forward in a progressive and honorable fashion. She hoped her son would emulate the values and ethics that were attached to his namesake, Guru Gobind Singh Ji's son. She expected her son to project the power of the Khalsa Panth and the morals and principles upon which it is based. She believed her dreams were coming true; all she had to do was keep a steadfast faith. She knew deep down that, if she held steady, not only would everything work out, but all her prayers would be answered. She knew that all she had to do was keep her trust rooted in Waheguru Akal Purakh (Wonderful Immortal Lord) and keep the recitation of Gurbani on her tongue.

What she didn't know was...

... her son would grow up to not only go against everything she stood for, but he would help spur an uncontrollable dysfunction on the local streets of his hometown, which would claim the lives of his best friends along with other boys who had no time to recognize the consequences of their actions.

What she didn't know was...

... her son would not only end up in prison, but be targeted again and again by shooters.

What she didn't know was...

… not only would he let her down, but he would drag the family name through the mud and dirt, again and again.

I am that son. The one who let her down.

I was born in Abbotsford BC, Canada, on 28 March 1987. I am currently serving an 18-year sentence for a crime that rocked a normally peaceful town. I have not seen my mum in over 7 years, and I don't know exactly how long it will be till I get to see her again. I gave up so many things without a second thought (more about that in the chapter "What I gave up").

There were many things I most certainly did not live up to. I was brought up to be an honorable sikh. I was also expected to be a Sikh, an honorable Singh (a lion-like warrior of Khalsa).[4] I was expected to be the bearer of good news and to help strengthen family roots in the community. I was supposed to carry the family name forward and be like a stitch that keeps bonds of relationships and responsibilities together.

MY MOTHER and father both planted valuable seeds, early, in my head and heart. My father spent most of his days and nights at work, to make a comfortable life for his family. He says in the end you'll be judged for your ethics, so stay vigilant and do right. If you're willing to put in the hard work, you'll reap the benefits – if God wills it, of course. Only God knows when the season's right. My father is a patient man, whose daily discipline is governed by the teachings of Guru Granth Sahib Ji. He strives to organize his life around the Gurbani and usually has on his tongue verses to share when faced with a practical or philosophical question. The will in him doesn't know how to give up, and the heart in him keeps him compassionately grounded in love. He is the type to let you speak, hear you out and offer advice or insight in a short and simple way. He freely shares what he has, and will give what he thinks you need more than he does. He faithfully keeps himself rooted in Guru Nanak's earliest teachings, "as you sow so shall you reap". He firmly believes that what goes around comes around. He is not one to dwell on the past, understanding that every moment is a moment to start anew. Starting anew and doing things differently will bring about corresponding circumstances and situations for better living. In a sense, that sums up "the law of attraction" without the need to read books like *The Power of Intention*, or *The Secret*.

My father knows this life experience is temporary, could end whenever, and so you should be ready for departure. This requires you to be and to have been: humble, kind, sincere, of service, and an uplifting light to others. It requires you to be free of hate, grief, pettiness, and envy. It requires a character that has been tirelessly improved upon, and an inner being rich in deposits of virtue, free of attachments and vices. It requires you to have harvested NAAM simran (remembrance of God, verbal recitation or quiet contemplation) – it matters not in what tongue it has been recited in, or where it has taken place. It requires that your eyes reflect a glow which can only be brought to light through the NAAM (remembering and meditating on God and God's name) which, once your heart has been immersed in it, will radiate outwards from your being.

Cause and effect.

He has an easy-going nature and it takes quite a bit to pull him out of balance. I have been hit with bullets on two separate occasions. The second occasion, a friend called my father and while he was on the line trying to figure out a way to tell my father what had happened, he basically sensed it and said, don't worry about it he is going to be fine – then went back to working.

Grit.

He is the eldest son of his family, and has been working since he was a young boy – about 60 years straight, now. He isn't one to shy away from a challenge or take no for an answer. If a task has been put before him that requires multiple people, he sets himself to it and, one way or another, gets it done. He has the utmost respect for his parents, something I am still learning.

To my mother, the practise of Sikhi is absolute. There is no wavering there. Staying true to the path is her ultimate goal. When she finds herself in a place where it is difficult to look back and uneasy to go forward, she requests courage from Waheguru and immerses herself in Gurbani – often, she finds her way into the comfort of a gurdwara (Sikh place of worship), listens to recitation of Gurbani, kirtan (laudation), or loses herself in sewa (service). When I was avoiding home, I too would find my way into the perimeter of a gurdwara, seeking comfort and refuge; seeking solace and peace; seeking direction and instruction.

She told me about the likes of Udham Singh, a hero of the Indian independence movement, at a very young age.[5] These figures etched themselves deep within my conscience. She exposed me to stories of courage of the Sikh faith. I know that I was supposed to absorb the lessons she was trying to teach, but along the way, and quite early really, I became lost. I became not only the talk of the town, but a laughing stock for the embarrassing acts I was suspected of and, eventually, convicted. I had not been brought up to be a thief, but a thief I became.

My mother's father was regarded as a leader of the pind (village) she grew up in. An honest and hardworking man who dealt out discipline (old school way) when and where warranted. He passed on when she was very young. He was known for his heroism while defending his community. What was he protecting the village from? Thieves.

From dakuus.[6]

My mother, daughter of an honest hero who stood up to dakuus, gave birth to a son – a son she wanted the world to know as a Singh – who would become a dakuu. I can't imagine the pain this must have caused her; but when she saw what her son had become, she told him again and again: he would only learn when he was given a rude awakening one day, when he would be violently targeted, end up dead – or in jail.

---

1. Waheguru means "wonderful God" and the greeting translates: "Khalsa belongs to Waheguru, victory belongs to Waheguru". Established by Guru Gobind Singh in 1699, when he gave birth to Khalsa, the community of the baptised (spiritually realized) Sikhs.

2. There are 10 historical (breathing body) gurus who sat on the Divine Throne. Sikhs believe God to be the highest, True Guru. Guru Granth Sahib – the holy text – is the 11th and final Guru to hold the Divine seat of Sikh Gurship.

3. Gurdwara – literally, "the door to God". This door is open to everyone equally. Anyone is welcome to enter the Gurdwara.

4. When it has a small s, "sikh" designates a disciple of Guru Granth Sahib Ji; when it's capitalized, it designates one who has drank Amrit – the nectar – and participated in the ceremony of initiation into the community of Khalsa. The significance of small s and capital S, the need for projecting both principles they are based upon, will be shared in another book, *Soldiers & Saints... Battle Formations of the Meek & Militant*.

5. Udham Singh (Shaheed/Martyr) witnessed the Jallianwala Bhag massacre in 1919 (Amritar, India) committed on direction of General Reginald Dyer. He vowed revenge. After years of determined planning, he arrived at Dyer's home. But, Reginald Dyer had long passed on. Udham Singh shared the intimate details of 1919 and his vow with Dyer's wife. She sympathized with Udham Singh and revealed Dyer had suffered before his death, suggesting that perhaps he paid for his wrong doing. She also told him Michael O'Dwyer, lieutenant governor to Punjab at that time, had authority over Dyer, and if he wanted to hold someone responsible, it should be him. Udham Singh tracked the former governor to the British Parliament where he was giving a speech, and on 13 March 1941, he executed him. Udham Singh was charged for murder, and when the Indian Government suggested he plead insanity, he refused. He was hanged for murder by British authorities in July 1941.

6. "Dakuu" – thief – also means "one who lives outside the law".

CHAPTER 2

DO NOT CONFORM, SAYS ZOLAAL

Speak from the heart.
It's risky.
It's unrehearsed.
It's spontaneous.
But it's honest.

—Anonymous

S o. My gut – or feelings from within, rather – said write in a way that isn't... conventional? Just write Jujhar, writing rules don't apply to those that live outside the law. Not that the purpose is to go against the grain, but instead to write in a way that feels like... well, *me*. Not to make a point or express an "I will have my day of reckoning" attitude, but rather to say things in a way that is *free* of... boundaries. *Free* from a set of rules that feel... limiting. Rule-breaker hey? Well, didn't need you to write it out for us, maybe you say.

But again – not exactly.

Fine. Yes, I have broken *some* man-made or, wait, correct that – mortal-made – rules. Ok, *and* some God-made ones too – but – the Almighty sent her or his feelings of disapproval, alright. Yup. Heard it loud and clear. Do not break God-made rules. K. Got it. Respect mortal-made ones too. K. Um, working on it. But no, the type of rules I am talking about are the ones that leave you feeling restricted. The kind that take the fun out of what lays ahead. If there is no fun in envisioning what is to come, will the touch of one's own will find its way into it? If one's will isn't in it, then one's heart won't be in it. If one's heart isn't in it, then what is the point? If one doesn't feel good from within while doing, or *being* rather... then how will the colour of love, the joy of *being*, or the sounds of inspiration find their way into the endeavour?

Ha! That is a rhetorical question. They will not. Yup, fancy shmancy words I know of too, you know. Not the blandest cookie in the jar, loved ones will tell you that much. I love them. My loved ones, obviously.

I have been given valuable advice by loved ones. One of whom is, weirdly, a lawyer of mine, who represented me in the not-too-distant past. One does certainly become a loved one when you see tears of concern, care and empathy in the eyes of another. Advice like, you need to organize your writing into "a coherent manner" and "it needs chapters". You can't just go from thought to thought, it needs a sense of... direction.

Way to clip my wings while in flight. *Thanks* pal(s).

Well, this... task has taken over a year! The sorting through the book to create headings and chapters, etc.. Not only did it feel unnatural, but it was working from behind. Should have done it in the beginning then, genius, right? Perhaps. My way of saying things has certainly matured as well, and looking at this 300-page-plus book in your hands, it is easy to see that I have a lot to say too!

Zolaal (aka Zelda), a friend of mine who is a poet, writer and gifted musician. Yup ladies, what a catch, right? I won't say tall, phenomenal football player (the one where you kick the ball on the ground) and hits the bag with a force that makes you turn your head and say – what in the world is he on? He definitely has a lot to say and for a year he has been saying stop dragging your heels and doubting what you have written, the book needs maybe three chapters. A beginning, a middle, and an end. Funny one he is. He asked me what I was doing now, and why? How was I going to tell the world not to mold to someone else's idea of format when it comes to reaching for dreams, if I caved and conformed? DO NOT CONFORM Jujhar! You're going to lose that authenticity that makes it you! Who cares about the highly educated anyway?

Hmm. Interesting.

He has a lot of sense in him, that one. What I have written isn't so intellectually advanced that it needs to be written so formally and in an intellectual manner, which speaks to the highly edumacated members of this "society". A society which, by the way, is supposed to be one big community. How will younger ones and my loved ones understand the book, then, anyway? No. It is written for the heart first. The mind second. Where matters of the heart are concerned, the bridges are *simple*.

We are advancing (society) in a way that is just... wow. We have Alexa in the world. Oh yes, I know of Alexa – BBC's *The Click* to thank for that. We are moving at a pace that is fast. Our collective level of sophistication potential is mind-boggling. But, at the core of us is a simplicity that will always be *simple*. Easy to understand. Refreshing to experience. That is what the simplicity of what flows through our heart signifies. Love. Oh you bet that is what permeates from within the heart, it isn't pink for no reason. Love is simple, kind, caring, it is thoughtful. It is *inclusive*. Maybe you're thinking, what does *love* have to do with it? What do you mean, what does LOVE have to do with it?

Everything.

Those who love, will realize God.

—Guru Gobind Singh Ji

Love *is* the answer.

Before I delve any further, out of *love* for my loved ones, I've heeded their advice – a little anyway. I have heeded their advice and created some headings. I hope it suffices, providing clarity and not confusion, for I like to "speak-write". Or write as I would speak, because for me, this is a conversational sharing of perspective. A sharing of perspective and opinion, coloured with thoughts, feelings, experience, and maybe a little bit of Awareness. However it's written, the conversation is directed towards one audience – *you*. The intention is to have words meant for you, reach you. Maybe it is only a sentence in this writing you are meant to read or hear, but that sentence is to be found within these pages, nonetheless. I do hope it doesn't offend anyone, for it wasn't the intention; my motivation is only to connect with the world in a way that, perhaps, lays the building blocks of a potential foundation from which something may emerge.

I do hope it is *coherent*!

Thank you now to everyone that's been there or "here" over these recent years. Thank you to those that are standing with me today, that have stood with me throughout the different phases of this journey. The care, the guidance, the love. Thank you.

Thank you to those that were also there in the past, in the earlier years of this life journey. It all mattered, it matters still and, in a way, will matter always. *Thank you.*

There are more ok thank yoouuuuu's coming. *Obviously.*

CHAPTER 3

WHY ARE WE HERE?

Your purpose is not to judge.
Your purpose is not to figure out if someone deserves something.
Your purpose is to lift the fallen, to restore the broken and
to heal the hurting.

—Anonymous

This quote was sent to me by a friend (Eddie F.) who said he read it, felt it and wanted to pass it on. Well, I read it, felt it, and now want to pass it on too. Want to pass it on to the all of you. "Why?" you say? Because it is fitting. Look how warm it is. Just reading it made a difference in my experience, as I am sure it did for some of you too. The warmer ones, or warm ones. Not the cold ones. Perhaps we can warm you up a bit somewhere throughout the journey of these here words.

I must admit the writing here has a sort of light, maybe even humorous feel to it, so I'd like to think anyway, but – don't let that take away from the importance of it! It matters, what I say, it truly does! And for you that like to tread in heavy waters, stay glued to your seat for the ride does get heavy at times, maybe even sullen, but you want to know why? Because it will have connected to a heavy, sullen part of you. If you realize it, that is awareness! If you can break it down to why you feel what you feel, what triggered it, are able to observe it, sit with it and use it for growth – well that is awareness with depth! So, enjoy the humour. Enjoy the laughter. I suppose you'll laugh a few times. At least once – you have to!

You better.

No one will know you did, not unless you tell! Muahaha. Enjoy it for what it is, because that is the beauty of enjoying life. *Contrast.* Enjoying the moment it brings. So, enjoy the sad too if you encounter it, including the sad parts of this book. I doubt you'll find any anger. Oh, perhaps flying off the handle *would* have happened, but the lawyer had to go and ruin that fun. I pretty much removed it before I even sent him the initial draft. "I will be saving you from a conspiracy charge, Jujhar". Oh you will, will you? Couldn't save me from this one, though. Thanks! And you think *I* have a career as a comedian.

Oh yes. Why are we here? Well, you are here to read what this silly boy has to say – duh! The main thing I am saying is, let's *wake up*. Let's enjoy the beauty of life unfolding around us and unlock our highest potentials. Let's recognize the importance of self-evaluating early, unlock the power of love and let's make a difference – *together*.

Reppid, a friend of mine, says that society has taken on a new point of identification bro – apparently everyone is "woke" these days and they sing it to the world while they – the unaware – snore away. Fast asleep at the wheel of a bus, yet they don't even know what they are here to do! Well, it is good that mortal beings are saying they have awoken even if, say, the eyes haven't fully opened... yet. That brings us, humanity, super-close to being collectively united for the betterment of our family. The mere dialogue revolving around being "woke" or treading that journey invites in that destination's possibility. If the seeds are there, warmth near and that intention is watered with rightful action – it is only a matter of time before it blossoms.

Oh, and the cool thing about it?

Once a trend has begun, who wants to be left behind? Who wants to be left out? That conditioned thinking-slash-behaviour thing that leaves many wanting to be part of whatever is perceived as... fashion-able. The desire to be included and the need to be accepted, to belong, and to be regarded in a way that puts one in a common, favourable light.

For some, the waking up process is more of a challenge than for others, taking them to points of extreme suffering and hardship. It might take years and years of pain and torment before they stumble across the thing that snaps them out of it. Hood guys usually need a few rounds to hit the headrest (of their vehicle) or maybe even a few in the buttocks before they start to... wake up. Um, actually, some-times it takes a little more than that. My mum used to say, when you catch a few shots to the butt cheek you'll learn. Well, that didn't work for me. Even after a few point-blank rounds to one butt cheek. Long story, that one. Maybe someone thought it was my head. Best leave that one for the movie and any events that seem non-fictional, a pure chance type of thing. (Yes, there's probably a movie on the way in the near future.)

A friend (Dgib) called me butt face not too long ago. He laughed "haha" saying your butt got mistaken for your face! Rude. No? Boundaries! Some need to get tagged with a life experience that leaves them at odds with everyone and everything, including oneself, before this urge from within beckons exploration and, possibly – a new destination. Others will not suffer like those around them, they'll get the awakening jolt out of someone else's experience(s). We could just read too! Expand awareness.

The take-time-to-learn thing.

Deepak Chopra says that we are here to fulfill a specific purpose, or purposes. In *The Seven Spiritual Laws of Success*, Chapter 7, "The Law of Dharma or Purpose in Life", he says:

> Dharma is a Sanskrit word that means "purpose in life". The Law of Dharma says that we have taken manifestation in the physical form to fulfill a purpose.

> [...] there are three components to the Law of Dharma. The first is to discover our true Self, to find out on our own that our true Self is spiritual. The second is to express our unique talents.

> [...] you have a talent that is unique in its expression, so unique that there's no one else alive on this planet that has that talent, or that expression of that talent.

> [...] the third component of The Law of Dharma is service to humanity – to serve your fellow human beings and to ask yourself the questions, "How can I help? How can I help all those that I come into contact with?" When you combine the ability to express your unique talent with service to humanity, then you make full use of the Law of Dharma.

So, I'd say we are here to make a difference.

To make use of the moments bestowed upon us. To love. To realize it's a God given gift, the gift of Life, and we should use it for our own betterment, certainly, but more so – the betterment of others. When we move in a way that is for the betterment of the world, the whole, we help ourselves too, for that is the power of service. A power that has within it the quality of a colour, full of light. That light is life energy itself. That light *is* the sparkle of Source, which has within it infinite potential, just as Creator is in the creation and the creation in the Creator. Cool way to put it, right?

Maybe some of you say, Hah! Sure, like you know what you're talking about. Here to make a difference. But, trust me, it is not a lie. "It is known", just like the Dothraki in *Game of Thrones* tell Khaleesi. It is known, indeed. *Trust.* The foundation of friendship. And maybe by the end of our journey together, you and I will have a formed a friendship of sorts, regardless of where we may stand on views, beliefs, and...

...the field (wink).

Just try it, because trust can help us let go of resistances that serve no purpose. If you don't want to take my word for it, take it from Bubu, who is no longer a girlfriend, but a treasured and trusted friend. Been years now, since – the girlfriend thing. But, years ago (maybe like 7) I said some things to her regarding spirituality and she neighed like a horse having its reins yanked. Bah! Aughhh! 'Spirituality'... yuck. Party, woohoo! Um. Well, my sense of spirituality, then, was... a bit lacking and flawed, and I see now I was trying to control her – more than a little. That is the truth. Result of insecurities. Oh... the ignorant days. No going back.

Fast forward.

Now she sees auras, relies on meditation, and finds solace in the quietness that has revealed to her the ability to direct healing energy. Where was this girl when I wanted to lock her away from the world and have her sit in a room with me, my partner-sufferer in this epic jail journey?! She was actually by my bedside, praying and sending me floods of energy filled with vibes of hope, faith and trust – while I lay in a coma for 28 days looking like a lab project. Tubes this way. Tubes that way. What a fool not to see things for what they were. Learning curves indeed. She sent a message a while back, saying, "See, *I told you* to try on spirituality, this life is *amazing!*" Cuteness in personality she definitely has, and that is why she is referred to as Bubu.

Trust.

It is a key ingredient of love, and absolutely necessary in a healthy relationship. So, if I am suggesting – or more so, *saying* – that we are here, and more specifically that *you* are here, to make a difference... I mean just that. Just trust it.

And.

We can all do a little something, in our own way, on our own terms – and in the very environment we spend our moments in – which contributes towards the betterment of ourselves, and those around us. We do not have to go to any other place, if we don't want to.

How convenient is that?

One aspect influences the other – the betterment of oneself and the betterment of others, that is – and they are connected to each other in ways that cannot be separated and we cannot ignore. Don't ignore it, I tell you; fools pay a heavy price for ignorance! The time to act, *it be now*. The fate of Humanity (capital H), the future of the innocent lights of the world (children), depend upon it.

Betterment of oneself doesn't have to come in the form of drastic changes to, say, one's attitude, behaviour, or actions. Change can be simple, subtle and can happen in small ways; these changes will accumulate as one grows. And then again, change can be as drastic as it needs to be.

That part is up to you.

The betterment of others doesn't mean one needs to go out of one's way, sacrificing time and limited resources, or that one should take up the fight for a cause. Instead, it too can happen in small and simple ways that accumulate a quality of energy that makes the Power generated – unstoppable. Yup yup, capital P.

Herein lie the secrets of the Universe and infinite potential. All it takes to harness their power is to align with the very principles that reflect the nature of that easy-breezy flow. The nature of that easy-breezy flow is one of harmonic balance, an equal exchange of give and take, which is essentially a quality of sharing and receiving that has in it the ingredients of love, of a fire, which is the binding energy of the universe. A power which can transcend any physical or non-physical barrier.

Teilhard de Chardin says:

> Love is the most universal, the most tremendous, and the most mysterious of the cosmic forces... the physical structure of the Universe is love.

Making a difference in this world in a way that puts out an uplifting, gentle, and high vibrating energy is simple. It can be done through action and non-action. There is an internal component in play for both aspects, but sometimes before some of us can make a difference in the life of another, we might need to make a difference in our own experience first, and taste the flavor that harmony brings.

We can only give away what we have.

That means, some of us need to heal, which means we may need to balance ourselves, and that process is triggered with a specific key – *awareness*. Each aspect – healing and balance – is intertwined and is intricately connected.

There is nothing to separate.

Nor is there a need to. Enough with this separation thing, anyway, this relentless push for division. Division in religious factions, schools, neighborhoods and within communities in general. Enough already. Things are more connected to one another, speaking both scientifically and philosophically, then we may have ever realized.

Like, seriously connected.

Why are we here? To make a difference (I hope that resonates). Where should we go, for now? Let's keep rolling along this journey, shall we?

Let's.

CHAPTER 4

HOW SIMPLE IT IS

Love and do what you will.

—Saint Augustine

At a young age, deep down, I knew what I wanted in life. I had a lot of alone time to reflect on my life situation and circumstances. I was always trying to figure out answers to questions that never fully revealed themselves because, what do you really know when you're so young? Very little, if anything at all.

But you learn slowly, of course.

I knew that I wanted to help. I wanted to help my family, and I wanted to help anyone and everyone that needed it. There was this time, grade 3 I think (age 8-ish), when I hid underneath a staircase during recess, wanting to be alone and away from everyone. I was the only brown kid in the class, and my mum decided that instead of putting a regular patka on my head, she would put this bulky, orange, wool-knit thing that I wanted *nothing* to do with. As if that wasn't enough, I stunk. My clothes had this weird smell to them. A Punjabi food smell would have been inviting, but no – that is *not* what they smelled like. I didn't even have to turn heads for being brown skinned or for what I was wearing, I was turning noses and it was as if those around me thought I couldn't catch their vibes or pick up on the energy they were giving off towards me. Unaware, or didn't care, it didn't matter – it felt the same. It hurt. Nor did I need to be told I was emitting an odour that made you step back, I knew I smelled. I hated being there. I got bit by mosquitos while I was tucked away from the world.

Thanks God. Solid. One for the books!

I did not eat lunch that day. It wasn't a "normal" lunch anyway. It only served to remind me how much of an outsider I was in this environment. To make my life easier, I would've had to burden my mum with my worries, but she was in and out of a somewhat fragile state, back then. I loved my mum, and so if I had to bear my troubles alone to keep her from extra burdens, then that was the way it was going to be.

Oh… how ungrateful we become at times. No concept of appreciation for the so called "little things" I've come to realize aren't little at all. The things we tend to label "little" or "small" turn out to be the things of greatest importance. That turned out to be true, again and again, for me anyway. Oh... what I would do for that lunch Mum used to make, right about now – how ungrateful I was, indeed.

I promised I would never make fun of others and that I would help people, especially those that felt like outcasts. I made huge slips along the way. One of my most regrettable moments, before spring 2017, was at school – Maharaja Dalip Singh Education Center, situated in Abbotsford, B.C. – home town, baby. I mimicked a girl in one of my Punjabi classes; she stuttered when she spoke, at times, probably brought on by the nervousness of having to read Gurbani out loud during Gurbani classes. I would make stupid noises to throw her off when it would be her turn to read, and even mimicked the way she recited the verses – it takes practise to get the pronunciations right. Takes even more concentration to say it in an uninterrupted flow with the added pauses and emphases. Yup – talk about a foolish kid trying *way* too hard to be the main focus in class.

Oh. And that kid?

He was an A-scoring student *and* close enough to the main class clown. Smacks from a stick at school and a broomstick at home will get you to both spots. In a sense, the negative energy I put out in class was returning to me pretty quickly. I regretted it, even then, and have thought about it a lot since; I was the jerk in her early experience during a critical phase of growth, who was a source of displeasure – unpleasant, rude, and disrespectful.

But.

Nothing is left to chance in this Universe of ours. Everything has its place in the world. Things happen when they are meant to happen. And only when they are meant to.

No accidents.

The same girl came to draw blood for a blood test I needed, while I was in the hospital in spring 2017, after a serious stomach surgery (reversal of colostomy). I was at a low-level vibrational alignment, the body ill and drained, fighting an infection which wasn't slowing down. It still hadn't hit its peak. To see her, after all those years, first left me in shock, then awe. There I was, crudely making fun of her all those moments ago, and here she was, gently drawing blood from me.

I felt lighter. I felt better.

I realized she brought with her an energy field of love. She brought with her a field of higher vibrations, which didn't subside, even after recognizing me. Her energy pattern didn't change or decline, despite the way I made her feel all those years ago. If anything, there was an added layer of tenderness, I sensed. This warmth that radiated. I can still feel it.

That is Love. *That* is Empathy. *That* is Caring. That is sharing warmth. *It is that simple.* Making a difference on the front lines. It really is.

I wanted to thank her, but knew it would create pandemonium – it would be taken as a security breach, coming into contact with someone I knew, and with a full-on emergency response team sitting outside the room (more of an elite rearrange-your-life-permanently-if-you-mess-around team) along with one in the room ready to act on any... weirdness – it was an easy 'not right now' decision. Time and place, right? Yup. This be that time.

So.

Thank you. So much. Thank you for helping me realize how simple it is.

It didn't seem to matter to her what I had done all those years ago, it didn't seem to matter how I had treated her in the past. In that moment, before her was someone who was suffering, someone who was sick, who was in need, and she responded with a quality of kindness that has in it the power to, indeed, *heal the hurting and lift the broken.* She was on the frontlines that day, and on that field she encountered someone who had once triggered a negative and unpleasant experience for her. She could have very well responded with a look of disdain, or anger, and yes I would have deserved it and certainly picked up on it. I would have sensed it in the way she held my arm, or in her expression, or the meaning her eyes would have conveyed.

But, no.

Something else came to the forefront. The inner child responding to the childlike needs of the being in front her. Hunched over in that chair, not able to straighten up, weighing 125 lbs, barely able to stand, I certainly felt as vulnerable as a child.

Vulnerability reflects a degree of innocence, and even if only temporarily, the innocence in her connected with the innocence of my vulnerability, and in that moment she answered her call to duty. Unconditionally. Her natural response was harmonic and in service for betterment. *This* is the energy we need on the front lines everywhere.

Every human being is on the front lines in some way. A question we need to answer, if only for ourselves, is: what is our individual contribution? We have much to do and the ones who can make a monumental impact are the ones reading these words. *You* are the boots on the ground, at ground zero, and each and every one of us, one of you, has a delicate and important responsibility to engage in a way that *is* for good, and that *is* for betterment. It is even more important that you yourself experience growth, which will bring out your inner humility, within the field of kindness, the unstoppable Power of Love, and the harmonized effect of balance and healing, which allows *being-ness* to just unfold naturally as you go.

The inner child understands these aspects, best.

So, this writing, all of it, is directed towards the child within us. It lives. So relax a little – if you're uptight that is. Take a few deep breaths, let your brain be oxygenated. Loosen up your neck and relax your shoulders, let any tension, if there is any, leave your body. Give this writing a chance to connect. It took a lot of maneuvering around (on part of the Universe) to finally get this book into your hands.

A lot.

The inner child – it never left. All we did was acquire adult-like traits with this desire to be adult-like. I read that somewhere, I forget where. Neat way to put it though, no? A child is naturally open to learning, and naturally relies on built-in guidance systems that strive for feel-good experiences. A child naturally experiences a quality of harmony, keeping close the medicine of laughter, and radiates happiness from within to those around them. Their natural instinct is to feel concerned for those around them. Try being hurt, or sad around a child, and see how the child reacts. Even if only momentarily, the child forgets its own strife and tunes into the other. Oh, and should you smile wholeheartedly during the exchange... well, you've seen the effects, haven't you? The child will summon the light of the sun and shine it upon you through their eyes, their smile, their face, and through the conversation conveyed. Apparently, in baby world anyway, the baby knows you understand what is being said.

Why should the child think otherwise, anyway?

Oh. That is right. It doesn't know *how* to think yet. It only knows how to *be*. Imagine that. And here we are *thinking* we know how to go about understanding this treasure trove of our experience.

They have much to teach us, the gods of our world. We have much to teach them, too. Learners learning, with *much to learn*, still. So, let's learn humility again. Learn kindness. Learn to relax a little more. Relearn (if we have forgotten) that the inner child is always there. Learn empathy. Learn respect, and let's regain the capacity to enjoy innocent humour like a child's spirit does, so the power and might of Love will flow through our experiences, our joys, and our laughter, with the glow and healing joyfulness of a child's light.

CHAPTER 5

IDENTITY

There is nothing noble about being superior to some other person. True nobility lies in being superior to your former self.

—Anonymous

W hen you are young, perception is easily influenced. It is easy to lose sight of what matters. It is easy to lose sight of what matters at any age, but there is a tender vulnerability when one is young and going through the earlier phases of development. The ones who drop on the street, who become a statistic, don't just drop because they fall victim to the 'lure' or 'push and pull' of money or lifestyle – because some come from wealthy families. Right? Yup. So, for many, it just comes down to the need to belong.

The factor it comes down to, for most, is *identity*.

When I was younger, I chased beliefs, needs and wants in the search – simply – for an identity. I chased an illusion only to look back and realize that I had given up, and missed, so much; I was so confused, despite being the embodiment of an idea, a pillar of strength for certain loved ones. Certain loved ones who turned to me for mental and emotional support, loved ones who turned to me when they couldn't sort through the things they were going through. I thought I knew it all – and they echoed back that illusion.

Happy, who passed on after catching one fluke round to the chest in a hasty drive-by, 3 months after I was charged for first-degree murder, is someone I really let down in his time of need.[1] He wasn't the brightest at typical school stuff, but he understood numbers. He knew how to hustle a dollar out of a penny. He occasionally – outright – lied to you, saying he was busy while he was really watching Hindi films on his bed, having a cheat day with his number 1 – his pup, Brick, a pure-bred, blue-nosed pit bull; easy-going, friendly, transforms into a dangerous beast if provoked... just like Happy. His pup was number 1. His girlfriend number 2 – maybe 3 or 4, depending on how he felt that day and how he felt towards certain.... bros. Sometimes he just didn't answer his phone because he was sleeping. Brick was in the car the day Happy caught that fluke round. The pup went haywire moments before, sensing the danger.

So... Happy wasn't always honest; hustler's nature and all – which was non-malicious, but. But. He would have given you, any one of you reading these words, the shirt off his back if you needed it. I never thought that he would ever not be here, walking around in this world. Or driving around somewhere. I never thought that I wouldn't go to his wedding, never thought that I wouldn't get the chance to be one of his best men. Never thought he wouldn't be around to *get* married, for that matter. Never thought I wouldn't get to take his children to the beach, to the park, or to the edge of the world just to teach them how to meditate. Never thought that he would never have children to whom I would become – by force if necessary – a favourite uncle.

I certainly never thought I would be sitting in jail on a first-degree murder charge, getting transported around the city in a convoy with occasional air support, along with little-to-no stopping at red lights. Never thought that one day I would be sitting at a jail desk, writing words filtered with opinions and feelings to share with the world.

Never thought that, after 3 months in custody and 1 month before Happy passed away, another loved one would pass on from the physical. A loved one who was more of a dear brother, really, and who moved on without a word, one evening. The result of medical distress his body experienced, triggered by a laced pill he consumed. Most certainly never thought I would never get to hear his contagious laugh again, ever. His name was Amar.[2]

But.

How can you control fire? We cannot control the invisible energies that are in play, at every moment. When you play with fire, when you toy around with it, trying to manipulate it with bare hands, ill-experienced, you will eventually get burned, and some are bound to lose more than just the use of their hands. And if we can't control fire, can we predict the future?

Maybe our journey is mapped out already. Maybe there are multiple possible outcomes. Maybe it isn't mapped out at all, and we are writing it as we go. No matter what, though, I believe one's journey can be affected at each pivotal moment of one's experience.

The difference? The one thing that makes the difference? The quality of consciousness. The quality of one's state of awareness. Conscious or unconscious participation.

Then.

No matter what the belief is, each individual journey comes primed with opportunities that could mean freedom from cycles of habits, of behaviours, that do not need to go on and on. Moments in experience that jolt awake awareness. Yup, awareness is a living thing. It is the substance from which all other substances are created. From that very field of intangibleness. From trial, error – learn, know that things can be fixed, things can come together, and we can grow...

...*evolve.*

Those wake-up moments don't always have to come in loud ways. One can often learn from others' experiences. From others' falls and stumbles. From others' bumps and bruises. Because that loud way might just be a loud BANG that is hard to recover from. That loud way could be an unwelcoming brush with a brute force that turns one's world upside down, with precious few moments left to correct anything.

Nothing is guaranteed.

Nothing, and we need to wake up to the mistake of not thinking things through, or we will make that mistake time and time again in ways that will leave one's life altered in a manner that... shreds the hearts right out of families. In ways that take the colourful light right out of a household. The fallback onto the whole "second chances" thing, the "not written on my palms" saying that many apply once time has run out, and the clock of the physical body has expired – that doesn't lead anywhere, and it's time we saw that. Finding a way to see through to the actuality of things, with a clearer and healthier perspective, is an individual process that needs to take place sooner rather than later.

If someone had told me that Sukhvir, my wife-to-be in October 2007, would pass on in the manner that she did, I would've dismissed it and maybe said something like – and I'm the one that's crazy?

If someone had told me that 7 months, 2 weeks and 2 days after her passing, a young homie would be jumped outside his home, that his mother would have to see him in that state of distress, and that he would succumb later that day because of injuries sustained to his neck, I'd have said – sure, *right*.

If someone had told me that Amar would suffer in the manner that he did, and that he would move on from this physical world without a word to anyone, I wouldn't have been able to imagine it.

If someone had told me that Happy would be hurt, and no one would take the initiative to rush him to the hospital, which was less than a 2 minute drive away, and that he would just... be left there, I wouldn't have been able to accept it, let alone anticipate coming to terms with it while locked in a cell.

If someone had told me that another young friend, who felt more like a younger cousin, would catch a fluke round through his garage door, let off blindly, and that his body wouldn't recover from the injuries sustained... it would've been difficult to imagine.

But.

That's what happens.

That is what happened.

Things happen that we cannot always control, but the one thing we can assume responsibility for, and gain some conscious control over – is ourselves.

Our actions.

Our behaviours.

We can make, and you can make – the choice to slow down and start self-reflecting, earlier. We can develop healthy habits, and not rush into things in ways that leave us cordoned off from life's simple, yet irreplaceable treasures. You can ask yourself certain questions earlier, and that my friends – may just be the answer.

---

1. Happy – loved one. Baby boy of the family. Bodybuilder. Hustler. Fighter. Kind. Compassionate. Empathetic. A light. A blessing. A symbol of courage. Unbreakable will. Punjabi and Hindi-speaking hunk.
2. Amar – loved one. Brother. Soulmate. Spontaneous. Spirit-enriching sound felt in his laughter. Seriously jacked. Heart of gold. Quietly intelligent. Less words more action. Loved saying the word SCCHHTEHKK. One word that describes him – DangerouslySex-c.

CHAPTER 6

REALIZING THE IMPORTANCE
OF QUESTIONS

Questions are the lasers of human consciousness.
Use their power to cut through any obstacle or challenge.

—Anthony Robbins

Q uestions are important. They are critical to honing in on specifics when pursuing internal growth. I don't know exactly when it was that I realized this, in a light-bulb-over-my-head moment, but in that sudden realization, it all made sense. I thought to myself, Jujhar, if you want answers, you have to ask the questions – then answer them truthfully. I came to see that questions are necessary when one is self-reflecting for the purpose of... growing and learning about ourselves. It is also a simple approach to what could seem daunting; that trek of inner-exploration. I read somewhere that in order to find the right answers, one must ask the right questions again and again, in the knowledge that these will change and continue to evolve as we, too, experience change.

Everything changes.

Nothing stays the same. Nothing that we perceive – hear, see, or touch – is a permanent physical. Down to the very hands that are holding this book. Just energy vibrating, constantly in an exchange pattern. Looks real right? Define "real".

Everything is always in motion, and this journey of becoming self-aware is in motion too. As our internal journey continues, the body experiences cycles of shedding and regenerating, too. On and on it goes as the expiry date gets closer. This physical body, that we're expressing ourselves through, certainly has an expiry date. A body that has its own purpose, own cycle, operating on a life energy, having its own cycle of expression to complete, that is really just a temporary vessel. Guru Nanak called it a piece of cloth and that is good enough for me.

What designed it? Um. Source? God? Infinite Intelligence? I guess it really matters not what we call it, does it? It doesn't require a label. Labels are limiting. Limited, in any sense, is measureable – a concept. The Infinite, the Unexplainable, is not limited. It is not measurable. It is unlimited. Unmeasurable. But, not unreachable.

We inherit belief systems, develop conditioned thinking patterns, and some of us have so much rigidness that we are unwilling to open ourselves up to new knowledge and new understandings, keeping many of us stuck in... limited thinking patterns.

For example: this cycle of birth and death.

If someone passes on when they are younger, they are unlucky to leave so early. If they pass on when they are older, but have been wanting to go for a while, they are unlucky to have endured the pain and suffering they were subjected to while they lived. Or if someone catches one bullet and dies, and if someone catches a little more and survives – it is summed up to luck.

I don't think luck has anything to do with it.

Choices:

> Souls who have become involved in these tragedies are not caught in the wrong place at the wrong time with a capricious God looking the other way. Every soul has a motive for the events in which it chooses to participate.
>
> —Michael Newton
>
> *Journey of Souls*

We all attract circumstances and situations into our life experience, and we are responsible for the energy we put out. That energy comes from our thoughts, our words, our actions, our deeds and misdeeds. We are responsible for what we bring into our experience, whether by this current cycle of expression or previous – it is all connected. By that same token, there is an Organizing Intelligence that is operating in synchronization with a tune that is responsible for what happens when a moment of cataclysmic energy exchange occurs. An exchange of energy with a result, which has in it the factoring of its own calculations, and its own Knowing.

That isn't luck.

That is a perfect accounting system. Deepak Chopra writes about it in *The Seven Spiritual Laws of Success,* in the third chapter, "The Law of Karma or Cause and Effect". The return of the boomerang.

Call it the boomerang effect.

Omraam Mikhaël Aïvanhov's oral teachings, converted into written words in a book entitled *True Alchemy or The Quest for Perfection,* put it like this:

> If it is ordained that you must die, where can you go to escape? People have been known to travel great distances in order to find a safe refuge, and just as they reached their destination death caught up with them in a totally unexpected way. Instead of being afraid we should tell ourselves that we are in God's hands and that whatever happens to us is His concern. If He finds that we are useful to Him here, He will save us, otherwise we shall have to go. It is pointless to think we can preserve our own life, it does not belong to us, it belongs to God.

Guru Arjun Dev Ji, 5th Guru of The Sikh Faith, said this:

> *The One preserves and destroys.*
> *Nothing at all is in the hands of mere mortals.*

Well, there you have it. Don't take it from me. Take it from the rarest of rarest beings to walk this blue-and-green planet we call Earth. Many have said it, continue to say it, in their own chosen words and from their level of Awareness and Higher States of Consciousness.

Do take what I write lightly, too. Pursue your own growth. Ask questions. Explore answers. What I write here is an opinion, an expression of thought in words as a best illustration of what is felt or understood within; understanding that comes from collected thoughts, opinions, reading, conversations, bits and pieces of knowledge heard, absorbed, learned, felt, and yes – experienced.

It took a lot to rid the programming that started early for me, but that 'it took a lot' was because of all the ways I tried to cling to what I thought I knew, what I believed I knew. In letting go, openings emerged that led to breakthroughs, and those that have shared their experience with "me, myself, and I" know that if I have an opportunity to go for things – I probably will. Once I saw that bright baby-blue sky and a land filled with multi-language-speaking women, you bet I went for it. Once I made it through, seduced I was. Seduced to stay put for a while, but then eventually I became accustomed to just... breathing deeply. Became accustomed to enjoying the splendor of the moment; of laughter. Laughing with the laughter, at times – uncontrollably. A laughter close friends and loved ones call a high-pitched giggle – it is not. And if it does resemble that in any way, well then, shrapnel nicking a vocal cord along with a small exit wound out the front of the neck *may* have something to do with it. Wait. Do we have one vocal cord? Or are there multiple vocal cords?

Hmm. Interesting.

If you think I might have a teen-like laugh at times, I definitely do not.

It is more childlike.

I stayed put long enough so that eventually I became accustomed to just enjoying conversations, letters, emptiness, fullness... quietness... so that, eventually, I forgot to look back. When I looked around, I saw only what surrounded me, this beautiful vastness of... everything. There was nothing to crawl back through, no other side. Just here and now and the experience of the power of presence, and the joy of being. How I perceive the feeling of abundance is mine to choose. How you choose to view it or not view it, if you have or do experience it – it be your bizz. Duh. That is the way I choose to say it, for now anyway. Oh, and trust me, once you see that opening – you're going for it too.

For now, where shall we go?

Oh yes, to some questions then.

CHAPTER 7

QUESTIONS DEFINITELY WORTH ASKING

Hardened children always suffer.

—Trinidadian saying
(courtesy of Dgib)

A re you doing it for the money?

What are you willing to do for it? Hustle? Set people up? Rip people off? A jack-boy doesn't make it long. Eventually get run up on. Guys in masks, them things pulled out, creeping up like a Rainbow 6 team, that can't be good for you.

What are you not willing to do for money?

Will you pre-set a moral compass? Have you set yourself one to keep you from straying?

Who are you willing to hurt in the process?

Parents? Family? Loved ones? Customers? Random people? Better yet, who are you not willing to hurt? Are there those that you will never cross? Or, is there someone you won't double cross? These questions are *muy importante* whether or not you care to explore them. Just reading them will create a ripple effect in your subconscious. They'll sit there in the mind somewhere and, then, at random times – bubble to the surface.

Who are you doing it for?

Who is, say, the paper chase for? "Family"? "Friends"? Yourself?

I thought I needed to chase paper for my family. The irony in it was that my parents wanted no part of any money that wasn't honestly earned. I was able to make up a story, at times, and slip a little bit to my Dad, but it seemed like, every time I did, something would break down or get lost, that cost the same amount. No room for that energy in a house where Guru Granth Sahib Ji was present. My mumma never accepted a dollar. Nor a gift. Now I understand why. I may have started doing certain things to accumulate funds for, say, my family as a whole, but it turned into a blind chase and nothing more. The justifications don't matter. Reflection revealed it for what it was – unconscious participation.

Unawareness.

Are you doing it for the name?

What type of name do you want? What type of reputation do you want? Or—

How do you want to be remembered?

Cold... warm... volatile... angry... greedy... even keeled... grimy... light-hearted... compassionate? Well-rounded? Virtuous? Trustworthy? No backbone? Strong principles? Black-and-white? Does it matter?

These things matter, and to gauge yourself early you must develop the ability to see, perceive and correct early shortcomings and weaknesses.

There are lessons in weaknesses and shortcomings. When we learn from them, we are not held hostage to them, and once we move beyond restraints that hold us back, from this emerges strength. One who exudes strength and strong character will certainly have an impact in the environment he or she ventures into. The quality of energy exchanged will leave impressions, even if they are faint, subtle, and sometimes unrealized.

What are you willing to do to get the "name"? Why is it important to you?

Go at the next man? Trash-talk the next man? So many go after the next man without any real insight as to why. What is the purpose? Are you doing it for stature in your own circle? Do they even want to recognize you as so important? Where are you living this idea of importance? Is it in your thoughts? There will always be the next man, you know. Always someone badder or more ruthless, more cunning and maybe even smarter.

Tread softly.

Shadows might follow your footprints around forever. Until they catch up with you at last. *Boo.* So – why not? – just give respect where it is due and avoid bringing into your experience – mayhem.

Are you willing to give up the dearest things to you?

What is dear to you? Your loved ones? Your friends and family? Are you willing to give up the ability to spend moments with them? Give up the ability to be around your loved ones, give up the ability to enjoy moments that do not repeat themselves?

Are you doing it to stand out in your school?

Are you doing it to be a hero? Are you trying to be cool? Is it for recognition from an older circle? Are you looking for someone's approval? If you are, why does it matter, the approval?

Are you doing it to gain the attention of a certain girl?

This one is usually what sets it off, right? Illusions on illusions.

Do you pillow talk?

Capital L, Lame.

Who are you?

Who or what are you trying to be? A 'G'? A fixer? Someone who unites people and has the charisma to bring everyone together? Or are you someone that divides those around you? Are you looking to be recognized as the most important out of the bunch, or do you point out the importance of everyone around you? Everyone has a uniqueness, a uniqueness that has its expression in the form of strengths and weaknesses. Weaknesses don't render someone useless, they open the door to opportunity for learning and, possibly – teamwork.

Who do you idolize?

Take a deep look into this, because the one you idolize will have an influence on your personality, your character, and provide you with glimpses into your awareness level.

Who do you look up to?

Many kids follow idiots and manipulators, taking on the same low-level awareness, getting pushed-and-pulled into a world some will not make it out of. Some ask where I went wrong. Ask, instead, where are you going right? And if you can't say you're right about those you look up to, it's time to put right that mistake. Are the ones you look up to making the mistake of putting money before everything, eyeing up each other's girlfriends or wives-to-be? Do your mentors turn on one another in the blink of an eye, with no understanding or appreciation of what a genuine friend is? The people you look up to matter a lot.

Choose them carefully.

How do you show respect?

Respect is a key ingredient for a lasting friendship. If there is no genuine respect between you and those you have relations with, the relationship won't last. One way or another, it will come to an end.

Is it your parents? Is it family?

Instead of putting them first, my mistake was to put them second. Instead of thinking about their well-being, I thought about satisfying distorted ideas of perceived wants and needs. Instead of protecting them and making sure nothing got in the way of their security, I jeopardized their sense of security by putting them second.

I didn't understand what I was risking.

Like, who doesn't want to be able to take his mum to the park? Who doesn't want to take their mum shopping? Who doesn't want to take their mum cruising through hills and valleys she's never seen? Who doesn't want to take his or her mum to an important appointment? Who doesn't want to take his mum to do something that means a lot to her? Who doesn't want to be able to drop Mumma off at a friend's or family member's home, and then come back to pick her up?

God knows I do.

But, I can't.

That's pretty Lame.

Whether or not I want to, that's secondary now. Whether she'll want to see me, at all – primary.

That's what misplacing the value of family got me.

What do you respect? Is it culture?

Is it a respectful, progressive culture? Are the traditions worth getting involved with? Are they traditions based upon love and inclusion?

Misplacing the value of family made it easier to let go of the value I put on culture. Khalsa culture. I valued Khalsa culture a lot growing up. An encounter with a member of a travelling group that I looked up to, that held devotional services in gurdwaras, played a role in my trading the culture I grew up with for the new one I was trying to fit into. I travelled with them for a while, until I was cornered in a room and subjected to a sexual advance. But it wasn't only that which led to me trimming my beard.[1]

I was trying to be someone else.

I covered myself by saying the trimming of my beard was a security precaution, but that was a lie. I wanted the women who didn't gravitate towards me to be attracted to me. But, regardless of what I said to others, the story of Ganga Singh was ringing in my head like a never-ending nightmare. Would you like to read about it, the story of Ganga Singh? Those of you that don't know the story, that is? Well, here it is anyway:

A Singh newly-immigrated to the United Kingdom meets a beautiful woman his age. Both have an instant attraction to one another. They spend many moments together, getting to know one another. He is mesmerized by her accent and she is constantly eyeing up his colour coordination and how it flows with his clothes. One day she notices that his belt matches his Turban and another day she notices that his Turban matches his tie. He notices that this girl's accent isn't the only thing that has him feeling stuck to her, but the insights she shares. He not only feels like her voice has cast a spell on him, but the attention she pays to her physique casts a similar spell. She can't get over his confidence in rocking that style and she likes it that he doesn't seem to mind her endless questions about his culture, such as why does he wear his beard so long, and never cuts it? When he tells her the story of the two young boys aged 7 and 9 who exchanged their lives for the values they believed in, and how they chose to be bricked in alive for standing up to a Mughal ruler for their principles, she is in tears.[2] One of those principles was to practise a way of life that preaches freedom of expression and religion. It breaks her heart she says, the thought of Guru Gobind Singh Ji's youngest boys being murdered. He tells her, for the Sikhi Kaum, it doesn't break their heart, but instead – it builds it.

It keeps the heart whole.

She is even more mesmerized after learning of the deep-rooted beliefs behind the identity of Khalsa he projects. Those boys made sure that, if someone ever needed to look for a Khalsa member, she or he could be spotted from half-a-mile away.

They fall in love. Head over heels.

They want to get married. They want to spend the rest of their lives together raising Khalsa/British babies. They would both need permission from their families. They talk at length about what their lives might look like and imagine what it would feel like to live out that vision. They fantasize about having children who can speak 3 languages. Punjabi. English. And Punglish. It happens. The cross-breed of languages.

When they meet the next day, however, the woman has a solemn look on her face. She is sad and looks like she has been crying all day, maybe all night. Her family has said no. His family has agreed and told him his wishes are his wishes and that if they both love one another, then that is enough for them to support the marriage. He is taken aback that her family won't allow it. She tells him how she became hysterical when her family denied her wishes, and that they had finally, in fact, agreed, but with conditions.

He would have to cut his beard and his hair.

He tells her he can't do it. She tells him that if the conditions cannot be met then she is to stay away from him. She tells him that this is probably the last time they will hang out together. It isn't right, they agree, or just. The conditions imposed upon the marriage were messed up and, in a way, they both knew that everything would end abruptly. They are both saddened and heartbroken. She tells him that they could meet one last time tomorrow, because she does want to see him again and, perhaps, for the sake of their love, he will reconsider what her family has proposed. He says he will meet tomorrow, but his position won't have changed. She says she knows, and with a deep, sadness-filled sigh, she hugs him and they part.

The next day, she arrives first at their usual spot. The spot itself has a very romantic feel to it. It overlooks a clear lake where ducks roam freely and birds swoop in and out of view, humming away. The sun reflects off the water, making the lake shimmer and shine, like diamonds are dancing off the surface. She is deep in thought when she senses him walking towards her. She turns in his direction intuitively, but doesn't see him. There are a few people walking on the path leading towards the spot where she is standing, but she can't make him out in the crowd. She ignores the feeling in her stomach that something isn't right, and keeps staring in the direction she thought she had felt something. She checks her watch and, with a sinking feeling, tries to push away the thought that she has been stood up. A figure breaks away from the crowd and starts in her direction. As the figure nears she can see he is male. She stares at the approaching figure, takes in his clothes, then his shoes, and then finally realizes who is approaching her.

He has no beard. He has no Turban on his head.

As he gets within arm's reach of her, he extends his arm. She pulls back. Who are you? She asks of him. What do you mean, who am I? As he steps forward to close the distance. She takes two steps back this time and asks again, who are you? It is me, Ganga Singh, do you not recognize me? Perhaps she actually can't make him out, he thinks, since he looks so different now. No, I do not recognize you, she says, what have you done? He starts to get frustrated, what do you mean what have I done? I have done what you asked of me. What is that, exactly, she asks? I have cut my beard and my hair. Why have you done that? So we can get married. So we can be together. His voice starts to lose confidence. You cut your beard and took off your turban for me, Ganga Singh? Yes, he tells her. I did it for you. I did it for us. We are in love with each other. He is near tears.

Yesterday I loved a man who said he couldn't trade his values and beliefs for marriage. I believed him, I didn't think he would. I decided to meet you here, today, to tell you that my family accepted the marriage. I was going to propose to you today, here look, I even brought a ring. A family member advised me to make sure I was making the right choice. I could think of no other way but to see if you would give up your identity to be with me, and that's why I told you my family had set those conditions. You told me that two young boys had given their lives to keep the Khalsa family alive, knowing that what it represents is something eternal. Yesterday I said to you, I love you Ganga Singh. Today I say, *you bloody fool Ganga Singh!*

He runs from that spot and keeps running. Crying too. In fact, they would marry eventually. 5 years down the road, though. It took him a while to find himself and grow back not only his beard and hair, but the dignity he knew he had traded.

THE FACT THAT SUKHVIR SAID, never change, went unremembered. Even got a tattoo of a Singh putting his sword down after a battle paying homage to a memory piece dedicated to Sukhvir. In my head it made sense like this: the days of being a Singh are over (made sense at the time). In reality, my days of being a fool had begun. Yes, I was an idiot – probably still am. But I am learning, and that's what matters.

The fact that Bubu was attracted to the style flex, went over my head too. I tried to preach to her one day about something and I will always remember the silence before her reaction. She first looked at my head, my face, and then my eyes. And you know about self-respect? was her response. At that, I became irate and angrily told her I cut my beard and hair because I didn't want to be recognized.

Duh.

Oh, yes. Cut my hair too. Two days after Happy passed away. New guy. New mission. New goals. All I could think about was... destruction.

But.

I do value culture. I have been growing my hair since August 2014, and the last time I cut my beard was in November of 2017. Never again will I forget what it represents, why it mattered to me as a kid, and why it matters to me today.

How were you raised?

I was raised by religious parents. Parents that strive to practise the Sikhi way of life. Gurbani is never far from their lips, nor the principles of a faith that has made itself a gentle home amongst humanity. I was raised to respect tradition, culture and religion. I did, until I started to lose faith in some of the beliefs I had inherited. Some of it lost meaning to me over time, but not everything. And for that I thank my parents and the way I was blessed to have been raised.

Were you raised to be part of a faith? What was it like? Do you still follow that faith, or have you moved away from it? Did you grow up in a secular home? What was that like? Did it offer you freedom to find your own way?

One of my most embarrassing moments took place on Happy's birthday, while out on Granville Street in Vancouver. We went to a club to celebrate his name day (*Game of Thrones* = dope). I was standing at the bar when a girl nudged my arm and said my name, questionly, and followed with "It *is* you". I asked her if she wanted a drink. She stared at me blanky and asked, "You drink?". Yes, sometimes, I said. She responded with an "ew" look, lost interest and strolled off. I got thrown out of the club that night for being disorderly, ended the night in a drunk tank, and then got scolded by my lawyer who couldn't believe he had to come get me out of such Lameness.

I have thought about that girl and her reaction many times, realizing that I couldn't have been further away from an aspect of myself I once understood. It wasn't for me, the drinking. Not only that, I wore the traditional long hair under a Turban or patka with a beard look, where raising a glass of liquor... just doesn't suit the outfit.[3] I was raised without a drinking culture, and raised to know better than to do it while wearing the image of Khalsa.

What are you worth?

Are you buyable? Do you have a price? Can you be swindled for dollars? Do you have what it takes to stick to certain principles or honour a code? What strengths signify your worth?

Are you observing?

Are you watching what goes on around you? Closely? Are you observing what is unfolding around you, or are you lost in the sandstorm of activity? Do you see the ones who shape-shift? Are you aware of the ones who tilt with the wind?

Fair-weather friends.

Much to learn from them. Are you aware of those around you who are only motivated by money? Are you aware of the ones who want to exert influence and gain control over everyone? Or how about the ones who want to exert control and influence over you?

How do you move?

Straightforward? Do you have good business ethics? Do you step strategically? Cleverly? Intelligently?

This matters, you know. You will leave footprints determined by how you move, and it is not easy to erase those prints. Some you cannot erase because they are not left in sand. They are etched into the happenings of this world, and have come to shape reality for you and those around you, and this has a ripple effect. I wish I had taken my time with certain steps; many steps I wish I could redirect because it would create a different story – but that isn't an option. Many steps led to much heartache – much heartbreak for those who weren't even related to me – and caused damage that can never really repair or restore itself. So, take your time. How you move will reflect your inner nature, and your inner nature will be but a reflection of your awareness level.

Unconscious acts resulting from low awareness cannot bring any good to this world. All they will do is leave behind pointers to look back to when you start to evaluate your journey. Evaluate those steps earlier. You will avoid much chaos and unnecessary heartache. It will save a lot of pain and tears – maybe even cuts, holes and final farewells.

Would the hood be better off without you?

A humbling question. Ponder it. If the hood would be better off without you, then what are you doing in the hood in the first place? If all that you're doing is destroying the hood, what benefit does the hood get for keeping you around? If you do not add anything of value to the hood... then you will not last.

You will not make it far.

You will not survive the rebound. The boomerang. If you do not affect the hood for the better... then what is the point? The return boomerang isn't forgiving, it comes looking to decapitate – it comes to finish. So, ask, would the hood be better off without you? If the answer is yes, what can you do to change that?

Are you a slow learner?

Learn from other idiots' mistakes and be mindful, otherwise you'll pay a heavy price for your ignorance and missteps. You don't want to die a dog's death, do you? Hands in your pockets, left face down on the ground, holes in the back of your head, or throat slit from behind. Yikes. Ouch. Getting hit up from the neck up, that can't be good for you.

The energy you emit will come back to you in one form or another. Was what I said above crudely put? Maybe. It may seem like a fun upward trek, the climb to a richer life, until the body is being dragged by its hands and feet to be left to rot. It isn't even yours anymore, you no longer belong to the body once the soul is knocked out of it. The body at that point is just a shell that once had life inside it. You might even get to watch it unfold, depending on what realm your soul ventures onto.

Draw a moral line.

Innocents are innocents. Don't make the mistake so many have made, because the rebound comes back to chew through your experience, and those closest to you. And, deep down, you know who the innocent are. Two wrongs don't make a right.

Snap out of it.

Does fear dictate what you do?

A while back, I read in a book (the title of which I cannot recall) that a Buddhist teacher was asked by a student, if an intruder came in here with a gun to harm everyone, and you had one – what would you do? The teacher said he would shoot him in the leg and then nurse his wound. Or the dialogue went something like that. One's approach can change. One's approach can evolve. I guess what I am saying is that, maybe, the lesson in the story should be taken, absorbed and, then, applied. Not every situation on the street should have to result in... life-ending harm. I think the lesson in the story is that the Buddhist teacher did not operate out of fear, yet an awareness of not only the necessity to preserve life, but the compassion needed to rebuild bonds with those who have come to harm or have done harm. Compassionate concern for both attacker and potential victims. And compassion is what will help move us towards one another, where we may be able to relate to each other from a place of higher understanding. Not just compassion, but empathy, both of which have healing capabilities.

Because...

Anyone can pull a trigger; so what? Do you know how easy it is? It takes a little pull, a few pounds of pressure – a baby can do it. I don't think it is G, to just go and pull a trigger. Perhaps some situations may call for it, but don't let the reasons be ill thought out, misinterpreted or fear-based cowardice ones. The world is in dire need of soldiers and warriors whom practice compassion and kindness.

So, are you acting out of fear?

Fear can make one do lots of things, and masking one's fear with a cause doesn't eliminate the fear factor – it creates more. The urge to be something is, many times, a misplaced fear of not existing. The fear of not being known unless one makes a point to stand out. Many use personal fears, then tie it in with others' fears all in furtherance of a goal which is the product of fear. Fear and weakness. Most individuals are usually unaware of their roles in others' fear-motivated and self-serving agendas. Fears and manipulation cloaked in an illusion of some form. In the construction of "the image". lol. No capitals for that. Lame that one.

Cleverness divides.

Always looking for angles. Always looking for an advantage. Cleverness separates, and those that are unable to see the dividers or divides for who or what they are, the unawareness will come with a price. It will cost you. It will cost those around you. Cleverness brings out the devious nature of the ego, brings about deceit and opens the door for discord. Instead of threading together possibilities, it tears apart opportunities and plucks at the roots of friendship. It puts distances between friends and brings into question the links necessary for longevity.

So, are you moving cleverly?

Intelligence includes.

It unites. It has an energy pattern of its own, carrying within it a quality that has the power to weave together differences and mend them into a bond. What those operating from the level of cleverness haven't realized is that there is no surer way to secure long lasting power than to do it as a whole. Individual outputs of energy can only go so far. Intelligence removes the element of struggle. A force-based struggle where vying for control of a lower operating energy field – this stands revealed for what it is: pointless. Intelligence is inclusive. It is strength. And if one can operate from there, well then you shall see what the wind blows your way and you'll see that what does comes your way, will come around to stay. So.

Does what you do have the touches of intelligence to it?

Don't just speed-read through the questions if you know they apply to you; ask them to yourself. Some answers may be lingering on the tip of your tongue, others will require some quiet contemplation. Constructive thinking. If you quiet your world down, the answers will emerge. Once you start to tap into that place of silence, the world starts to reveal itself. It may be easier to overlook some of the questions and not pay any mind to them, for now anyway. One day, though, the questions will be relevant. The questions relevant, and the answers simple. So simple, and the realization of how ill thought out and confused your original approach was – a humbling contemplation. An approach for many, which goes past the point of recovery, because it is impossible to summon back a released arrow. It doesn't have to get there. Are you conscious enough to become aware of where you are headed? This is a question worth reflecting on. Question worth reflecting on indeed.

---

1. There is more coming on this a little later in the book. It's a big deal for a Khalsa Sikh to trim his beard.
2. I return to this moment in history in the upcoming chapter, "Remembering what being brave means".
3. Uncut Hair (Kes) – one of the 5 Ks and part of the mandatory uniform of Khalsa.

CHAPTER 8

WHERE ARE YOU HEADED?

Between stimulus and response there is a space.
In that space exists our freedom to choose.
In that choice lies our ability to become the person we were meant to be.

—Di Know

W here are your choices leading you?

What price are you willing to pay? Only a few succeed at getting rich, staying under the radar and away from drama. Most find themselves in the thick of some BS that just follows them around like a cloud. Maybe a few get away with a bag full of riches, jewels, laid back on a beach on a tropical island with a lot of Spanish girls around. OK, that was my definition of "making it". Money. Jewels. Tropical beach. Key word: *was* the definition.

What is yours?

Some are going to catch lead and not survive, but you already know that. Right. Some are aware, that's cool. At least you have come to terms with it, and have accepted this as your destiny. OK. That isn't the only outcome though, right? Nope. Lead or dead isn't the only one. Left bleeding from a few holes or suffocating from punctured lungs. Nope. Some go to jail. Others realize... I cannot do this.

Do you have what it takes to do the time?

When you look in the mirror, you know who is staring back at you. Meaning, if anyone knows how you feel internally about certain things, it is you. The guys that are playing roles, driven by fear, are motivated more by wanting to belong, driven more by the urge to be recognized, are pushed more by the fear of not being perceived as a 100 per cent, than by the internal state which reflects who they are. Some things are ingrained in you – principles. Principles are principles, and one sticks to them, not for others, but for what they are in themselves.

The guy that turns into an informant or becomes a cooperating witness knows he will turn long before the pressure system designed to actually "break" them. One is already aware of what the breaking point is. Why are you going to let it get to that point? Why are you going to live a lie and then cave when it gets rough? Why are you going to turn on someone in exchange for something and lie in the process if need be? What are you going to get out of it?

A Canucks jersey? Lame.

A million dollars? Weak. A new life outfitted with a new identity? Will you be able to sleep peacefully with the new last name? Will it eliminate the fear of having to be cautious – forever? That is what acting will lead to.

So... are you acting?

If you're acting and you know it, it is not shameful and degrading to admit to yourself, and maybe even those you trust, that you are not meant for something, or that you are not a certain way. Living a lie isn't going to have good results. You are playing with fire. You are going to get burned. Caught in the middle. Sandwiched between two flames, when you could just step away from it all before it is too late. How will one ever expect peace of mind if one is living a lie? How do you even go about finding the balance necessary to experience harmony, which is interrelated with that peace?

An individual willing to give up testimony in exchange for money, for a lighter sentence, for "freedom" – what freedom? Freedom from what exactly? Testimony in exchange for "coming clean" under the guise of doing "the right thing", starting anew, or "having found God" when beneath the surface something else is going on. The fight to stay alive.

The desperate fight to survive.

The fight to come out of a situation as unscathed as possible, knowing full well the truth deep down of what one has found or not found. That lie has its own rebound. It may not even come directly into your own experience, but the experience of your loved ones, leaving you torn mentally and emotionally. That is just the way it goes.

Ripple effects.

You already know deep down what you are cut out, or not cut out for, and if you are able to do the time. If you're not cut out to do the time, then admit it to yourself, and tweak your life-path a little. Save everyone the torment and the headache. Why bring about the possibility of physical chaos and mental agony? The stresses, the pain, and the suffering? Why bring about the kind of negative energy that influences your mental and emotional state in such a way that it starts to deteriorate your physical body?

What type of life do you envision for you and your family?

Can you see what your life looks like 5 years down the road? 10? 15? What does it look like in your thoughts? Is it comforting? Have you imagined what it would feel like to be constantly looking over your shoulder? Paranoid at the slightest movement? Erratically paranoid, sketching out at the slightest thing that seems out of place? Constantly worried that someone may have recognized you, or whether or not you truly recognized the face that left you worried? Have you thought long and hard about what that would really feel like? Constantly worried that maybe your children aren't safe, even after moving away? Constantly draining yourself mentally, emotionally to the point where the physical organism that is the body, is physically ill, "sick" again and again?

Think about it.

It can't be good for your health in any respect, nor for the ones who are connected to your experience, the ones that mean something to you. Put their care and concern before your small wants and needs.

Sooner or later cuffs find their way onto wrists, and those that lack the quality of mental strength – crack. They burn. Many turning to substances that erode them from within, all because the "reality" of their situation was or is… bleak. Is hard. So…

Are you substance dependant?

Many who are idolized on the streets are substance dependant. Their security, feeling of well-being, is at the whim of a substance, some at the whim of – basically – poison. The coping mechanism of their life situation comes down to a continued reliance on the support it provides. They hold it together externally by using that substance to ease the "pain" and "suffering" internally. Is that G? Is that hood?

Many of those that are substance dependant today, started early. It isn't so bad in the early years. It is easier to curb the vice, too. Nothing good can from it. How can it? One isn't even in a right state of mind, one is continually in an affected state of mind, and that state of mind has a huge impact on one's emotional well-being.

So.

If you're young and reading this, and you are already leaning toward vices – be mindful. Be careful. Be aware. Don't be the one that doesn't have an appreciation of what paths certain choices lay for you. Or – at least – some idea of the sorts of paths. Paths of self-destruction. Choices that bring about self-defeating habits and behaviours; don't be the one that doesn't have an appreciation of it. Become aware. Self-destruction, in the form of addiction, doesn't happen overnight. It happens with repetition. Repetition that starts with one initial decision.

But.

That one decision doesn't have to set in stone all the choices that come after it, not if you tweak your inner co-ordinates a little bit. Not if one becomes aware of the negatives and adjusts accordingly. If that first choice was a stupid one, it doesn't have to have any absolute control over what comes after it. Only a fool continues to do that which is self-destructive (like I did). Become a conscious participant, make mindful choices. Don't be the one who gets dragged around by their choices and thrown into the bottom of a pit, again and again.

It comes down to awareness and making an awareness-based choice. Moderation is a big word, yet it is overlooked. Don't. Don't be afraid to ask for help if you need it, seek out the ones who would have your best interests at heart, seek out someone you feel comfortable talking to. Don't become a statistic; you're better than that. The life-energy inside of you is worth more than that. You have a grand purpose to fulfill in this world and you were given this opportunity to add something of color to this dance of life – so don't waste it.

Are you an ethical addict?

A certain type of addict, street guy/girl, a certain breed of addict will adhere to a code of conduct that would rather see them suffer mental agony, emotional torture, and physical distress than trade certain ethics, values and morals when stuck in certain situations. Most don't live by that standard; no such code exists for them. Theirs (unethical) is only survival mode. What do I need to do to get out of this and who do I need to do it to? That is the question that gets answered, and very quickly, usually. That is what happens when one is lost in the cycles of addiction. Don't let it get to that point.

Do you know someone who is trying to do better?

There are many who do wake up and snap out of it, moving in a way that is not only better for them, but better for everyone around them too. They do so humbly, not selfishly, and they aren't looking to intrude on the well-being of others. For the liars who act like they are turning over a new leaf, that hide behind veils of dishonesty – for them – morals, values and principles just become a constrained battle of wants, of needs, and compromising them becomes relatively easy. When one is already in an unhealthy state of mind, one is fighting an internal mental battle, and a tug of war ensues of "what to do, what to do" which is emotionally and mentally draining. It is what brings about physical illnesses in short order. Because that is the effect of having toxic substances in the body. Substances which erode not only the physical, but leak poison into the non-physical.

We need new approaches, friends; and we need to reach out to those that may be potentially on the brink of complete destruction, faced with dilemmas that they may not make it out of in one piece. Be supportive of those trying to do better, don't eat away at them with your words and actions. Just help them out. Some words filtered with awareness, a little support, a little love may be all someone around you might need to see things from a different perspective. It may just be enough to make a difference, in a life-changing way.

Am I trying to change you? *Nada homez.*

I am not trying to "change you". I can't change you and nor is it my life purpose to change you. I am only expressing. Only you can change you. Only you can come to realize whether you need to change, if change is even required, and what it is that you need to change. You can take what I say for what it is. Literally or figuratively. It will only matter if you let it matter.

But.

Through these words I may just connect with an aspect of you which starts to see something else. Or help see something else. Which, maybe, starts to see something a little clearer. I may not know you personally but, then again, I don't have to – for we are all connected in unimaginable ways. It does matter to me if and when a young body drops on the streets, but I am no hero here to save it from dropping. Only you will dictate your destiny. Dropping doesn't mean a bullet to the dome or the face, it can mean falling short of your dreams. It can mean falling into a cycle of self-destruction in the form of addiction(s), substance abuse and repeat reckless behaviour.

I am saying that there is so much potential in your ability to create and do good for this world. I say this because it is now easily understood. We are all capable of doing good, being good, and spreading good. Of that, *you* most certainly are.

CHAPTER 9

MAS PREGUNTAS (MORE QUESTIONS)

Iron rusts from disuse.
Stagnant water loses its purity, and in cold weather becomes frozen,
even so does inaction sap the vigor of the mind.

—Leonardo da Vinci

Here are some questions for young women. They are universal, really, and can apply to anyone, as the questions in the "boys" section could too (even though the questions there were meant to take swings at the interior headspace and hearts of them boys).

Do you influence those around you for the better?

What effect do you have on those that come into your experience? What effect do you have on those whose experience you venture into? Do you know whether they feel better or feel worse? Does it matter to you if your presence makes others feel better?

Guess what?

You already *do* influence the boys whether you are aware of it or not. Some do it to bring out the good, some do it to bring out the worst. Some do it for the good of others, others do it to manipulate and get what they want.

We all have the potential to unlock the good around us, and more importantly, the good *in* us. The highest good within ourselves is awaiting to be discovered, fields and fields and fields of it. We have the potential and, more so, *you* have the potential to trigger good things to happen just by being a bit better than yesterday. By maybe shifting, even slightly – ideals, desires and objectives.

Bad boy chase?

What fuels your chase? What satisfies your inner mental and emotional needs? Is it the feeling of being regarded as important, and an increased idea of status, because of your name being mentioned alongside a specific person? Is it the increased value you put on your material accumulations? Is the chase just to become materially afflu-ent? Are you willing to hurt those around you while on the chase? Are you running around blindly trying to fill an internal jar of wants and needs that may have a hole at the bottom? How do you fill up a jar that has no bottom? Are you willing to go from boy to boy, to satisfy your perceived wants and needs? How many will you hurt in the process? How many will you double cross? How many friendships will you toss into the wind? How many relationships will you walk away from while on this... chase?

What value will you put on the chase when you imagine where you're gonna be 10 years ahead?

Think on it.

Powerful words these ones below certainly are.

> There's no fire like passion, no seizure like anger,
> no snare like delusion, no river like craving.

> —*The Dhammapada 18*

Perspective.

Are you manipulative?

Intelligence and manipulation do not go hand in hand. They don't vibe. Yes, maybe it is an opinion. But. Manipulation is destructive and corrosive. Yes, you might think it harmless. But it can be damaging beyond repair.

What then?

Manipulation is fear-based. Manipulation causes destruction. It destroys the threads necessary to knit together genuine friendships. At times, those threads are not easy to just... replace. Manipulation causes heartache because there is no way to avoid the energy it contains. Your hidden agenda(s) and motive(s) don't matter. It doesn't matter if you are playing the "game" for yourself, it doesn't matter what front you put up and what you do to try and conceal it. The energy you emit from within has a vibration, and it will materialize for you exactly what you asked for. Thoughts, feelings, actions, emotions... all *vibrations*.

It will materialize an outer picture that matches your inner picture in the form of your life situations and circumstances. It will literally do it in vibrations. You literally get what you give. You literally receive what you put out. You literally attract into your experience chaos or harmony. You attract into your experience truth or lies. You attract the quality of what you are putting out – or what you lack. You literally attract love into your experience or you don't. Easiest way to do it?

To acquire love... fill yourself up with it until you become a magnet.

—Charles Haanel

Easy, I'd say.

You can't harbour non-love and then expect love to find its way into your experience. It is an oxymoron. It cannot happen, that one. Only love attracts love. Love. Real love. Not the made-up idea of love.

Have you tasted it yet?

Focus, Jujhar.

Boys try to impress girls, and if it is your approval they seek, then bring out their best qualities. Don't manipulate a boy or man into a position where his actions could, or will, cause destruction. Don't do it. You're displaying a level of control in that exchange, and if your energy is higher than the energy you exert influence over, don't mistake that for true power. That energy isn't power-based. It is force based.

And yes. There *is* a difference.

That which flows from force will wreak havoc, cause damage and destruction. It is law. It must. That which flows from power – true power – will repair and heal wounds. If you find yourself with a little control – use it for good.

Use that power for good. It will come back to you tenfold. Your power – internal power – will increase and it will affect your experience in a way that words cannot fully describe. Attempts at explaining it are just scratches on a glass surface while trying to feel what is on the other side of the glass.

Like eating a mango, it is an experience.

On a hot sunny day, you take a big piece of chilled mango fresh out of the fridge and manjah. Yup. Mmhmm. Good. Delicious. In that moment it's like the best thing you've tasted, the only thing you have had in hours. Can you imagine that feeling of contentment? That feeling of enjoying it? Don't be smart with me and say, well I don't even like mango. For those of you that would suggest such blasphemy, imagine a piece of fruit that you would favor on a hot sunny day that you *would* enjoy on the beach, or just steps away from your back porch, perhaps. It is way beyond just physical taste – it doesn't even come close. That feeling you'll bring forward, or out from within, rather. The quality and potency of the energy that flows from you when your power is turned toward good, will be... beyond any flavor one can imagine. It will be intoxicatingly enriching.

So be the one who keeps it real.

You'll make more friends and, years down the road, the level of respect that comes your way, will be intensely genuine. It will be tasty and flavored with love. Because that is what you'll have attracted into your experience. *Power and love.*

And it will attract more of it.

Enjoy it.

Humbly of course.

And so, ask yourself, am I manipulative?

Are you destructive?

Do you construct, or tear down? Do your words and actions have the touches of negativity all over them? Do you sow hopelessness with your words, or do you create hope? Do you help construct ambition with what you do or say, or step all over aspirations? Are you helping those around you grow in self-confidence, or are you tearing away at the seams of their emotional and mental fabric?

Are you a healer?

Does your presence mend wounds or make them fester? Does your presence and energy help heal wounds, or tear them up? Is it your intention to have a healing effect on those around you, or are you indifferent? Most of us want to help someone in this world. On what does the help you provide, or intend to provide, rest upon? What conditions are necessary for you to help someone else heal? Are you aware enough to pin-point it?

Do you inspire?

Are you aware of the effect you even have on those around you? Do you know whether you spark someone else's creativity to rise and come to life, or do you stunt that process in some way? You can inspire by being in close physical proximity to someone; it can be done when you are nowhere near them physically, too.

Time and time again I have said to Giggles, you are an inspiration – but she has no clue as to the extent or depth the sparks of the flames she helped light, actually go. Sparks from the deepest fires have been ignited because of her effect on my experience and this unfolding journey. *This* is how it happens.

When we engage those we care about in loving, caring, sharing and healing ways – we trigger into motion the energy of love. The effects are unstoppable. There is no way to reverse the effect. Yes, it is a two-way exchange. And yes, an environment does need to be readied to absorb certain effects.

But.

You can kick start that process. Like Giggles did. Something said to her, in a voice only she understood, that she should enjoy a part of this life journey with me and that she should help heal and make a difference in my experience. Her intention was enough. Her intentions were unconditional. And when we step past the filters of ego and ill-intentions – we create magic. And magic is what we created. You can find traces of it throughout the journey of these words.

So. Do *you* inspire?

Do you pit guys against each other?

That's not cool. Don't set guys up. Don't give up information on them. Don't be ignorant. If you want to play in a certain field you're going to have to pay sooner or later. How long before you're found suffocating from wounds, having been left to bleed out? How long before you're choking on your own spit? How long before you're falling asleep never to wake up again (in this dimension and this human form)? Not long.

Not long at all.

Why?

Because the energy will return to you. It has to. The law of karma is adjusting to your deeds, your thoughts, your words, your actions – and don't forget, there is possibly karma following you from a previous life cycle which is continuously being calculated into the equation. The law of attraction is what is bringing it to you.

But.

It literally is. So be aware. Become aware of what it is you're truly doing. Do think things through. Some things might seem beneficial to you, may seem like an advantage, when they're really not. All the while those things are zinging around invisibly.

Boomerangs.

Are you thinking of setting someone up?

Some might set someone up for money. Others just out of desperation. Some will knowingly do it for free, playing the 'oh I am just a blonde' card, tid bit here, tad bit there. Think it through. If something comes of what you have said, you may not live long to continue on talking. So before you go telling all... ask yourself. Is it worth it?

If it is money you're after... it is the easiest thing to manifest. It's readily available – on request. So how about tap into that realm? If you have done things that have caused destruction... correct that energy. Put out uplifting, healing... loving energy and change your ways. Change your chase. Change your small-minded pursuits. Because if you don't... you will suffer, and so will those that love you. You're at ground zero, girls... why not make a difference while you're there?

If you don't, then who will? Make a difference, that is?

Giggles asked me three questions in a face-to-face, through-the-glass visit at the Regional Reception Assessment Center, at the beginning of this federal bit (end of May, start of June 2018, I believe). It was the first time I had seen her in 4 years, aside from seeing her through a computer screen – Skype styles! With all these things swirling around inside to say or not to say, she posed 3 questions. *Yeah, take the lead why don't you, go right ahead Giggles,* I thought.

1. Who are you?
2. What is your purpose?
3. What do you desire?

Answers came to mind and I almost blurted out some words, but then I realized how significant these questions were. I smiled at myself inside because the first two questions I had used as titles to pieces I had written before the transfer over from the provincial system.

Synchronicity.

I then smiled at her and said let me sit with this for a little and get back to you, which was apparently her cue to giggle. It really is infectious when she does that. Giggle – not ask awareness-jolting questions.

Duh.

It mattered not that I had just been writing about the first two questions; I couldn't answer them on the spot. These weren't questions to be rushed. Later, in the days and moments to come, I thought back to that visit and broke into a smile – more than once. I couldn't conceal it even if I had wanted to. It came from within. Still makes me smile. Probably always will.

A smile of realization does that.

I thought, interesting, this bubble of joy that has helped trigger so much good to unfold, so much joy to happen in my experience and the experience of those around me, someone who has helped me learn so much, has become the teacher – *again.*

Thank you, Universe.

This one female presence has made so much of a difference in my experience. Female presences continue to make a difference and, where they make a difference in mine, they most certainly make a difference elsewhere too. They have to. By the law of attraction, they certainly do. Because they are just exchanges of energy.

But.

Don't let the word "just" take away from its priceless value. I say "just" because it as simple as that, exchanging uplifting energy. But that uplifting and loving energy, however, has in it the colour, the quality, to heal, to mend, and to lift not only spirits, but summon inspiration of ideals, purposes and desires to climb to higher levels. It has the potential to take the exchanges of energy onto the highest field possible – *Love.*

That is what we need, girls, Love. We – as in humanity. Nuestra Familia. So much of it.

Will you be the one to spread it?

To share it?

To create it?

To make a difference?

CHAPTER 10

RESPONSES TO A CURIOUS PERSON

Good people strengthen themselves ceaselessly.

—Confucius

I was recently asked if I was done with "the game". What game? The game of life? Life isn't a game. It is a gift. It is a treasure. A blessing. It is a karmic fruition of deeds and misdeeds, an opportunity to get it right this time, to make a difference, to share and spread love, and to enjoy its warmth. It is an opportunity, to not only enjoy this human experience and uncover the ability to tap into the cosmic energy from which we have blossomed, but it is an opportunity to adjust our coordinates. It is an opportunity to experience harmony. It is an opportunity to become aware (wake up – become conscious). It is an opportunity to tune into our life-purpose or purposes, to really do something wonderful.

I knew what I was being asked, though.

I will do what I have to do to protect my loved ones and their loved ones, by connecting with enough individuals to ensure we all transcend cycles of self-destruction, relying on the guidance from our teachers to do what is necessary, when and where it is needed. When loss of life happens because of an immature understanding of things, of actions, of causes and effects that go unevaluated – it is a sign to become part of something new.

And so, yes, I am done with "games" this life experience, in a sense, has begun anew.

Have you given up your lifestyle, Jujhar?

What lifestyle? What are you even talking about? What actually signifies the lifestyle?

Well, the lifestyle that influences your choices and your decisions, young man.

Which aspects of the lifestyle then?

Well, staying out late and hanging with the wrong crowds...

.... the drinking, the partying, the money-making, and the fornicating, all of which lead to – and are the result of – really bad choices.

Ahh. It is *definitely* the fornicating that leads to bad choices. I agree.

Drinking has never been me. I was an awkward fit amongst the drinkers, felt out of place. Would have rather been chilling on the beach under the stars by the water, with or without company. Somewhere quiet and inspiring. Making money, we have expanded our awareness on how to grow one's bank account – mindfully. Fornicating – Mum, I have *never* done such a thing.

Waheguru. Waheguru. Waheguru (sweating face emoji).

I have, however, given up beliefs I held dear for all the wrong reasons, and have realized that...

... I don't know anything.

I've accepted that this journey is a continual process of growth. A growth that has its own cycles and stages. I am open to learning, listening and understanding, having realized that I may not have many answers just yet (if there are any answers to be had) but trusting that they'll emerge as the journey continues. Whether that journey is an individual one, or the collective journey shared by all of Humanity.

"The Great Big Family" as Martin Sheen put it.[1]

I *have* realized and understood that life isn't a game; it is a gift, but by that same token, whatever label I attach to it, that doesn't make it so.

How you come to understand life, and what it means to you, is your own journey. It is your own perception. It is your own experience. Know, though, that there is a difference between experiencing this human dimension from the perspective of being – of genuine, embodied awareness – versus just doing. Know, that there is a difference between conscious, and unconscious participation. Know, that there is a difference between experiencing with awareness, versus just.... sleeping.

No depth.

How does one experience this treasure of a gift in depth? Depends how it comes to take meaning in your life. Depends what you let it mean to you, I guess. What does it mean to me? Smiling. Enjoying the company of loved ones. Laughing. Enjoying the company of those that may be in our experience for no more than a brief moment. Receiving a letter. Receiving pictures, or funny and inspiring quotes. Engaging in an upbeat conversation – even if it consists of a smile and a 'Hi, have a nice day'. Or just a 'Hi' with a smile – it is an exchange of energy. Receiving a hug from a loved one. A phone conversation. Intentions to make a difference in the experience of another, a positive one, and knowing that – it could actually be the person who will make a big difference in my experience.

I am sort of a self-proclaimed problem solver, or so I'd like to think. Well, that and, I guess, because loved ones have turned to me to solve things. Yup. D-time boys. Kidding. So, this self-proclaimed problem solver looks for opportunities where he can be a part of something uplifting, and be a part of creating something that is in vibrational alignment with a higher energy field. I guess he looks for the positive while learning.

We're all learning, you know.

Individually, sure – the journey will continue.

But.

We can learn to live together. Grow together. Love together. We can do something to make a difference. Together. That's how I see it, anyway. What about you? What do you guys and gals think? Is it worth the pondering? Can we do it? This together thing? I think we can. We can do anything we put our minds to. Better yet, we can do anything we put our hearts into. So you see, it is simple really. And, isn't it though?

I'd say so.

———————————————————

1. I read that in Tony Robbins' book, *Notes from a Friend*. Thanks, Mr Robbins'. He's pretty kool. Yup. Kool with a K.

CHAPTER 11
WHAT I GAVE UP

Without blessings, Satsang[1] is not accessible,
Without Satsang the filth cannot be removed.

————————

Bin bhagan, Satsang Na Labai,
Bin Sangat mal Ne Theejay Jeo.

—Guru Granth Sahib Ji

N ow *this* is a better question to focus on:

What did you give up Jujhar?

Oh, what did I give up? *What didn't I give up?*

I gave up the ability to hug my Mumma. No moments to hand deliver flowers and give her smooches, or attempt to give her smooches while she tries to swat me with whatever it is she is cooking with. Walked away from Mum's food. Not being able to eat something she has cooked with her own hands, put love into, to make her son feel good: *that* is a prison sentence of its own. I gave up my mum's cooking without thinking twice, and time and time again I am reminded of the difference between what I eat here in jail and what I ate in the comfort of her care. I dream of it too, sometimes. I would like to eat it very much. Oh, you would agree it was something else too if you got the chance to enjoy it. It is definitely restaurant-worthy, something you would find in a small, cozy, little homey place with a sign hanging above the entrance saying "Mum's Cooking". Who knows? maybe one day there will be such a place.

What else? Let's see… sound of Dad's laughter echoing about; for no apparent reason, at times. The ability to hug him, talk to him, and/or get told straight by him from time to time. Takes a lot to push his buttons – a lot. Should you manage it… he won't need to raise his voice nor lash out in anger to convey it – you'll feel it. Gave up the ability to put out his clothes for the day – I miss that. Clothes he would find a way to save for another day, opting for whatever he wore yesterday – they're going to get dirty, he would say.

Creatures of habit we can be, at times.

I gave up the ability to give him a hand with something from time to time while he worked through the night and into the new day. The sounds of him hammering away or using blow torches still fills my ears when I think of those times. I can smell the metal, the burning odour, and if I close my eyes, I can see it all. I can see the way the welder crackles and comes to life when he starts stitching things together. It doesn't matter to him if his knee is swollen or if his hand is bruised from accidently hammering it. It doesn't matter to him if his eyes sting because wearing protective lenses obscures his vision. Man on a mission. He will do what he needs to do to fulfill his duty. I gave up the ability to be around him and that is a feeling of emptiness that cannot be filled with anything else.

That's what I gave up.

Haven't seen my mum in 6+ years. That is quite a bit of time. Hadn't seen a current picture of her for years, too, until I was sent one in the spring of 2019. Staring at her face, her eyes – I do truly realize what I gave away without second guessing it. Haven't actually seen any family members in well over 6 years now. Truth be told, family is now more comfortable keeping a distance, without risking getting too close. I don't blame them, it isn't even about that – nor do I have any right to blame them. I know what steps I took, and those steps, in a sense, led me away from them; away from some of them forever.

No weddings. No receptions. No funerals, for that matter. No hospital visits when a loved one isn't feeling well. No way to physically be there for a loved one in times of need – many of those moments passed by indeed. No way to be there for anyone, other than just a voice on the phone.

One day Bubu and I were arguing over the phone and being all crazy while she was trying to cross the road. There she was trying to hold it together and keep from crying, and here I was attempting to trigger it when she bumped her foot or knee, and fell. I think she fell over the divider thing in the road. Clumsy cute. It sobered the fight out of me, brought about her tears, and it didn't matter how much I wanted to be there for her or see if she was OK – wasn't happening. Not being able to be there for your loved ones: that is jail too. Not an aspect of jail, but a sentence of its own. That is how I feel about it anyway.

Loved ones have certainly passed on during this time of incarceration, but the day our family baby, a pure-bred Presa named Tiger, passed on, the helplessness and inability to really do anything for my parents, along with the realization that I could not be there for them in their time of need – sunk in like never before.

Tiger came into our collective experience in the winter of 2006 while I was incarcerated on my first set of charges. I met him in May of 2007 after making bail. He had been a constant companion around the house since, a source of smiles for the household, and the rest of the family too. He was more than a dog; he was the baby of the family.

I got into working out while I was incarcerated, something Happy drilled into me in those early years, and I continued that pursuit once I had made bail. I was out on house arrest so we ended up turning the sundeck of the home into a workout space. We filled it with free weights, a bench and a couple pieces of equipment. Some of my most memorable moments of that summer were created there.

Sukhvir loved to talk. Well, if she felt comfortable, then she talked. She would talk away while I worked out. I didn't mind. The sound of her voice was like everything I ever wanted to hear. Apparently, it was everything Tiger wanted to hear too. I remember quite clearly his cute little paws on the table listening with fascination to the voice coming from, well – the table. Many days, and weeks, went by like that. Tiny little pup growing fast wagging his tail to the music in the air made by Sukhvir's voice. The day Sukhvir met my Mumma, Tiger hid behind my mum's leg. He got *shy* at the sound of her voice. I was so choked. I was like: this is your sister! Why are you getting shy?!

His antics didn't end there.

One day I decided the yard needed professional trimming. Keep up with the neighbours, I thought. I gave very specific instructions to the guy who came to get it done. One of those instructions was: should you need to go into the backyard, come get me or my mum. *OK?* Yes, OK sir. I kid you not, 5 minutes, not *even* 5 minutes later, I hear this scream and by the time I've bolted towards the sound I hear my mum's voice and little barks from Tiger. That was fast, I thought. I can't remember if Mum had ran down the back steps or if she was already in the garden, but she had a flip-flop in her hand and young Tiger was trying to hide behind the pillar he was tied to.

En route to the location of my mum's verbal assault on Tiger, I pass the labourer as he's headed towards the street, apparently looking for safety. This guy's limp-running, screaming, possibly crying, and I see blood leaking down his leg. Uh-oh ***** I thought. And then there is Tiger, who is not only successfully dodging my mum's attempts to smack him with a flip-flop, but he is wearing the biggest grin on his face as if he has never been happier. When my mum stops trying to smack him (it may have taken a few attempts to tell or, rather, suggest this to her) he sits down. Tail wagging triumphantly with a look of, *See what I did?* No doubt thinking in his head, *I guarded – be damned if that fool tries coming around here again, bro.* Meanwhile all I am thinking about is how to get Tiger out of there before he gets hauled away by the dog police.

The night Sukhvir sustained injuries he went ballistic. My father told me he didn't stop till I finally came home. And I remember it, the minute that I came home he went all quiet. He knew.

Connection.

He refused to walk past a certain point where I would go to light candles. He knew. I didn't even need to put him on a leash, it didn't matter who walked by, he sat there perfectly still – he knew.

Connection.

The evening he passed away I called Dad at a time I don't usually call home. I was in the middle of cooking a sauce, and something made me put the sauce on pause and I went to my assigned room. More of a home than a mere room, actually, though it's intended to be a jail cell, I guess. In the room I looked around as if I was looking for something, freshened up and grabbed my phone card on the way out.[2]

My father was in the car when he answered the phone and, within a few seconds, I heard this shrill of a cry that made something inside me churn. What is that? I asked, trying to keep from freaking out. When he told me it was Tiger, it felt like someone had just driven a bus into my midsection. I asked to be put on speaker – getting out the words that usually push Tiger into joy overdrive, in the right tone, were hard. They didn't have the same confidence to them, because they had to squeeze past the lump in my throat. My father said Tiger would be fine and that he was headed home from the vet. He said not to worry because he was going to give him the medication the vet had just provided as soon as he was home. I took that as my cue and said I would call back then – it was almost lock-up anyway – something inside me wanted to be off the phone and alone.

After the call, I walked around aimlessly for a little and then went into my room when the last lock-up of the evening was called. It was a Saturday. Cultural and religious programs are aired on Saturdays. I collected myself mentally and sat down to meditate, to rid the… unsettling feeling I felt in the pit of my stomach. I knew kirtan was most likely going to be played at 8pm on Taur Punjab Di, aired on Vision TV.[3] The Shabad that was played is one I recite every day.[4] Within a moment, a meditative state was induced, and then I focused on Tiger. Moments passed; a calmness came over me, and not just over me – but around me. As that calmness came, the Shabad ended, and my eyes opened to the click of the door unlocking.

It was the final unlock of the evening. The lock-up schedule is fixed and is broken up into approximately 2-hour increments: morning, afternoon, evening, and late evening. There are roughly eight hours a day when an inmate is free from the confines of a locked cell, room or home, whatever one considers it, I guess. When doors are unlocked, one may walk out into a concrete yard (accessible on the unit) with a high ceiling that has multiple security meshes so one can't just up and decide to climb away. The somewhat open ceiling of the yard allows for the sun to come through, and that my friends, is a necessity in jail. It helps elevate not only the mood, but the vibration of the entire building. The sun does that. One may do body workouts in the yard or play handball. There is access to a workout space in a separate room, with a pull-up bar and dip machine, too. One may use the phone, shower, socialize, play cards, sit around, and even... cook food. Yup. Yum. Well, one can cook with what ingredients (and spices) are available off the canteen or commissary.

This is what I went back to doing – cooking.

I went back to tending the sauce I'd started earlier, and then at 9pm, I picked up the phone again. We made small talk first, and then I finally asked the question. How's Tiger, Dad? I already knew the answer though... I didn't have to ask. Oh him, my father said as he chuckled his signature chuckle... he is onto the next journey, Son. Ya? I said calmly, more of a reflexive reply than a question. That hurts, I said – ouch. Then I told my father I felt him move on while I was meditating. He chuckled and said, he made his rounds. He saw everyone he was supposed to see today, and talked to everyone he was supposed to talk to. He even got you to call.

Connection.

That shriek of a cry that I had heard, wasn't a cry at all. It was him saying bye. And then my father echoed that by saying, he wasn't in pain, Son. He was saying, it is time to go, I am leaving. And you know, he wanted to hear from you. I thought, yup. Because I felt it when I was pulled towards the phone, and felt the peace in the farewell as I meditated.

Connection.

Not being able to take my loved ones to any appointments, or drag them there if need be, is something I can no longer physically do. My father is a hardworking man, has been his entire life, and to get him to commit to a pamper session would be quite a detour from his daily grind. It is not on the itinerary – ever. There were times I was able to slip him away for a little bit, but I had to force it. Knowing that he needs to be looked after and that I cannot be part of that experience physically, is something I have to not only endure, but continuously make peace with.

I have nieces and nephews whom I will probably never get to see, never get a chance to hold and hug till I am long gone from the chains of the system. Even then, it could be a while. Footsteps taken and all. That isn't a very welcoming feeling. I won't get a chance to enjoy their company in the most innocent phases of life. And, honestly? That's not cool. Why would anyone want to trade that off, ever? Being able to share moments with the gods of our world, being able to exchange energy with the purest forms of the Infinite in expression, is healing... is uplifting, and it is an experience that is indeed a God-given gift. Not being able to share those moments.... is, well – is what it is. But oh, what I would do to hang out with them, for even a moment What I would give up.

But.

Who thinks of that while walking around lost and blind?

---

1. Satsang – Company of the holy. Company of Guru Granth Sahib Ji.
2. Every inmate is assigned a phone card with a personalized pin code to place collect or paid calls. An inmate must load money onto his or her card, funds for which are sent in or earned from a handful of available jobs.
3. If it weren't for shows like Taur Punjab Di, I would not have experienced the healing that I did. It influenced my journey in an inspiring and uplifting way.
4. Kirtan – singing of Gurbani with instruments; Shabad – the prose of Gurbani, sung during the kirtan.

CHAPTER 12

UNCOOL AND CAPITAL K KOOL

When you lose, don't lose the lesson.

—The Dalai Lama

I've heard it said that young ones, these days, are so much grimier, shadier and slimier than previous generations. No back bone, no character, no originality or personality. Really? Is that how guys are these days? Hood guys? Neighbourhood, street guys?

No.

Don't think so. Even if someone did something yesterday, *it doesn't have to define you today*. Don't waste the precious moment before you, do not let those you care for waste the precious moment either.

It is not cool to intrude on the well-being of others. It is not cool to pick on others. It is not cool to bully others. It is not cool to make up lies about someone and start stupid rumours. It is not cool to sit there on camera talking away, playing double roles. It is not cool to turn on your friends over anything, let alone some chump change.

It is not cool to sit in prison waiting for mail to show up (trust me on this one), for pictures to show up, for any outside connection to make its way through the boundaries of the prison so one can escape for a bit. So one can "get away" for a little bit. It is not cool to have to give away precious privileges and deprive yourself, your loved ones and friends of moments which will never repeat themselves.

It is sort of, capital L – Lame.

It is not cool to give up the ability to share a kiss with a lover, give up the ability to hug a loved one. Give up the ability to hang onto your mother and give her kisses all over her face. It is not cool to give up the ability to give your dad a hand, a hand he could really use. It is not cool to not be able to be there for your loved ones in times of need, which could even be life and death situations. Times of need where the presence of a loved one could avert something life-ending or prevent loss from happening – in whatever form that loss is inching its way closer into your experience. It is not cool being unable to spend moments with your children or your newborn(s). It is definitely not cool to be unable to enjoy the delicate touches of your niece or nephew's fingers all over your face and to listen to the music they make with their voice – the sounds of the gods.

It is not cool to put your friends behind bars, or to play a part in someone ending up behind bars, not when you're playing the role of a non-civilian. If you're playing a role, knowing full well that when the time comes you will just... cut your losses and move on, know that those cold calculations will have some dire consequences for you. The energy you put out will come back to affect you in ways you couldn't even imagine. It doesn't matter how much you try to do to cover up your deceitful ways because in the world of vibrations, the law of karma is deciphering, tallying, and then re-applying the rebound.

The universe is doing calculations of its own.

It doesn't matter how much you cry or project the pain and torment you are experiencing into the universe, it will only help feed that destructive cycle. It will bring you more of it. Because that is what you are manifesting again and again – suffering. So, recognize it isn't cool to lie and weasel your way around the hood; you will have to pay a price for it sooner or later.

It is not cool to endanger the lives of your loved ones. It is not cool to put them at risk for getting caught up in some drama, in some nonsense... in some BS. It is not cool to not make it to your sister's wedding, your cousins' weddings, or your friend's wedding. It is not cool to not think things through – it is so old and lame.

It is definitely not cool to not make it to your high school prom. Gone with the wind at an age where one should be picking out prom suits and planning for the next steps of the journey. One's family shouldn't be planning the next farewell, planning a service at a Gurdwara, or a Church, and one's family certainly shouldn't be sitting in a funeral home going through the motions of doing what is presumed necessary after one physically ceases to be in this world.

That isn't cool.

That is heartbreaking. It is gut-wrenching. There are no stripes involved in that. Not when innocence is being stripped from the world, when one is at the age when the planning of college and university courses is natural – innocence is certainly being stripped.

It happens.

It has happened. It doesn't have to happen again. It isn't hood. It isn't G. It is heartbroken mothers. Heartbroken sisters. Ever heard a shriek from a sister or a mother when they have been told their brother or child was injured in a violent way? It's heartbreaking, but then it doesn't come close to the cry that rings your soul when they are told that the brother or child has passed on. It is just really, really sad. Heartbroken sisters – same sisters who, having read this book up until this point, realize that the words above were written with them in mind. The call for something different is written in the memory of those who have had to experience... the pain and... heartbreak that comes from learning that their brother(s) passed on. (But. It isn't the end. Know that.) Mentally tormented mothers and fathers. The type of pain and torment that... sort of just sticks around.

That's not cool.

It's sort of sad. No, it is truly sad. Let the ones who have passed on too soon be a reminder of where things aren't supposed to get to at a certain phase of this life journey. Let it be a reminder of what the world can learn from, and grow from.

It is not cool to just turn to a weapon – where is the tough in that? Many turn to a weapon out of fear, and then let others' fear-projected agendas influence their own thought process. What about the factor that keeps one tossing and turning at night? Because it does for many. What about the cold sweats and the inability to sleep sober? What about factoring in the snorting of lines of dope, at a time when some are rinsing their bodies with water? What about the substances used as cushions from an onslaught of thought, the process triggered by a reminder of some sort? A reminder that was started by a thought. Ew.

Is there a standard in that?

It is not cool to set up your friends, and getting a girl involved in some way is equally dumb. Why are you going to put that evil on someone else? You'll pay for the negative energy you help manifest in their experience. It is not cool to just hate on someone who was once your friend over money; over any form of jealousy, over some smallness. No good that can come from it. You're trading away values and replacing them with a type of darkness that will suck the life-juice right out of your soul. That darkness will eat at you, and eat at you till there is nothing left for it to feed off. It will pull at the threads that hold together the idea of sanity, and you will eventually unravel. You are putting out into the universe an energy that will return to you, in exact proportion, and that boomerang you will certainly feel.

It is not cool to do a drive-by on someone's home, or to go after someone when they are with their family. It isn't cool to just roll through a hood and light up someone just because they're from a different "hood". That is dangerous. Brothers from the 6 certainly have much to say about the type of suffering it has brought, and brings.[1] Two wrongs don't make a right. Someone has to take steps to do things differently, otherwise... who will?

Don't be the one who gets struck with realizations 10, 20 even 30 years down the line. Don't be the one to realize late that some things will follow you around like a plague until they've had their say. Don't be the one who finally realizes and understands that some things just don't leave you much room for peace of mind. Don't be the ignorant one whose thinking is short-sighted. Don't be the one who is found, hands in pockets, bullets to the back of the head, sprawled out across the ground, or slumped up over a steering wheel.

Karmic cycle.

Un-avoidable. Energy balancing itself out, is all.

Boomerang.

And...

The guys that truly respect their parents, respect their loved ones... those are the Kool ones. The ones who treat others with respect, with respect and love, those are the Kool ones. The ones who respect their girlfriends, who treat them like princesses, who respect the essence housed inside the body... they are the Kool ones.

The ones who look after their loved ones, the ones who look after one another, who praise their loved ones and build them up, they are the Kool ones. The ones who are responsible enough to assume independent, and collective, responsibility for their family's needs, loved ones' needs, others' needs... they are the Kool ones.

The ones who are confident enough to walk their own path, a path that doesn't bring any destruction to anyone around them... they are the Kool ones.

Those that move humbly, striving to create an honest living, putting their hearts into honest endeavours; the ones who forgo greed, step past the barriers of envy, of hate, the ones who embrace the energy of Love... they are the Kool ones. The ones who approach others with warm intentions, the ones who look to help someone up – they are the heroes. Heroes are pretty Kool.

The ones who won't kick someone when they are down, won't manipulate innocence, won't take advantage of someone who is hurting... someone who is already suffering... they are the heroes.

Those who recognize a sense of duty to move in a way that is for the betterment of those around them, moving in a way that isn't triggering a negative experience for others, they are the strong ones. The ones who understand the strength of humility and who understand the energy in kindness, they are the heroes.

Compassionate beings who add colour to neighbourhoods and to this dance of life; the ones who add a colorful vibration to the energy field of those who have made it their life purpose to do good and spread hope, spread warmth... *they* are the heroes.

The ones who take a moment to listen to that inner voice which beckons them to do good, to be of service for the good of humanity, to be quiet and humble leaders... they are the heroes. They are the role models the world needs. *They* are the Voice of Humanity (yes let's capitalize) and they are the ones who are making a qualitative difference in the lives of not only their loved ones, but the world as a whole.

Be one of the #Kool ones.

---

1. 6 – How friends and brothers reference Toronto ON, Canada. They have experienced the pain and the senseless carnage.

CHAPTER 13

THE REMEDY

The secret of change is to focus all of your energy not on
fighting the old,
but on building the new.

—Socrates
Saint and philosopher

If you've done things that cause you unrest; if you've hurt people, bringing about destruction... it's time to start along another path. Start spreading goodness. Start making a difference. If you're true in your heart – not scumbagging around with ill intentions – if you regain your moral compass and bring ethical, highly principled, value-led qualities to the forefront of what you do... then spiritual, invisible, and *potent* energies will come to your aid.

Angels will come to your aid.

They'll be by your side. They'll be dispatched to you by the Creator, because they too have a purpose to fulfill, and part of that purpose is to guide the likes of those who have aligned themselves – vibrationally – to receive them.

If you're out there street hustling on the frontlines today, the d-boys and some rare d-girls, serving customers, and you're hell bent on being whatever it is you are trying to become – then be mindful. Realize that, in the exchange of energy that occurs, there are two totally different dynamics in play. Building and accumulating versus destroying and depleting.

Find a balance.

Whether that comes in the form of you looking out for your customer a little by bringing them food or water, or spending moments doing the Dr Phil thing, it *will* matter. If you see your customer starting to fall apart, or see that he or she is seriously destroying his or her life... don't be ignorant of that. Build a connection with them. Recognize that someone is suffering and you are profiting from that suffering.

It *will* make a difference.

It could be just the thing (energy output) that prevents a shell from finding the side of your face, and your bone fragments from sliding down the side of the opposite door. It could be just the thing that prevents pieces of your bone structure from shredding the inside of the vehicle you possibly spend so much time in.

If.

If you realize that, on one end of the scale, there's an individual who is destroying not only him or herself, but who is affecting everyone touched by their destructionist ways; and on the other end, there's someone who is looking to gain and secure riches for themselves; if you realize there will be a price to pay for the "luxury" accumulated – then you will self-correct some of your ways. You won't look to take everything your customer has, even if the customer is desperate to hand it over. You'll look to make sure that they are doing OK.

There is no way to escape the destruction that occurs on the other end of the exchange, because you are part of it. You are triggering energy into motion by involving yourself in it. If you can realize the simple facts, the reality of the relationship, and become aware of its effects, then you will find ways to make a difference while still in pursuit of monetary riches. Because that difference you make – inner and outer qualities – is what will keep the most intense waves of energy from putting you 6 feet underground or into an incinerator.

If you are on the front lines taking and taking, destroying and destroying, and if these words make no difference to the way you move, have no impact upon you and the way you relate to your customer – this is a sign of unconscious participation. You may have read the words, you may even think you understand the words, and that there is a karmic thing in play, but at a deeper level – there is unawareness.

If you genuinely take steps to make amends, to correct things, from a shifted and realized state of awareness... humility will flow into what you do. Harmony and balance will be at the center of what you do – *the Power of the Universe will then flow through what you do.*

That is just how it works.

This cosmic energy dance and its rhythmic tune thing. Take your time with things. Don't rush into things. At times, I wish I had taken my time with things.

But here I be.

I'm one of those guys who is sharing a perspective with the underlying insight of "I wish I had taken my time and not tried to pelt the ones who were trying to speak in assemblies at school with anything my mind jumped upon". But, on the flip side of that – I be *being*. So, that be all good. ADD – I veer off at times – I sometimes forget what I am saying or, in mid-sentence, I ask, what was I saying? And the person is usually looking back at me with an expression that says, what in the ****** world have you been trying to say for the last 5 minutes? You want *me* to tell *you* what you were saying? Dunno is usually the verbal response that comes back. It's in the eyes though. That's where the meaning is when verbal words don't convey.

They speak a language too.

Don't look to create issues or problems, look to create solutions. Look to create answers, positive opportunities. *It is impossible to extend a hand and make a fist at the same time.* I read that quote a while back and smiled, like duh. I also thought hmm, perspective. Not every response has to be one of aggression. Not every step has to be un-evaluated and destructive. Not every reaction to someone's actions has to be in haste or countered with low-level awareness. Not everything that leaves you feeling offended needs to be responded to with anger or a toxic vindictiveness.

Let some things just be. You know? Need to let go of some of the things we hang onto, at times, and let them lose importance, or the very things you might be hanging onto could be the very things that leave you mashed right up, in the end.

Love and be done with the rest, said a brilliant mind, a name I cannot recall. Love and use that brilliant mind of yours for good, and for the betterment of Humanity. Create rather than destroy. Assist and help rather than intrude. Be upfront rather than backstabbing.

Share rather than penny-pinch.

CHAPTER 14

WHAT DO YOU WANT TO BE?

My dreams and my hopes are still the same, and I'm hopeful that I will be able to continue my journey and to be what I always wanted to be, to help people, to put every child into school.

—Malala Yousafzai
To her editor, Judy Clain
I Am Malala

W rite it down. We're constantly growing this is a continuous process of growth. Those of you who are in high school, you write it down for sure. Take a moment. Think about it. Sit with it, and after you have written it down, put it away somewhere. Cool?

Kool.

Growing up, I didn't just want to be the guy my loved ones and close friends could rely on, but someone that anyone in my school could call on. Could depend upon. Everyone in school I felt a sense of connection with, because it was "my" school and it was where "my" friends and I were growing up. I wanted to be a low-key hero. That's the truth. Who doesn't? A hero in some form or another. Probably ingrained into our DNA just as much as it is shared in the collective field of consciousness.

The opportunity to connect with those incarcerated at Okanagan Correctional Center (OCC) brought with it an eye-opening experience which helped me realize how blind I really was during high school. It made me realize how delusional the world I had lived in was.

While at OCC, a handful of us were getting together for weekly "awareness/meditation" sessions for self-help. One evening, we engaged in the topic of high school, drug abuse, and its detrimental effects. During this group discussion, a young man said he started using meth at the age of 11. *Eleven.* Others said, 12, 13, and 14. One had his first taste of cocaine at the age of 10.

Ten.

When I hear of children in high school experimenting with and even getting addicted to opioids, cocaine, and substances like meth – I get rattled. I get rattled at the fact that there are those who are willing to let loose such poisons into such vulnerable environments.

Not cool.

Some of the guys at the OCC sessions became addicted to drinking as early as grade seven and eight. Every one of them said they were trying to escape a reality they didn't want to be in, even if it was masked with the intent to have fun, experiment and fool around. All of them said, deep down I was miserable, disconnected, lonely, depressed, angry, sad and unhappy with life in general.

Some weren't seeing eye-to-eye with their parents, others felt out cast by their peers, by their classmates, and that feeling of alienation made it easier to isolate and, eventually, trap themselves in harmful behaviours. Some felt left out by not having nice things, or cool things others commented on or gave others attention for. Some never had the things other children had, which automatically created this void for those who didn't fit certain... criterion. It created a gap for those who didn't fit the idea of "cool enough". Cool enough to be identified with certain circles of friends that seemed to be enjoying their lives so much. The non-inclusion however, wasn't the only pre-requisite.

For some, inclusion itself was the catalyst.

Every one of them said, *I wish I listened to the other voice in my head*, or *I wish I listened to myself and not to other people – it only messed up my life, and those who were affected by my choices.* Almost all of them said they knew the choices they were making were bad for them, but it felt good to rebel.

It felt liberating.

It felt good to self-harm, because it made others concerned for their well-being. It felt good to create feelings of guilt and sympathy toward them and, when it didn't work, they rebelled harder. But these strategies led to so many getting pushed and pulled into a world in which self-destruction *seemed* to be about finding an autonomous phase, but without the know-how to step away from it and save themselves, time and time again it ended up with them being abused, taken advantage of, and/or thrown in jail.

Many of them said that, in a sense, they were addicts and stuck. *I didn't want to be this, I wanted to be a famous singer*. Another said he never imagined living the life he had been living; and not just him, his girlfriend said the same. *We didn't want this, we wanted something else. We didn't want to be what we are to each other, we wanted to be better than this. Our children are suffering because of it*. He added that they both knew that, if something didn't change quickly, their children were going to suffer and struggle, just the same.

When I heard them share their experiences, thoughts and feelings, I found myself asking whether this took place while I was in high school. Nah... it couldn't have. We went there, it wasn't like that. Yeah, we were there and we said we would look after those in our school so, no. But.

Yup.

That is exactly what was happening. Flashes of memories, of faces, of children, both boys and girls, who were in such sensitive phases of their life journey that were just starting out on paths of self-destruction, came to me as I travelled back in my mind. I realized how much I missed because of ignorance. Missed because of my own dysfunctional behaviours, insecurities and misplaced sense of self. Missed because of unawareness.

I accept that I cannot go back and redo the high school experience, cannot go back with these 10-plus years of lessons, realizations and new awareness. But. That is ok. What about you? Well, here you be – right on the front lines. Right at ground zero. Each and every one of you can make a difference in the environment you are in. *You can make a quality difference* in your own experience. You can even start by making a difference in someone else's experience in some way, if you don't know how or where to start in your own. That step you take for someone else, will release energy, lots of it. Energy that will rebound like a boomerang and come right back to affect your experience in some form, in the same exchange. Maybe not right away. But it surely will.

The law of attraction says it must.

Substance abuse in the earlier phases of life is toxic and dangerous. It is dangerous for mental, emotional, physical and spiritual health. Abusing dangerous substances hinders the natural growth of the brain. Emotional and mental growth are linked to one another. A healthy emotional state will influence a healthy mental state. They complement each other.

But.

An imbalance in any of those fields of energy and you have serious issues. These fields all affect one another, and so imbalances will have a drastic affect across the whole system, and on and on it goes. Cycles, remember? A continued mental or emotional imbalance will infect the physical organism. The energy of one's thoughts and feelings, of one's emotions, will trickle their way into the body, and then it's "uh-oh". Houston, we have a little bit of the prawlum.

I am not saying don't do this or that, that this is bad for you, etc.. Not at all. What I am saying is, *become aware* of the fact that the body and its organs, the mind and this life journey, have stages which revolve around growth, and to *become mindful* of the processwith sense and knowledge. No one, and I do mean no one, will live your life for you. Only *you* can do that. Only you will take the steps you take, but those steps don't have to be ones that were ill-thought out, or made to fit someone else's idea of what is cool or right or what a good time is. I am saying you have the *power of choice* to take steps you feel are truly beneficial for you, and not steps taken to please someone else. Not steps taken under pressure or to look a certain way.

Most of the people in pressurized group settings won't be around years later. The ones who might be there are the ones who aren't asking anything of you, who aren't demanding anything from you. The ones who don't keep you around to fix their insecurities. The ones who aren't trying to manipulate you for their own benefit. The ones who have good intentions for you and who encourage you in the direction of the dreams you speak about.

Role models.

Some of the guys I shared brief moments of genuine friendship with became the older homies that I only came to appreciate later – much later. Only recently, actually. Older homies that weren't looking to be recognized, homies that could enjoy laughter, pulling off innocent pranks but knowing when and where to stop; or slow down, at least.

Self-control.

I had a close call with an "innocent prank". I skipped class to snowball vehicles with two friends. Here we are, fresh enough snow, at one of our favorite spots. We jump over the hedges as we hear the vehicle come within striking range, and we let our carefully-made snowballs fly. We're all running before they even connect. Why? We recognized the vehicle. We hear them connect, the brakes screech and a slur of profanities follow.

It was my dad.

Never again did I let a snowball go in that manner, with the possible danger it created. I kept thinking over and over that I could have caused my dad to have an accident. If it wasn't OK for me to put my dad at risk of having an accident, it wasn't OK for me to put someone else at risk of having one either.

See? Learned a little self-control, that boy did.

The ones who became older homies, they lived with this… higher awareness, and they are the ones who were smiling inside. They are the ones who have always been smiling inside. Through their life circumstances and situations, they experienced heartache and hard times too, but they made quality choices early. They chose to take things slow, to be patient. They chose to take time to understand things and not get ahead of themselves or put themselves into stupid situations. They surrounded themselves with those who had their best intentions at heart. They took moments to self-reflect and understand the difference between unawareness and appreciation of what they had or didn't have.

They started to understand, early, what negative and positive meant.

They knew what they wanted to be. They knew they wanted to be part of the solution, and give answers without creating issues for others. They knew that where they wanted to get to was going to require walking a certain path (walking your own path). They knew who they could rely on to help support them with their decisions. Most importantly – *they were humble.*

Nothing is guaranteed.

This dance of physical experience, it is temporary. Things happen that bring beings in and out of our experience. Things happen that take us in and out of others' experiences. Which means even the ones who are sincere, loving, caring, and a source of inspiration, may not always be there.

The guy I took my first couple of weed-tokes with (high school), the guy that showed me how to smoke a joint, is someone who was in my experience for a brief moment. I asked him for ecstasy pills one day, and he responded in an angry and aggressive way. He even took a few steps in my direction as he spoke:

> What are your dumb friends asking you to go and find? Don't listen to the idiots around you, they're only going to get you in trouble. I had a couple of tokes with you, because it's not that harmful, and even then – once in a while. Don't be an idiot. Don't listen to the guys who aren't looking out for you. Stay away from them. If I find out they are trying to get you to do dumb things, I am going to come looking for them. You're a young Singh. Singhs don't do drugs. Drugs change you. Stay a Singh. It suits you.

He was a genuine friend to me.

He isn't around anymore.

He was gunned down.

R. Nutt was his name.

He is someone who will always be remembered. What he was saying will be remembered too. What he was saying was, don't be a fool.

So.

Don't be one. I was a fool once. I was a fool many times. A fool was definitely not what I wanted to be, but because of my rigidness in critical years of growth, it is what I became. I became identified with the idea of the reality I thought I lived in, to the point where I continuously invested in thoughts and feelings that supported the distorted reality I saw. The distorted picture I saw was the sign of suffering, the suffering was the effect, and the cause was unawareness: the inability to step back and actually take my time with things. The inability to recognize what I really needed to do; this led to a path which triggered chaos and self-destruction to unfold in ways I never imagined possible.

Well, consciously anyway.

Because in some way, and in some form, I envisioned the very pictures that came to form my "reality". The inner pictures did go on to create the outer pictures.

As within so without indeed.

I got caught up in a whole bunch of nonsense and a cycle of self-destruction, so much so that I forgot to slow down and remember what I wanted to be. The nonsense became more important to me than the things that mattered most to me when I was a child, but they also matter to me today.

Family. Values. Tradition. Culture.

I walked a path that eventually ripped me away from my family and ended up with me in prison by the age of 19 on charges the judge, at sentencing, called senseless. It was fitting, what she said, because it *didn't* make any sense. The charges played their part in a cycle of events that eventually led to me walking into the Surrey Court House late for sentencing, on 31 October, 2007 – 11 days before a would-be wedding date. Sukhvir had passed on a few weeks before, on 8 October. I walked in with assistance – I was recovering from a suicide attempt on 9 October (I stepped in front of an SUV). In front of the court house, news reporters snapped pictures and recorded video footage that would circulate in newspapers and on television for the next decade, putting me and my loved ones on blast (in the lime light) in communities locally and internationally, again and again.

So much happened so fast that, when I blinked away the fog and looked around, I was sitting in a prison cell again. My family had been put through the shredder, along with other loved ones, their families and everyone that was connected to the turmoil of my energy output; all had felt its consequences.

In one sense, I completely accept that this is the way things had to play out. But, then again, what can I do other than accept it? I am not going to resist it. Not now. Resistance is completely contradictory to the spiritual principles I have learnt.

In another sense, it didn't have to be this way, it could have been different. But. Choices. And this is what the moment has brought out of my choices. This is reality. What I choose to do, here and now, is what I will look back to in a decade; which just happens to be about how long I have to wait until the system no longer has its fingers dipping into my personal experience. A decade is a long time; I went a minute too long without self-reflecting or evaluating.

Not cool.

All the opportunities were there, I just didn't recognize them. Each missed moment – each missed, pivotal moment – reset things and reassembled the coordinates, assembling another moment, another phase, another stage (and another choice) within the journey that led here. This is what has been assembled today.

I would be a fool not to recognize it.

What I wanted to be was – a warrior. Someone who could be relied upon and called upon by anyone who needed help. And I don't mean that in an aggressive sort of way. I wanted to be someone who affected those around him for the better, and did what he had to do without needing praise or the spotlight.

Awareness.

It took much suffering, much hardship, many stumbles, and much ridicule to realize, finally, what I had wanted to be. Because I had forgotten. Don't forget. Remind yourself. Keep that note handy. Be a hero of sorts. Be a hero for those that matter most to you. Take time to understand what being a hero means.

And.

I still want to be that person.

But.

What about you, what do *you* want to be?

CHAPTER 15
WALK YOUR OWN PATH

*Those who maintain a clear sense of purpose in life
are strengthened by hardship.*

—F Diddy

B e your own person. Practise good manners. Follow a clear code of honour. Cultivate strong values. You don't have to follow someone else's idea of what acceptable behaviour is, or what is perceived as "normal".

Practise being quiet and observe those around you. If you encounter vulnerability, offer sound advice. Acknowledging another's vulnerability is a strength. It is an empathetic-based strength. Be a friend to others. Set your own standards and set the course of your own path. Walk in step to a beat only you hear. You'll be the one to make a difference in the world. That said, it is also important to listen to others; to actively hear them.

Listen to their intentions – *that's* awareness.

You have the power of the moment and you can use that moment for foresight. Awareness. If you contemplate where you are, what choices you're making, you can foresee where your path is headed. Don't be the one who looks back years later and says, wish I did *that* different, or *if*. If only I had taken my time. Don't be the one who stares back over the years that passed by in a blur, thinking... why didn't I self-evaluate earlier? What was I doing? Why did I do that? How come I didn't see certain things coming? Awareness. That's why. Be aware. Don't be ignorant. You're an amazing miracle, a manifestation of Life.

It took a lot to get you here.

Um, the act itself may have been easy for your parents. Actually, what if it was awkward? Why did I even go there, what are we even doing talking or reading about this? My mum's *not* going to approve. I am catching a couple different coloured flip-flops across the side of my head for sure. Not only have I dropped the word sex in here, but the fact I am bringing light to the fact that it took the act of sex to get you here – she will definitely have a few colour flip-flops waiting for me. Oh wait. Have I dropped the word sex yet? *See.* Where is a Bubu when you need one to check the order of things? Oh. Actually. I guess I just did drop the word sex.

Waheguru.

Be aware. Not like "oh no… dangers lurk". But – take a moment. Take a moment to think about things while you sit with them. Sit with them in silence. Alone. That's when your awareness will make a jump. Through the process of self-reflection.

Through the utilization of the power of silence.

And, it did take a lot to bring you into this world, respect that process. You are not here by chance. You are not reading these words today by chance. You are reading them because you were meant to. I am writing them… because I was meant to. A part of my purpose in this world was to get these words into print and there is a purpose in you having received them. You have a purpose in this world that is totally unique to you. That can only be fulfilled by you. If there were no need for you in the world, you wouldn't be here. We are spiritual beings having a human experience, here to do something specific, we didn't just end up here by chance., said Deepak Chopra. I agree. Teilhard de Chardin said it before him. I agree; it is not by chance at all.

A younger friend of mine was trying to walk his own path. He was a favourite choice with girls, because his good looks and swag were unmatchable. He didn't care about trying to make money on the street. But, he brawled like he was from the street. He had the "not backing down" street mentality. The courage in me doesn't come close to the courage in him.

I got jumped one time in my high school lobby, 3-on-1. I was young and really dumb, and had my mind made up that I was going to be waiting for one of the kids when he would least expect it, and show him what it really felt like to be ambushed. But my younger friend got to him first. They fought at a spot that had become popular for fights. They were both bloodied and bruised by the end of it. But my friend was the one left standing.

Harmless – just a fist fight, right?

His path was indeed a different one, but others intruded on it. I intruded on it. I didn't give the right advice. In May of 2008 I was serving out the sentence handed to me on 31 October, 2007 – related to kidnapping charges I incurred in May 2006 at the age of 19. I was watching the news in the a.m., waiting for the doors to be unlocked for breakfast. The news report showed the scene of a stabbing incident that had unfolded during the night outside a home in Abbotsford. I recognized the home. I knew it was him. I wanted it to be someone else, but deep down, I knew it was him. I learned that he was just getting home when he was run up on by multiple kids. But he didn't run. Even after a weapon was produced, he stood and fought. I wanted to call him stupid. I wanted to tell him he was dumb for not reading the situation right. But I couldn't. He never recovered from the injuries sustained.

The innocence in him didn't understand that there are those in this world that will eat that innocence up. He didn't understand that there were those who would take it past a 1-on-1 fist fight. And there is no way to replace a lost life. There is no way to bring back a loved one that has passed on.

Be the one that doesn't put others in vulnerable positions, be the one that isn't looking to jump an innocent kid. It doesn't matter how things started or what point they have gotten to, some things can be put to rest. Things happen, it is not the end of the world.

Don't intrude on others' paths.

Be the bold one who has the will to say no, to say, hey, spiking that girl's drink – that's bad action. Be the courageous one who says, no we shouldn't jump this kid. For what? He is already defeated. Be the one that has the strength to say – it's not worth it. If the guy is beat, and helpless – it is done.

Do things differently.

If you seek glory, glory as perfection, then let it be perfection in the image of what the One, the Source, has already created on this Earth for us to learn from. The harmonizing ingredients of nature – when we are in harmony with nature, we move in a way that binds, mends and creates. Strength flows from this harmony, use it for the purpose of something good. There is no strength in beating a defeated person. There are scores of generals who won battles and, in turn, wars, without having to order an attack. The mere fact of having the advantage – of troops, territory or technology – was enough to prevent senseless destruction. There is no glory in putting down a defeated person, or a person who is shorthanded.

Also.

Surrendering small wants and needs, small opinions and the gratification of ego by retreating from a battlefront that serves no purpose... isn't accepting defeat.

Because it's not always harmless.

The younger friend who had been jumped outside his home had just received a new vehicle as a gift. He was supposed to pick me up when I was to be released in August of 2008.

The wounds from Sukhvir passing on 6 months earlier weren't even fully explored yet, let alone near healing or healed, and then this happened. At a personal level, it helped me spiral a little more. I continued to tumble out of control, becoming more and more lost. Scanning back over the years that have passed, I don't know where all the years went. I didn't know what path I was headed down. I don't know how many paths I interrupted. I have lost count of how many times I could have given different advice to someone around me.

The path did lead me here, though.

A friend of mine, an older homie when I was in high school, almost slapped me in the parking lot of Rick Hansen Secondary (in Abbotsford, Canada) when I said I wanted to hustle. I was in grade 10. Stay in school, he said. Get good grades. Don't be a fool. Look at the 100 idiots around you, don't bother with them. A few years from now, if you want to hustle, then do it, but remember this shit isn't cool, and it doesn't last. You're just a kid, learn something useful first. OK, I said.

He was gunned down that same year.

A lot changed. But that advice – take that advice. The power and wisdom in the advice doesn't change. He was a G. And he knew what he was talking about. I just didn't realize it till now, how much he was really looking out for me.

H. Bassi was his name.

Forever and always in the hearts of his loved ones. But another memory at a very young age, too. Too soon, much too soon. All these years later I realize that... even if I had wanted to hustle, I didn't have to be so loud about it. I didn't have to take certain steps. I didn't have to be so loud and attract attention.

I could have been the quiet one.

I went looking for security from those who never had my best interests at heart. They didn't have any good intentions for me at all, actually. They saw a young kid willing to step up, and that kid became an expendable resource. I strayed from home, from the ones that would lay down their lives, and step in front of a moving train to save me. I opted to spend my time and put my trust in those that would throw me in front of that moving train if it would save them.

Does that make any sense to you?

I was moving too fast. Unable to see the blaring signs whizzing by. I strayed. But. If *you* just slow down a little and remind yourself what truly matters, and why it matters – you won't stray too far. You won't fall down as hard, or maybe as many times as I did. By all means, explore and enjoy life... but explore it in a way that brings you, and those around you, joy. Keep in mind the things that matter to you. Don't exchange the things that mean something to you deep down for the things that will tear you away from what truly matters to you.

And, remember you're on the front lines every day – don't forget that.

Every environment you venture into, you put yourself on the frontline in some way. There is no way to avoid it. Any moment you're exchanging energy with someone else, you have the ability to make a difference. Be aware of your impact.

Awareness.

Awareness.

Awareness.

How you talk to others, what you say to them, why you say it to them, has in it the potential to build or destroy. It has the power to heal and mend or hurt and cause pain. It has the power to help steer the course of their life through life-changing turns.

Help someone up if they fall. Those exchanges of energy will never be forgotten. Be the bigger person in situations and the reward of that energy returned will be... limitless.

Years ago I self-destructed. Very slowly. I took everyone around me and everything that was connected to me, to a point of complete anni-hilation. Through it all the one that endured the most was my then-girlfriend (yup that would be Bubu).

This girl stood with me. She didn't pull away. She stayed shoulder-to-shoulder to keep me from falling over. I behaved in a manner towards her I could never have thought possible – until I had done it, that is. I said things that felt gross when I reflected on the words later. I kept shoving all the negativity towards her, but she stood by me. She was aware of what I was doing to her. She was aware that I was pulling her apart slowly too. She was the bigger person, though. She was the better person. She cared. I was mangled and a wreck and clearly not right in the head.

I was a mess.

She understood that we had lost loved ones, one after another – in May, then June 2013 – and that the after-effects hadn't fully been felt, yet. It is... different adjusting to such drastic change when you're locked up, especially when it involves... loss. She made sure I could stay standing before she pulled away. She didn't just let me drop. Her quality of awareness wouldn't let her be that type of person – that leaves a loved one hanging. That brings an attitude of indifference towards another human being in the face of suffering. No, she relied on her inner strengths, led with her heart and kept her resolve to see me through the hard times, letting herself be destroyed in the process. Oh, she came apart too, brick-by-brick. Then she moved to Australia to put herself back together.

But.

What has come of it since is... Love. Joy. Care. Laughter. For the friendship will last forever and it matters not if we even speak to each other again, we will forever have that bond. We will always have that energy we shared. And that's what matters.

Difference made.

I am not saying stick it out with your bf or gf. I am saying take a moment to reflect and be there for one another, especially through the hard times. Be there for your friends. Be there for your loved ones. Don't just let them fall. Do what you can without letting it destroy you, but if you know you can put yourself back together, difficult as it may be, and know that the other person may not have it as easy as you... then be there.

Be the better person.

If you are aware, you will know your limits. You'll know how much you can take before it affects you for the worst. Keep your eyes on your own path and be mindful of the steps you take, is all. The journey is unfolding and *you* have the power to take it where you really want it to go. Deep down you know where you want to go. Where you want to be. If you be still, you'll hear it.

And then.

Then that destination, that purpose beckoning you, will become energized and, like magic – it will pull you toward it. The seeker who seeks will be attracted by that which is sought. And then it is that which is sought which has actually found – and is drawing in – the seeker. Said something similar, did Mr. David Hawkins. Fitting words.

Attraction.

Create a feeling of optimism for those around you. Create the energy of Love and care for those around you. Create feelings of empathy and recognize when someone is in need. The simplest gesture could change someone's life. It could, in turn, maybe change yours. Be the quiet one. Smile while you do it and look around you, for you can take your path anywhere you want to.

Just go for it.

CHAPTER 16

REMEMBERING WHAT BEING BRAVE MEANS

Fear Not.
Frighten Not.

———————

Pai kahu kao dait nai.
Nai pai manat aan.

—Guru Tegh Bahadur
9th Divine Master, Sikh Faith

W hat does being brave mean to you?

Do you identify with the word "tough"? How? I think at times we misconstrue what being tough means. When the idea is misconstrued, it becomes something else entirely. Something that is, actually, weakness. I think we constantly find ourselves in situations where we are trying to prove ourselves worthy, to look worthy in front of others, and when broken down – it is a mechanism utilized to exist and even, feel relevant.

At what cost, though?

Some set out to prove themselves, or to show others they have what it takes; these others they might not even know, and they may hold no personal significance for them on, say, a fun night out.

Does that make any sense?

Isn't going out about having a good time and enjoying the company of others? Maybe sharing moments with strangers in a connecting way? Isn't strength best displayed through attributes and character? Why does a fun night out, in the blink of a moment, have to turn into something dangerous? When does it end?

When do we grow up?

We wouldn't all be here today if it weren't for the real bravery of those who stood up as one to fight to keep generations to come – alive. They stood up as one, because it was the right thing to do, they knew they had to fight, and for all the right reasons. It is needed today. Raw courage. Humble leadership. Gentle yet veracious fire in leaders.

I would like to share a piece of history, which is a source of strength for Sikhs worldwide, yes, but also Muslims, Hindus and those who have an appreciation of what unfolded in Delhi, India, years ago.

Guru Gobind Singh Ji, 10th Guru and Leader of The Sikh Faith, had 4 sons. The 2 youngest were put to the test by a ruler in the Mughal Empire who was in direct opposition to the Guru Ji in the early 1700s.

The children, aged 7 and 9, along with their grandmother (Matha Gujri), were handed over to the local authorities by a trusted member of the Guru's family for a bounty, as well as a bag of jewels swiped off the grandmother by the same person. While in captivity, they were kept in a cold room at the top of a tower. Both location and setting were deliberate and were meant to break the will of the children and the grandmother. The ruler felt he had gained an advantage, having captured the children and grandmother of Guru Gobind Singh Ji, and believed that once he had broken them he would inch towards total victory.

The Guru Ji's opponent summoned the children. As they entered, they showed their contempt by entering the ruler's court feet first – a sign of straight disrespect at that time. The ruler had ordered a small door to be made for them to enter through, the idea being that, when the children entered, they would be forced to bow their heads. So much for his first attempt at displaying his superiority to the spectators who had filled his court. Then the children ignored the customs by which the ruler was greeted and spoken to, by opening up their communication with a spirit-filled Fateh,[1] which filled the ears of those present with the sound that was already driving the ruler insane. They ignored the warnings from those who voiced their disapproval of their actions thus far towards their ruler.

The children were requested – and then told – to convert to the Mughal ruler's idea of Islam, and enjoy splendour – denounce the Sikh faith, its traditions, and take up refuge in the comfort of the ruler's kingdom (no capitals here).

No thanks, said the boys.

They were told they would be given lavish riches, sparkling jewels, any and all luxuries and comforts. They were promised beautiful women beyond imagination. All they had to do was denounce Sikhi and convert to the ruler's idea of religion. All they had to do was let go of the beliefs that were instilled in them, and take up new beliefs. All they had to do was take off their uniform and put on clothes more suited to the surrounding tradition and culture.

Nah.

They were told they would suffer the same fate as their older brothers if they didn't comply. The ruler thought news of their older brothers falling in battle would shake them. The boys didn't even know they had passed on from this physical world. The ruler thought it would sap the lively radiance out of their soul.

It didn't.

Their courage grew. Their confidence grew. We want to join them, they told the ruler, not in death, but in spirit – literally. They were given ultimatums: convert or perish. But they held steady. The children said, we don't fear death and we don't fear you. The ruler told them they had the night to think things over. They told him, we are the sons of Guru Gobind Singh.

Zoravar Singh and Fateh Singh are our names.

On the final day of summoning, the children were asked to reconsider their position. The ruler, having took a beating to his pride in front of a packed crowd, brought his ultimatums down a few notches, hoping he could save face, and lessened the intensity of his demands.

Negotiation tactics, right.

Just give up your faith, take off your uniforms and we will figure out the rest. You will get to keep your lives. He tried coddling them with words, telling them that they were too young to realize what the consequences of their actions would bring them. Just let go of this Sikhi and everything else will work itself out. This road you are trying to stick to will only lead to one place.

Zoravar Singh said, we are going to preserve this Sikhi faith soobayah (mughal ruler) by giving up our lives here. You try to entice us? Then you try to force us? Don't consider us some little children. We are soldiers of the Sikh faith, and we understand very clearly what you're implying and where this road leads. We don't fear death, you don't scare us, and today, we will stand tall like our grandfather did. The world will condemn you, and will never forget what you did here. Our lives will be sacrificed, not lost, we will live for eternity through our faith. We will be remembered as our grandfather, Guru Tegh Bahadur, was. Why would we give up our faith anyway, when our grandfather sacrificed his own life while defending a neighbouring faith? they asked the ruler.

Guru Tegh Bahadur Sahib Ji, 9th Guru of the Sikh Faith, father of Guru Gobind Singh Ji, had been beheaded (on 11 November 1675) while standing up for the rights of fellow beings to practise the religion they believed in. He also refused to convert, or perform miracles. He had *given* his head rather, it wasn't taken. He gave it because the energy released from that exchange fortified the foundational blueprint on which the Sikh faith stands today. The likes of Guru Tegh Bahadur Sahib Ji saw what the moments to come would bring. Colour. Love.

Strength.

His 9-year-old son, Gobind Rai, the one who would become Guru Gobind Singh Ji, had been the one to ask: who better to stand up and sacrifice his life for a faith than the leader of a faith whose philosophy is to stand up to tyrants and the injustice they spread? This sacrifice solidified the emerging Sikhi faith as a faith that was here to stay, and with it, the creation of the Khalsa Panth moved one step closer to manifestation.

Deep, hey? Yes, deep roots.

The children were then asked, what they would do if they were released? They said, we will raise an army and break down the walls of tyrants like you.

Blasphemy! said some of the ruler's trusted men. Blasphemy! said the ruler. The Qazi (a magister and judge) suggested that the most severe punishment should be dealt out to these boys. Others present agreed.

So did the ruler. A death sentence was announced, to be carried out the next day. Death by being bricked in alive – death by suffocation. The ruler turned to a warrior in his court, and asked him to take on the honor of the sentence. The ruler said, here, avenge your fallen brother, and carry out the sentence.

The Muslim warrior said no.

He said, my brother fell on the battlefield. But this here, is haram (that which is forbidden in Islam), Allah does not approve of this, because killing them here, for any reason, is murder. And it would be the murder of two innocent boys whose only crime, it seems, is that they are the sons of the Guru Gobind Singh. Should there be a time when I meet their father on the field, I will challenge him. This here, however, I cannot and will not do.

The Muslim warrior made a plea to Allah for the Mughal ruler to see his actions for what they were.

Back in the tower, the children and their grandmother shared the cold cell, filling it with warmth and the energy that radiated amongst them. Warmth of love, energy of strength, courage, will, and glowing souls. A glow that shone brighter and brighter as the new day loomed closer. That is what happens when Consciousness is starting to make the transition. With beings of heightened awareness, anyway. Their souls glow and that is the Light that is reflected back into humanity.

A Light that affects humanity for the better.

Grandmothers and mothers ready their children for weddings, when the time comes. They prepare them for the journey ahead with all the advice, love and care they can pass on.

This grandmother readied the young boys too. She dressed them for a wedding, but this wasn't going to be the conventional celebration of bliss between two lovers uniting paths. Her words weren't about looking ahead to the years to come and the family you will build one day. Instead, the message was... don't sway, young boys.

The world is watching.

In the years to come, the children of this faith will look back at what you did, and your resolve will stand as the testament of this family's strength. The Sikhi family and all its relatives.

So stand tall, young ones.

That day, after refusing the Mughal ruler one last time, the children were buried alive while standing. Literally boxed in with four brick walls raised around them, in open view so the town's people could watch it happen. The older brother looked down at the younger brother as the wall rose around him, with a tear in his eye. The younger brother looked up and asked, why the tears? You're not losing resolve, are you? You're not faltering, are you?

No.

Never falter, echoed the older brother. He smiled and said that he came into this world first, yet he would have to see his younger brother leave in the name of sacrifice before him. He would have to wait his turn, as the wall would take longer to enclose around him. I came into this world first, and should have left first – that is all, brother.

They were bricked in alive by two individuals awaiting execution for sinister crimes committed – who were then pardoned. The ruler had ignored the advice of his close counsel, and chosen to bury the two boys. He ignored the advice of spiritual and religious advisors who told him that what he was doing was not only wrong, but was strictly forbidden in the Koran (Islamic religion scriptures and life guide). Nowhere is the murder of two young boys deemed acceptable or redeemable.

They are *children*.

As the young warriors, one by one, took their last breath, and the light of life moved on from their bodies, completing the cycle of life and the purpose instilled within their souls – so did the grandmother.

This sacrifice is where many beings derive their strength from, their energy of courage, in times of need. There have been moments in my life when I wish I had shown more courage. I was becoming disconnected, though, and that disconnection drove me further and further from the root that held a blueprint of courage I could rely on.

I forgot.

I had neglected to remember the warrior history that is the backbone of the Sikh faith. Neglected to remember the tales of warriors stepping into battle. Tales of young warriors stepping up to meet the challenges of past times. Tales of mothers who looked on while their children were tortured and put to the sword – tests of will. Tales of soldiers staying true to a code, who did what they had to do, never losing sight of the good.

As a young child, when I listened to the history, listened to the cultural music, it used to make me heat up inside, like a fire. This is the culture from which my blood flows. One aspect of it anyway. I forgot it all, it seemed. Forgot the principles there were instilled within me at a young age, forgot the lessons I was meant to absorb through stories that portrayed examples of will, courage and... goodness. And then I realized one day that I hadn't forgotten, just veered off course. It was still a part of me. I had become a little lost, is all. But, I am remembering.

I am remembering, and that's what matters.

Those two children had a quality of character deeply rooted in a strength imbedded in non-negotiable principles. Those two children had a quality of character developed as a product of their environment. They absorbed the energy around them because that is what happens. We absorb the energy around us and it comes to take meaning in our experience in a unique language, and we then apply it in unique ways. Those two possessed a quality of leadership that didn't crack, paving the way for not only the entire Sikh faith to remain alive, but the Khalsa's identity to stay intact. The footsteps they left behind left permanent imprints of a type of strength that is much needed today, here and now in many corners of the world.

Zoravar Singh and Fateh Singh – names that will always be remembered.

Let's be the ones to spread the colour of that strength, the will of that courage, and the harmony of that inner balance everywhere we go. Love is indeed all we need. Because that is what they had at the root of it all. Love.

That is what being brave is—

—the ability to react to situations that challenge us with the only fire needed to put out the cold ways of the ego – Love. What I was reminded of was: maybe it is foolish to think that a punch should be answered with a punch. Maybe it isn't about puffing out our chests to portray strength, but more about keeping our eyes lowered, words genuine, thoughts loving, and attitude humble. Maybe it isn't about pushing force outwards, but absorbing lashes to the ego and even body, letting them transform into a completely different type of Power. The Imam (Islamic Teacher) here at Mountain Institution suggested recently (28 January 2020, to be exact) that the test is in whether or not you can take someone's harsh words, or aggression, without reacting to it with the same counter force – that always stems from low awareness. Will you be able to ask Allah to grant the aggressor guidance or bless the aggressor with love?

That is the real question, my brothers, he said.

I was instructed to make revisions by a God-sent editor. Ironic that this chapter is ending with words from an Imam, after the Sikhi story of the two young boys shared earlier. When you strip everything away, those words emanate from the truth at the core of – him, me, and you as well. Let's remember that we're all here to help one another along this journey of life – together.

Look for that truth in yourself. I guarantee you will find it. It will not hide from you, though you may find *you* have been hiding from *it* for a while.

Be bold. Be brave. Be true.

---

1. Fateh – A customary greeting, established by the 10th Guru himself. "Waheguru Ji Ka Khalsa, Waheguru Ji Ki Fateh". It translates literally as "Khalsa belongs to Waheguru. Victory belongs to Waheguru". Waheguru means wonderful God. Source Energy. Supreme Energy.

CHAPTER 17

THE STORY IN SHORT PART 2

The Immaculate, the Manifest and Omnipotent,
Bestower of Eminence and universally present.
The Gracious Bestower, the Supernal Nourisher,
The Compassionate Being and universal Provider.

———————

Jahan pak zabarast o zahir zahur,
Atha mai dihad humchu hazir hazur.
Ataa bakhsh o pak parvardigar,
Rahim ast o rozi dihe har diyar.

—Guru Gobind Singh
Zafarnamah
(The Epistle of Victory)

A ll through my early years I was being primed to be a young Singh – a "lion" and a warrior.

I was expected to be an obedient boy. I was obedient, and I believed in everything that was being engraved in me. I believed blindly in the Sikh faith, because I trusted the sources I was learning it from. My mum was a major influence, because she was the one who was at home with me. She was the one injecting Sikh culture into me, and she was the one I was always trying to please. Something from within said I couldn't let her down – because I was afraid that I might. I had the feeling that I wasn't good enough, and this made me go "above and beyond" to get her praise. And when I got it, I became accustomed to it, and so that need for praise took root. As the years unfolded, praise became more and more important to me.

The need for praise later turned into the need for recognition.

Didn't have a TV with any cable till around age 10. Any chance I got at watching TV, either at a friend's or family member's home, I took full advantage of. It was like... *The Matrix* effect. I was soaking up everything I was seeing. Why was it being kept from me? I thought.

A lot didn't make sense when I was a kid. There was a huge gap between the world my mum grew up in – a village in Punjab – and the culture and teachings I was being exposed to in school. A distance between me and mum was beginning to grow, even then, in early elementary. Communication was a little easier with my father. He grew up in India too, but knew the hustle and bustle of the city, went to college and had earned his engineering degree. When he arrived in Canada, he hit the ground running. He could speak English, and got better at it as he went. I have seen surprised faces when he has responded back without any accent. It wasn't as easy for my mother. I could see, even then, that she was struggling, and I wasn't about to say anything. I was trying to make sense of the Indian-Punjabi-Sikhi life culture, and to reconcile it with what I was seeing around me. The two didn't fit with one another. How could I make them fit? Would I have to... juggle personalities? Yup. Would I have to compartmentalize my life? Yup. And so the secret worlds began.

Umm...

I didn't feel like I had to prove myself to my father in the same manner. Something said to me that I couldn't let him down – as long as I didn't hurt him, he would never be disappointed in me. I did want to prove to him that I could excel at sports and be smart. My father spent as many waking hours as he could at work. If there was something that could be done today, then it wasn't about to be left till tomorrow. Many days I would only see him right before falling asleep. Other days I would fall asleep as he was getting home – "now that I know he is home and safe, I can go to sleep". When he told me stories of Sikh lore, history, and the world in general, I absorbed everything. To me he was the smartest, strongest and bravest person, and I wanted to be like him.

But, then again, I sometimes thought, what if my father didn't know everything about this world?

I would have to go find out for myself.

I attended Punjabi School (as I mentioned earlier). The school's name was Maharaja Dalip Singh Education Center, named after the last Prince of Punjab – Maharaja Dalip Singh. He was the son of the last ruling king, Sher-e-Punjab (Lion of Punjab), Maharaja Ranjit Singh. I did well at Punjabi school. I also caused a ruckus in class, but I scored high marks and was able to set a couple of records – I nabbed a few trophies for performing well in studies, and in mental competitions (sitting cross-legged without moving for long periods of time) at the yearly graduation ceremonies. It takes real focus to sit in a cross-legged position and not move at all, 60 minutes into the competition. Yup. That means ignoring all itches and scratches – or flies, for that matter. Smacks from a stick at home ensured I performed well, and smacks from sticks in class kept me quiet (for the most part). Deep down I wanted to be involved in my culture and religion, and when the opportunity came for me to participate with a group that had travelled from India to perform and hold lectures, I jumped on it.

It was common for groups to travel from India to perform, but the method this group used and the following they attracted was out of the ordinary. This group was unique. Typically, we were used to seeing a team of 3 on stage, the norm for a kirtan jatha.[1] There would be 2 harmonium players and 1 tabla player. The leader or head kirtani usually sat in the middle playing a harmonium, the second harmonium player to his right and the tabla player to his left. The kirtanis usually wore matching attire, a Turban, kurdtha pajamas, and matching Kirpan gatras.

This group however, had between 5 and 8 members. The leader sat to the side, at the edge of the stage, flanked by the rest of his group. There was one dhol player who sat relatively close to the head of the group, and then around 4 to 6 chimta players.[2] The leader of the group was usually called a 'sant' (saint) and that had a lot to do with the way he was regarded, by not only his team, but the public at large. Instead of the conventional Turbans (a pointy one with the hint of second colour revealed at the front of the forehead), they wore one colour and they were rounded. To me they looked like 'saint-soldiers', guys I had heard so much of in Sikh stories, books and lectures, seen in pictures and videos, and even from my mum – I idolized them. Jarnail Singh Ji – a leader amongst Sikh warriors, dubbed an extremist by a biased and tainted Indian government – was a saint-soldier. I had seen pictures and videos growing up, and now here was a group who resembled saint-soldiers in what looked like every fashion.

I wanted to be a saint-soldier too.

I was allowed to play a chimta, first in front of the stage and then on stage with them. I felt special. Not only that; I began to be treated differently by the Punjabi community. So did my mum. Wherever she went in the city, she was asked: *Isn't that your son?* She would answer, with pride: *Yes, that is my son.* I wanted to perfect playing the chimta, so I practised again and again at home. I had a small chimta, though, and it made a different sound then the heavier and lankier ones the performers used. So, once I got the hang of it, the group – who were visiting for a month – gave me one of theirs. Woohoo! They held private sessions in people's homes, and since they had limited time, it became a privilege to have them attend your home. The leader was regarded as a saint too, so that heightened the... blessings when they attended your home. I eventually began joining them for their home visits. It was an intrusion to my mum's schedules, but how could she say no? This is sort of what she wanted, and here I was doing the dutiful thing. She obliged. Sometimes she had to leave me in the care of the group and I was all for it, because I got to spend time away from home (I was always running away from home anyway – not cool).

I was on track to performing with the group across Canada and maybe even India – but a couple of experiences eliminated that possibility.

At a private home performance, the dhol player of the group cornered me in a room and tried to undo my nala – the drawstring that holds the kashera in place.[3] If it wasn't for not knowing how to tie it properly – I was scolded for again and again making the knot impossible to untie – the incident could have been much more than a failed sexual advance.

I was able to get away and hide in the bathroom.

I forgot how long I hid, but I remember clutching my kirpan tightly in my hand and reciting Chaupai Sahib again and again, trying to figure out how I was going to get out of there unharmed.[4] I remember pressing the blade against my face with the sinking feeling that it wasn't going to be of much use – it was dull. I would have to hit him in the eye if I wanted to hurt him enough to deter another advance. I knew I could probably make it to the front door, but I wouldn't know where to go. A knock and a voice at the door from the lady whose home it was, made me quickly open the door and run into her arms and tell her I wasn't feeling well.

That day affected me forever. What must it be like for someone who goes through unimaginable trauma related to being a victim of unwanted sexual or predatory advances? Especially from someone who is in a position of trust, someone guardians and parents feel secure and confident leaving their children in the care of?

How did it affect me?

From that day on, I made it a point to know where I was and how I was going to get out of there. I cannot stop myself taking note of the exits when I walk into a place. It happens automatically. I have seen friends go from being completely comfortable to nervous and jittery, because they catch a glimpse of my eyes scanning the area and memorizing the layout.

What to tell them?

One of the group's members tried to reassure me that the other guy wouldn't have done anything to me, and that nothing of this sort would ever happen again. I wanted to trust him, but I knew he was just saying words to calm me down.

The damage was done.

After this, I began to see that the leader of the group was condoning idol worship, of himself included. He was also manipulating the minds of the vulnerable – mainly women's, behind closed doors. Allowing heads and hands to touch his feet for blessings, and his calves to be grasped in the "save me, save me" plea. Either others ignored it, or they were just ignorant in general. Whatever the case, I could not ignore it once I had seen it.

When I saw the lie in those who were furthering the voice of Sikh culture and religion... and especially in anyone regarded as a "saint"... it rocked my reality. When I contemplated what I had seen – the gap between what this saint was saying and doing – it made me question other preachers and so-called saints. A story my mum use to tell me, involving Jarnail Singh Bhindrinwale, would always ring off in my head (he was dubbed a terrorist by the Indian government). She said that ladies and others were trying to get through the barrage of soldiers to touch his feet and be blessed by him, and he put his feet in mud, saying here, kiss them now. Touch them now. He bluntly told them, if any head bows, it should be to Guru Granth Sahib.

I was a young and naïve kid, sure, but not stupid. I saw the violations taking place, and there was no way to escape the after-effects of that raw... exposure. I revolted against it. I was told to be obedient to... a lie; by those who had no right to be telling anyone to be obedient. I knew without a doubt that if one of the warriors from the previous generations were around today, like Bhai Mani Singh or Baba Deep Singh, they would resort to chopping off at least a few hands – if not heads.

Extreme?

Idol worship was forbidden, but I have come to realize that, in many ways, we were being groomed for idol worship through what was being taught to us, and how it was being taught. For example: we were told, here is a picture of Guru Nanak, the founder of Sikhism – and then we saw our teachers and elders bowing to these pictures, whether it was in the langar hall, or anywhere – will this behaviour, then, not be mimicked by their pupils and children? The reality of it is: here is the *Mool Mantar* (basic belief – the first teaching) composed by Guru Nanak. The teachings: they are the Guru, not pictures meant to depict the First Divine Guru and founder of Sikhism. Art is enjoyable, but don't mistake it for anything more than that, because it isn't.

> The Bani is the Guru, the Guru is the Bani.
> (Bani Guru, Guru hai Bani.)
>
> **—Guru Granth Sahib**

The truth and power of the Guru and the teachings are centered on the Supremacy of the Word. Because it is said that the Word came from On High and is the Universal Teacher. Meant to spark, instill and promote the inner connection with the Formless One God. Kirtan is a medium. Not a picture.[5] A picture becomes the idea of a medium, and the loyalty and reliance is divided or reduced to something that is... what exactly? Perhaps it was done unintentionally by those who were sleeping (unaware) themselves, but that doesn't matter. I myself also only realized recently that, in many ways, we were being groomed to idol worship Guru Granth Sahib Ji too.

How?

Through the importance given to the rituals, the adorning of the scriptures, and even directing ardaas to Guru Granth Sahib.[6] Guru Nanak took steps (he walked all over India and even into China) to help spark beings' awareness levels to make a jump. He revealed the absurdity of idol worship and used the Supremacy of the Word to trigger realizations, awakenings and the attainment of higher realities for a nation in the thick of kal-yug (dark age).

The fact that expressions of idol worship wasn't exposed way back then at a mass scale when the Indian, Punjabi and Sikhi communities were very intimately connected to one another, and connected without all the differences that started to surface over small wants and opinions, is something that can be corrected today.[7]

How do we expect the younger generation to get along when they see the divide and pettiness present?

My interest in following the group waned. The leader was faulty, and I had almost been taken advantage of by someone I looked up to as an older brother. But before I left, my eyes turned toward the piles of money that was "donated" for "Godly services" performed.

I became a thief.

The money allowed me to buy as many chocolate bars as I wanted. By grade 8 (age 13), I was a fully-fledged thief. And when the travelling group left, my stealing moved onto to other targets. Trips to the corner stores turned into standing in line for tater tots and French fries from the high school cafeteria, and candy from vending machines. Abbotsford Junior – Home of the Huskies – whoop whoop! It did feel cool to be able to buy things when others couldn't. I began to garner attention, like: *Yo... this guy is up to something.* And so it had begun.

The creation of this "other-guy".

On reflection, I didn't openly revolt against the lie I saw in those I had been taught to look up to. It was a silent attack. It was better to remain meek, passive. I was just a kid, I couldn't hold my own, not yet, and I was just beginning to learn how to manipulate things in my favor. I looked harmless, but, I was becoming dangerous. I realize now that I was becoming dangerous not only to myself, but to everyone around me.

After so much disappointment at the hands of teachers, elders and self-appointed spiritual leaders, I had to look to create my own ideals. If leaders were out for themselves, and they were willing to walk over innocents to do it, then it was follow the herd or try to carve your own way in the world. I thought I could carve a way that wouldn't trample over innocents. But I caused more hurt, pain and... carnage then I could have imagined.

Back then I also knew I needed a filter. A moral code. Why? Because I feared the wrath of God. It is not that I didn't think God was there, it was more: what will God let me get away with, and if he lets me get away with it, what am I going to do to make up for it? I kept in mind the Sikh history my mum taught me, and what I got from it was... do not steal from an innocent person. Do not hurt an innocent person. Do not take advantage of an innocent person. Never be the aggressor or cause harm to a humble and saintly soul. So, I made promises that I wouldn't do a good person wrong. If you preached one thing but did another, then you were just an imposter and a hypocrite, you didn't qualify as "good". If you were putting forward an image, preaching values and merits to go along with the image, but you were a fraud...

then I was going to turn you into a mark. If you put yourself forward as a friend, but your actions were showing me you weren't, then I was going to take advantage of you. If you felt you had a right to take advantage of me, then I had every right to do it to you.

I thought I could navigate the toughest of terrains – I was wrong.

I also thought it OK to steal if I thought you could afford it, and not notice it; this is how I first really hurt my family.

I stole from my aunt. So low. I know. And, I miss her.

I stole from her when I was a kid, and then, when the walls were closing in, I tried to divert suspicion to another family member – *I know... not cool.* Don't worry, I got dealt with right quick – *believe that* (Martin Lawrence's tone from movie *Blue Streak*). My aunt had also been like a second mother to me, and as a baby I was always running into her arms for comfort. Um yes, despite the many years that have passed, I can still recall remnants of that lingering feeling. She introduced me to scrambled eggs... Ummm... wait, I meant to say Yum. Mum, if and when you are told this – sorry. I take full blame. I loved eating the eggs she made.

Also, on a side note, while at OCC in 2017, I wasn't in a healthy state. I had a major surgery to my stomach, the reversal of a colostomy. A large skin graft had to be removed from my stomach, which was serving as my abdomen wall. The graft was temporarily serving as the outer skin of my stomach, holding my midsection together since February 2013. The graft was removed and my abdomen closed back up, *after* reconnecting the colon back to its regular functioning spot – down low. It was a surgery that happened on my 30th "birthdate" (think about it, it's just a similar date, not the actual day, right?) 28 March.

Signs and gifts from the Universe.

The chaplain at OCC expressed concern about my overall health. I told her I wasn't getting enough protein and that I couldn't rely on beans, lentils and chickpeas again and again, it was too hard on my intestines. They were irritating them to the point where I was feeling more and more sick, not wanting to eat, which contributed to the... unwell feeling, and the underweight physical state. She asked me if I was eating eggs, and I said I have, but I am not eating them at this time. Why not? I am a vegetarian, I said, I cannot eat another life form. She said that she lived on a farm growing up and could say for certain that the eggs supplied to this jail had no chance for life.

Huh?

She said, because the rooster never comes in contact with the hen, there is no chance for the life spark to enter the egg. The hen will lay eggs regardless, so you're not eating an alive or dead animal. It is neither. It isn't meat. To this day I hold this to be true. If it is other-wise, please let me know. Recently read translations of Gurbani, particularly Guru Nanak, some of which said, there is life in plants and water, led me to realize that the argument of not eating another "life form" no longer stands. I do not eat meat, though.

Where were we? Oh yes, aunt and the stealing.

Stealing from my aunt left me feeling shameful and guilty for a long time, and... I had damaged not only the trust between her and me, but the rest of the family too. My dad was pretty hurt by it. He couldn't understand how I could steal from her. He could get past me stealing from him, but her? He didn't talk to me properly for a very long time. I had royally messed up.

Oh.

Yes. I stole from my dad. I was in grade 6 or 7 (age 10-11) when I did. I had gotten accustomed to having upwards of a few hundred dollars in my pocket, by stealing from the money donated to the group I had been performing with; the itch to always have money and this feeling of needing to have money had begun.

I remember the day I started stealing from my dad. I wanted to treat my friends to a good time at Wonderland, a local amusement park, and eat with them afterwards. I had some money, but I wanted more, just in case, plus I needed to make sure I could afford a taxi. I knew my father would have *some* money, but when I saw the amount he had in his pocket, it left me confused. I was hesitant to take more than I needed, so I took a little bit. I think it was a couple of 20s. At this point in life, my father would buy a few cars that needed to be fixed up, and then sell them for a profit (handy-man that he is). He had just sold one. I thought we were rich, and his optimistic attitude convinced me that the days of struggling to pay bills were over. I don't know in what world I thought it justified stealing money from him, but in my head I had convinced myself that I wasn't stealing, just borrowing, and when I had money, I would give it all back to him. I couldn't tell him that I had taken the money, obviously, but somehow I would get it back to him.

So yes, I knew it was wrong.

How it made me feel when I was with my friends, was and is precisely the inner dysfunctional need to feel "accepted" and to "belong" – regarded as someone important – that would come back to haunt me. That feeling drove me to steal from him again and again. I went from taking a few 20s to thinking, hmm... if I took a 50 or a 100, it is less bills, he won't notice, and in this manner, I won't have to do it so often.

Dumb kid.

Have to call it the way it is. I could no longer support myself through stealing from the group – they had left and were continuing on with their tour. I guess I ignored the fact that my father could count the money and tell that he was short. The day he found out, he came to pick me up from school. I was sitting in class enjoying myself, immersed in the role of my "other-guy" identity, when something made me look to the right, towards the door (usually left open); the hallway parents usually waited in for their children to finish class. I don't know what it was that made me look at the door, but something did (now I know it was energy that made me look), and one sight of my father told me something was wrong.

Very wrong. Gulp.

To this day I remember his expression and his attire. He was wearing a long coat, might have even been the fancy London Fog coat that had been gifted to him (by whom I do not recall), and it covered him almost to his toes. The expression he had set on his face… was… one that had me making up every excuse to delay getting into that hallway.

My father has only hit me once in my life.

That day he didn't say anything to me but drove me to his place of work. I had tried conversing with him, but I hadn't gotten much of a response. Finally, when we were in his work bay (where he fixed and re-painted cars), he said he was going to ask me one time and he hoped that I would tell the truth. I knew right away that I had messed up bad. As his belt was coming off, my head turned into a garble of a mess. Nothing came out. No words came out of my mouth. He said he would know if I lied, and this was one of those times when, if a father asks his son a very specific question, it was time to tell the truth. He asked me the question. I forget exactly what words he used. I lied. He hit me.

It knocked me out cold.

I woke up in his arms. I don't recall how long I was out for, maybe 3-5 seconds. Maybe a little longer. He hit me only once. When I woke up I confessed most of it. I wasn't lying at this point, but withholding. I was trying to keep from hurting him further. That is why I couldn't get the words out of my mouth. I had hurt him. I had said to myself that I would never hurt my father, and I had just hurt him in the worst way. I had taken money from his pocket. I had stolen from a dad who was working day and night to not only feed his family, but clothe and provide a better life for them.

I never stole from him again.

The effects of the dysfunctional thinking I was developing lingered with me for a very long time. It wasn't until very recently, through contemplation and self-reflection, that I came to realize why I did certain things. I realized that, while the effects were many and damage uncountable, the cause was incorrect thinking. Dysfunctional thinking patterns. It was unconscious participation (in a sleep-unawareness-state) which was simply expressing ignorance from a place of little-to-no understanding.

I hadn't learned this yet, though.

I needed more money to keep up with this role I was trying to play, especially when grade 8 began. The stealing had to increase, and I would have to find other ways to make money too. So, when the opportunity came to deal in firecrackers, I jumped on it. What I didn't realize back then was that I was being used and manipulated, every step of the way.

I operated on trust.

To this day, family and friends scold me for this trust. I was scolded all through high school by my dad, because he saw through the guys I thought I knew, especially certain older ones. Later in life, my closest friends warned me about blind trust. They said, it is naïve, and it opens up the door for someone to seriously hurt you, because you see only one side of a person, and then you *only* catch onto how someone really is *after* you have been wronged. So when I finally caught bullets to my back from point-blank range (15 January 2013), they didn't hesitate to yell at me and say, *DIDN'T WE TELL YOU? Look at where naïve trust has got you!* Many of those voices are no longer around to tell me anything, they have passed on. Most of them have been shot and killed themselves. I miss them.

A lot.

Not a day goes by that I don't think of them and miss them in some way. But, it is ok. This was part of the journey too. Their memories can be projected in a light that puts forward a healthier exchange of energy. Wouldn't be writing these words today if it weren't for their support, their love, and their encouragement to get us all to a Bollywood stage. Perhaps it will be Hollywood, who knows. Maybe it will be both.

Deep down, I was beginning to hold serious resentment towards my mother for exposing me to the lies I saw in temples and in the characters of those who were selling themselves as religious and cultural icons.

The fact that she was not able to see this for herself made it worse. I began to resent her for her controlling nature and for all the restrictions she had put on me through the years. Just how much I was holding against her wouldn't come to light until July 2016. It was the words of Deepak Chopra that triggered the epiphany (made possible by Giggles).[8] It was during a guided healing meditation. The words were about letting go of grievances.

Grievances… grievances… What's a grievance?

I learned it was a long-standing resentment. Built-up resentment that was being held onto and stored somewhere in the body. For me it got to the point where it became poisonous and corrosive. My body was becoming more and more susceptible to infections, and it led to the forming of a "disease" I was diagnosed with in late 2014. Then, in 2016, I finally realized that it wasn't my mum's fault. It wasn't her fault that I had made certain choices in life – because *I* had made the choices that led me to prison, *not her*. I was responsible for ending up in prison – not her. It wasn't anyone's fault, really.

As soon as I had this realization, I could feel deep acceptance in me, complete forgiveness, and then finally, I could feel the letting go of the energy I had been holding onto inside. This triggered a new phase of healing to unfold, and with the release of this built-up toxic energy, the body moved one step closer to perfect health.

---

1. Kirtan Jatha: artists (jatha) singing Gurbani in praise of God (kirtan); kurdtha pajamas: long-sleeved buttoned top, looks like a dress shirt, usually hangs down to the knees, with a matching pair of ankle-length pants. Looks like an ajkun (worn by males, usually at weddings). Not as decked out as an ajkun, though. A kirpan gatra is a holster for the Kirpan (mini-sword), worn as part of the 'five articles of faith' or five K's by all observing Sikhs.
2. Dhol: produces similar sounds to that of a tabla. Comes in one piece, though, and instead of standing upright like a tabla, sits on its side and is played with two hands, on either side. A chimta is three-quarters of a metre in length. Made of metal. Produces bell and jingle-like sounds.
3. Kashera: long drawers, another of the "five articles" or "5 Ks".
4. Chaupai Sahib: Gurbani written by Guru Gobind Singh Ji. A go-to when asking for protection from the Lord of the Universe.
5. There are no pictures of the Gurus. It is all created in imagination. Anyone who prays to a picture of a Guru is a fool. Also – Guru Granth Sahib Ji is now the Guru. Guru Gobind Singh bowed before Guru Granth Sahib and transferred the Guru-ship along with the lineage of Pontificate to the 11th Final Sikh Guru.
6. Ardaas: supplications and prayers. How one is to walk, what and how much one should donate, how and for how long one is to bow the head, what one is to wear, why one is to ask the guru for something. There is only *One* that can answer any prayer or request: the True Guru – God.
7. Over what is deemed appropriate for Gurdwaras in Canada. There had been much debate, and many things remain unresolved. Fundamentals or moderns. Pangat or dining. Shoes or no shoes. Langar hall or cafeteria. Social gathering or awareness heightening environment.
8. Who is Giggles? We'll get to her shortly. Stay tuned!

CHAPTER 18

LIFE IN PRISON

Maybe the journey isn't so much about becoming anything.
Maybe it's about unbecoming everything that isn't really you,
so you can be who you were meant to be in the first place.

—Paulo Coehlo

How are you enjoying this journey so far? Are you enjoying it? Even if you're only enjoying it a little bit – woohoo! Mission accomplished. I've said quite a bit, haven't I? Getting warmed up we certainly are. Finally! Finally get to just say things and not worry about interruptions. One-way conversations (eheheh). OK. We're switching gears here a little. If it doesn't seem like a smooth transition, well... I am a first-time author. If it does, well... woohoo x2 and thanks to the editor!

So, life in prison.

Hmm... what is it like? Now? It is amazing. It has never been so much fun. And that is exactly what it is. Fun. Is it supposed to be? Yup. Life is meant to be enjoyed. This human experience is meant to be savoured. Isn't it? I think it is.

In this federal environment, post-sentencing, "time" is navigated via a routine. Usually a much-disciplined routine. Wake up early. Stretch the neck out. Stretch the back out. Hit play on the Bose so the low sound of kirtan starts filling the mind with healing and harmonious vibrations. Cold water on the face, then the feet, and sometimes – the body. Have to wake up with a kick. Almost always wake up rested and ready for the day. Wake up even more rested if an early 3-4 a.m. meditation has been enjoyed. No feeling to compare it to. Maybe I shouldn't have mentioned it. Ego said share it. Ahhh the workings of the ego.

Doors are usually buzzed open by 7:20 a.m., at which point one may walk out of the living unit to the kitchen for breakfast. The kitchen is usually a calm and easy-going place. Occasional fight might take place. Most don't qualify as a fight. Not very many stabbings here – medium security and all. Quite a contrast from the max prison that is about 100 feet away from here (Kent Institution). Someone just got airlifted out of there a few days ago. Not here. Nope. Well, it's not like the medivac helicopter has never been called to carry someone off in a hurry from here; because it has. But, you'll get guys putting their head in the soup more times than someone getting shanked up over an uneven oatmeal portion.

The doors stay open for about 8 hours a day. On a weekday the call to school, programs and work usually takes place at 8:30 a.m. You have about 5-10 minutes to get to where you need to be, and it lasts until 10:45 a.m. Lunch is 12:30 p.m. Another call for work, program and school takes place at 1:30-3:45 p.m. We're locked in our rooms (cells) from 4 p.m. until dinner. Dinner call happens between 5 and 5:30 p.m.

Then comes leisure time.

First free movement – where one may go to the gym or yard – takes place at 6:45 p.m., and then again at 7:45 and 8:45 p.m. The call to return to living units takes place at 9:45 p.m., which leaves enough time to shower and grab a bite for the night before making our way into our rooms for the final lock-up at 10:10 p.m. If someone wishes to stay outside the living unit from 6:45-9:45 p.m., it's their choice.

There is also access to a library and chapel sanctuary off the unit in the small yard. The main yard has a full soccer field, a running track, and a baseball diamond with bleachers. The entrance to the gym is also in the main yard. Through the gym one may access the music room, that contains instruments, drums and a few cool (outdated) gadgets. The gym itself has a weight pit (no free weights), a cardio machine section, punching and kicking bags, and a full basketball court. The court floor itself can be turned into an indoor volleyball or soccer ground.

Soccer rocks.[1]

Wherever you choose to go, you will not be able to return to the living unit for at least an hour, as the movements are "controlled", versus "open". The calls for movement, once again, take place at 6:45, 7:45, and 8:45 p.m. The reason for this is a riot that took place about 10 years ago, which left, I believe, at least one person dead. Perhaps the scars haven't been replaced with any sense of... security.

Been a long time, perhaps it is time for a change.

The prison is made up of 4 units (1 of which is currently closed due to renovations) and can house approximately 100 inmates each. A unit itself has 3 separate sections which contain 2 tiers (floors). Each floor is its own designated range. 6 ranges per unit. On the living unit, there is access to phones, fridges, toasters, microwaves, sinks, and laundry machines. One may store food in a fridge and cook it in the microwave. The Mountain Community even has its very own... master chef. He resides on one of the units here. Yup, he is an "inmate". One day the mouth-watering dishes he makes will make their way into some fancy magazine. Oh. And *the cakes*. Wow status. All made with limited ingredients. Frosty's would go out of business if he set up shop next to theirs.[2]

Yup... he is just that good.

Let's see... there are artists with mind-boggling talents here. Just had an Ironman necklace made out of small beads for a young boy in my family that looked like something you would find in a display case at a Marvel convention. I wanted to keep it. Should have. Because it got confiscated. I asked if I could mail it out. Yup, you can. Then I got told that I broke institutional rules. How? Got set up by the staff in visits and correspondence – *duh*. The maliciousness it takes to do such a thing! Where is the kindness, people? Where is the compassion? How exactly did I break the rules? By mailing out something I didn't make and couldn't have made, because I didn't have an art permit for beading, apparently. I was asked if I made it. I said, no sir I did not (and thought, *you think if I could make this I would be sitting in prison?*). Instead of receiving a picture of the necklace around the young boy, I will be getting a letter with a warning to not break rules. 30 hours of effort, attention and time on the part of the artist went into that one piece. It wasn't the only piece of art that got confiscated, either. But that's another story.

Grrrr...

But.

How *was* life in prison? In the provincial system, pre-sentencing?

Hmmm...

Gruelling at one point. Excruciatingly painful and extremely unde-sired. It was treacherous. It was punishment indeed. And we hadn't even been sentenced yet! I guess I was serving a prison sentence while deemed innocent waiting to be proved guilty. Trapped in the mind. Trapped at the level of ego, and mostly just ego. I guess there were rare glimpses of blue skies, but fleeting. And even that may have just been in the form of laughter and momentary happiness due to changes in circumstances.

It was the one place I did not want to be. Prison. I wanted to be free. I wanted to be out and about. I wanted to be beside the ocean and under the sun, not stuck in a grey dungeon. I wanted to be cruising through city streets and hills, not walking up and down grey halls for a court hearing. I wanted to be in a gurdwara and be able to soak up the energy that potently lingers in the atmosphere while kirtan is played or Gurbani recited in the early a.m., not waiting for Saturday to come around so I could hear it on TV. I didn't want to feel trapped or restricted. I wanted to be *free*.

But.

The freedom I was seeking, I would realize as minutes turned into hours, hours into days, and days into months, was not from the walls and locked doors that kept the body cordoned off from the world; it was freedom from the mind and the suffering I was experiencing because of it. I wanted to be free from feeling trapped in a place that at times became claustrophobic, and to be able to enjoy the scent that comes off the sun and the freshness of each inhaled breath. I didn't want to be lost, troubled and confused, but purposeful, at ease, and... free.

The mind had to be conquered.

How does one do that? It seemed impossible. I mean, I had heard of it before, but only as an idea. Certainly not as a pursuit; but I guess it sort of became that without me really realizing it till the journey was well underway. The pursuit of conquering the mind, freeing the spirit, and connecting with the soul.

The being within.

And if it wasn't for the loving presence and friendship of female energy in my experience, I would have been stuck, lost, troubled, and confused. If it weren't for the loving energy injected into my journey from the females in my experience, I wouldn't have been able to understand the difference between light and darkness. I wouldn't have been able to tune out the cold ways of the ego and begin to understand that unconditional love has within it unstoppable energy. That love in itself has within it an immeasurable power.

Unfathomable power.

This life in prison would have been just a dull life, if it weren't for the female influences in my experience; and because of the energy exchanged... it is anything but dull.

Now I am by the ocean and on the beach when I want to be. Now I am at a gurdwara of my choosing when I want to be, and if I concentrate hard enough... I can even feel the buzz that zaps your soul to tune into something very... powerful. Maybe it is a memory of a feeling experienced in earlier years at a kirtan darbar at Dashmesh Darbar, that is tucked away behind a door that can be opened and enjoyed when my vibrational alignment experiences a certain shift.[3] Maybe it isn't and I am experiencing it in real time.

Imagine that.

But. All that is secondary. The fact that this journey has become as enjoyable and tasteful as it has, primary.

I am very grateful for the female influences that have been helping me along this journey (incarceration and spiritual). I don't know where I would be today without their help. Not sitting here in front of this computer writing words in this manner, that is for sure.

In 2013, one female influence wrote out powerful words – the Chaupai Sahib hymn, written by Guru Gobind Singh (10ᵗʰ Master of the Sikh Faith), in hopes the vibrations within it would become a protective barrier around me. She hoped that I would find solace and strength to surpass the challenges that lay ahead on the road to recovery and inner freedom.

I did.

Another female influence would play kirtan over the phone, at times as early as 7:30 a.m. She knew it created a feeling of peace. She knew the importance of starting each day on the right foot, and that there was no better way than to start it relaxed and listening to sounds that carry in them harmonious vibrations. It just so happened that the kirtan she played was the very kirtan my mother used to leave playing in the house. It helped me appreciate what my mother was trying to convey to me in those early years, and to appreciate all that she has done on a deeper level.

Both of these female influences guided me through challenging times. With their support and unconditional love, I was able to navigate rough and uncharted terrain, with the feeling that I could go at it with my eyes closed. The unfolding path started to feel like a familiar one. A path that has been continuously adjusting coordinates in a most welcome way, turning this journey from a gruelling trek, to something that is... unexplainable in words at times.

So, onto the effects of female influences, then.

- Because of the COVID-19 pandemic, the remaining unit at Mountain Institution was opened up to house inmates from a neighbouring institution. The schedules and routines were drastically altered as well. No school or programs. Essential services employment only. To date – May 2020 – there hasn't been a single case here. That is pretty blessed. There is a tireless effort on part of everyone to ensure that the environment stays clean, healthy and outbreak-free. May those who have been affected by this pandemic be blessed with perfect health, comfort and solace. Let us see through to the simplicity of our lives and do our part emitting back energy filled with the power to see this outbreak subdued. Thank you to all frontline beings for keeping essential services rolling. Thank you to the nurses, doctors and health services who have continuously put themselves in the face of this pandemic. May the ones who have loved ones that have passed on, find peace and refuge in their hearts. Thank you to all health services at Mountain Institution for staying vigilant and ever-ready to respond. Together, the impossible says *I'm possible.*

---

1. Messi. Neymar 'cause it's Brazil. And... Ronaldo... well because there is only one Ronaldo.
2. Frosty's – custom cake shop in Langely, BC.
3. Kirtan Darbar: continuous singing (laudation) of Gurbani by multiple beings and, even, kirtan groups. Dashmesh Darbar: gurdwara located in Surrey, BC, Canada.

CHAPTER 19

EFFECTS OF FEMALE INFLUENCES (EOFI)

BUBU

The beauty you see in me, is the beauty in you.
And, so are the flaws.

—Angel B

I met Bubu in the spring of 2011. It was a long time since I had felt deep feelings for someone, and instantly deep too. I have always had a pull towards Spanish music, Spanish food (beans, eggs, cheese, tortilla wraps), and this loving, dancing and chilling on the beach culture that leaves me smiling in observation. We initially met in passing, but... an impression of that encounter lingered and I found myself thinking about her a lot and at random times.

All these years later – I fully believe – that she was thinking about me in those moments too.

One should certainly not judge a book by its cover. She wasn't taken seriously at times. Maybe because of an easy going personality, a big smile and this friendly energy that draws you in. Until you had crossed a line that is. *Uh-oh* for you after that. Because then came a sophisticated reply and a collection of thoughts arranged in neat sentences that might as well have been 2-3 punch combos. I picked the wrong fight at times too, and found myself wondering *why* did I even try to argue with her?

Waheguru.

She was interrogated following my arrest and charges. The approach was to intimidate her and back her into a corner. What did the cop think of her? Not much. A girl who did all the right things, went to the right schools, had the right sort of career, but – hands down – made the wrong selection of boy choice. He thought he could push her around a little bit and then sit back while she told him what he thought she would be able to tell him. We hadn't start dating till a year after the events for which I am charged for had transpired... So, no help there. But, still, being Bubu, she did have some things to say...

What did she say?

He opened my doors for me. He brought me flowers when I didn't ask for them. He brought me ice packs when I was hurt. He says nice things to me...

These things, were not the things he wanted to hear. He got irritated and said, so you're basically saying he was a *gentleman*?! Yes, I am, she said. The interview ended there. Maybe I shouldn't have shared these details. Ego said share it. Ahhh... the workings of the ego.

Her skillset is in paying very detailed attention to an intricate and complicated web of logistics. You think I have ADHD and operate in a weird and un-understandable fashion? It would have taken a team of FBI code analysts to crack the tracking system of paperwork for the operations that were under her control, laid out all over her desk.

Does this make you want to know more about her career choice? Obviously there is an official title for it, but... it isn't something I am at liberty to share – choices made and all.

I guess I could tell you that she is two years younger than I am. That she has an intensely alive energy within her, one that is filled with a child-like spirit, and I feel that from here is where healing energy flows through her at certain moments. My dad was the first to meet her – the gulp reaction when I learned of this after waking up from a 28-day coma, was very real – and then my mumma. Bubu is the second girl to have met my parents. Despite the language barrier (for my mum) and differences in culture... they were team Bubu. In May of 2020 I was told by my mum that I was responsible for driving her away.

Yes Mum, I agreed.

Bubu influenced a very sensitive phase of this journey in a most positive way. She, helped me realize many things, and in a sense, she became a critical piece of the puzzle involved in waking me up to how things really were – meaning – learning to truly trust those whom care for me and recognizing when and where that care is genuine.

A guy that backstabbed a few close friends, is someone whom she met in passing. Literally, in passing. We were driving through a parking lot and this guy was there too, so we pulled up to him for a moment. He had heard about Bubu, but hadn't met her yet, and here she was. I introduced him to her, and her to him, and he leaned in a little further from the driver's side window to shake her hand. We parted ways within seconds of that exchange, but I had already noticed a change in her. She had gone a little quiet, and by the time we pulled away, she was really quiet. When I looked at her, she looked... off. She almost looked like she was going to be sick. She said, who is that, I don't feel good, something is not right about him.

I took offence to it.

He is my bro I said. She said, I don't know... something didn't feel right, and whether she was aware of it or not, she was holding her hand in a manner that suggested it had perhaps taken impact or had been hurt in some fashion. I saw it. Ignored it. And then in a light bulb over the head – Aha – moment, recalled it after everything had played out. She didn't have to say anything.

Empath.

That is the term for one who can intuitively pick up on energy signals to the point where it affects the physical body. It does so, because it registers with the being in a negative response and its instant reaction is to alert the body to set off all the right warning signals. So, from her, I have learned a lot. About myself too.

When did I realize Bubu was teaching me about myself?

Sitting in segregation on a 21-day bit for attempting to kick down a staff door to get through to the next unit. It was an attempt to help a kid who would sucker punch me from behind months later. The kid was trying to get off the unit, and I was in a weak physical state making me the easiest – high value – target to ensure a transfer to a different range. He received a 'duty to warn' (life in jeopardy) within hours of the incident out of an "abundance of caution". Valuable lesson learned though.

Be aware of who is around you in a 2 arm radius.

I had just finished serving a 28-day sentence for a separate incident, and if not for those days already spent, the Warden would have given 28, because *if* the door had been kicked down, it would have posed a serious security concern. Had someone else kicked it, it probably would have been breached. But not by me. Not in the state I was in then, anyway.

I thought the kid was getting jumped and stomped out. Turned out, it was someone who couldn't get his toast out of the toaster. He snapped and slammed the toaster into the counter a few times, after holding it inches from his face and yelling *do you know who you are messing with!* At it.

Oh.

Um. Warden, if you read this… yup. You were right when you thought I was lying about my reasons. I guess the drop kicks caught on camera from a few different angles didn't lend much credence towards the bullshit reasons I provided. I remember him looking at me like… really… nice try. He did give credit for attempting to help a friend though.

That sucker punch? It happened in healthcare. The kid hit me twice. The first one knocked me out standing and the second one, which followed in quick succession, woke me right back up. My hands were still draped over the staff counter and, instinctively, my fingers closed around the edge of the counter to keep me from tipping over. It took a moment to make out the female correctional officer's voice. It sounded like she was talking from the other end of the room, when she was only standing a foot away from me, with a serious look on her face. As her face came back into focus, I made out a second voice from behind. It was the kid yelling from the corner of the room. Took a few more moments before I realized what had happened.

What is segregation like?

Depends what your overall mental and emotional state is. If it isn't healthy, then the chances of it being a healthy experience is pretty slim. When you are locked up 23 hours a day, with 1 hour to use the phone, shower, stretch your legs a little, and inhale some fresh air... it catches up with you quick. For those with unhealthy relationships, or imbalanced personal lives, segregation is not a good ingredient to throw into the pressure cooker of one's mind.

I used to be one of those individuals.

But this 21-day bit in segregation changed things for the better. I was barely hanging onto a friendship with my then girlfriend (Bubu), let alone a romantic relationship. We talked less and less on the phone. I knew less and less about her personal life, what she was doing and who she was or wasn't talking to. We were becoming less and less involved in one another's personal lives and, no, it didn't feel good. But, that is what I got back in return of the energy I put out. Valentine's Day had recently passed, and I hadn't even acknowledged it, let alone got her flowers.

Who doesn't get their "girlfriend" flowers *on* VALENTINE'S DAY??

This buffoon didn't.

I would later realize that I was beginning to respond to a tune I was hearing that was coming from a place deeper than the surface layer of emotions and mental mind fury. I would realize that my inner coordinates were beginning to reassemble to a different and healthier alignment.

In segregation I started to come to terms with the change that was taking place. A change that I had not only invited, but was helping further along. It didn't feel like a good change, at first, though. I played it off like I wasn't sweating it, the distance that was growing between Bubu and me, but I was.

It had happened.

The journey of growing into something fresher, had begun. It wasn't easy. It never got to the point where I wanted to cause harm to me or anyone around me, which is what many do; that is the way some cope with the extreme forms of suffering and hardships they experience. Some bang their head off the door or try to put their head into the wall, probably trying to put a dent in the wall. Others use their hands to try and bust up the wall(s). Some pull their hair, or at least, try to pull it out.

But nah...

What I wanted more than anything, was to be rid of the feelings I was experiencing. Those feelings I now easily understand as attachment, and thank Wayne Dyer and Deepak Chopra for that. Oh, Giggles too. Have to thank her. We're getting to her, just hold up a minute and keep reading.

I played it off like I wasn't attached to Bubu, but yup, I was. Couldn't get mad at her anymore, though. I did feel like I was left stranded, but that was my interpretation of the situation. And, it was distorted. Who leaves a girlfriend hanging on Valentine's Day? Someone who is trying to convey... that it isn't like that. And for me, I guess it was... not like that anymore.

So, I first remembered all the ways I had showed her and told her, that I was the one who went and changed (romantically) on her first. I then remembered all that she had done to not only show me how much she loved me and how much she cared, but how many times she showed me it was like that for her. She suffered when I suffered and she hurt when I hurt. And, when I started to break down actions, words and analyzed behaviour, I found that I was grateful for her presence in my experience, and that she was helping me change.

I started to feel closer to her than ever.

Through contemplation and reflection, I found that I should actually be very appreciative that she was still willing to answer my phone calls and help with things that make one's life a little easier in prison.

Through a deeper reflection I realized that she was the one affecting my journey for the better. Not only that, she was teaching me about my flaws. Not only was she teaching me about my flaws, but helping shine a light upon shortcomings. And not only helping me see those shortcomings, but the positive in me as well.

I no longer needed to be on the phone with her to feel like she was part of my life. I no longer felt a sense of rejection or disappointment if we went longer and longer periods without talking. I had finally realized that, we were in a healing phase. When I meditated at times, I could feel her energy so close, that it never felt like she was far away. Friends never are. Genuine friends stay connected, always. I finally realized that I will always have her friendship in my experience and the feeling of warmth it provides.

I have yet to meet someone with the grade of strength she has, the courage that keeps her going and the determination that doesn't let her stray from what matters most.

CHAPTER 20
EOFI
GIGGLES

*There is an intoxicating pull between two fields of energy
which are attracted to each other, and in that magnetism
exists a power which has in it the potential to influence much
good to happen.*

W hen did I realize I needed to change and pursue self-improvement?

The day I was diagnosed with what the doctors first thought was Crohn's disease. Not only diagnosed – cautioned that it could potentially be fatal because of the rate the inflammation had developed and what my insides looked like. It was towards the end of 2014, late summer or early fall.

I thought… what? Are you crazy? Die? From this? After *everything* I went through? Yeah right. Damned if I let that happen. No way. But I lacked a little confidence inside. I couldn't find the feeling of, no… *I will* be alright. The doctors gave me information and advice. I heard some of it. Mostly what I heard was a dial-tone-like sound that muffled what was making its way in between my ears. Die? I am not going to die. I wasn't going to let it happen. Deep down I had this gnawing feeling that, maybe it could. That maybe this was how I was supposed to pay back the karma I owed for all the negative energy I had emitted. For all the pain and suffering I had caused.

Uh-oh.

Another part of me that holds onto a steadfast faith in times of turmoil and intense need, said, chill, it will be OK… if it is meant to be… but, how? How was it going to be, I thought?

I changed my attitude that day. I was going to be positive. I was going to try to be positive all the time and not just the times I thought I needed to, or for the sake of keeping others out of a mood. I was going to try and live by it. There was no reason why I couldn't be positive all the time, and somehow I would figure out how.

Enter Giggles.

Giggles parachuted into my experience in spring 2014, and she did so on a life raft, with a life vest in hand. She popped up out of nowhere when I felt like I was drowning; little by little, too. I was scrambling to stay afloat. The air and energy around me, for the most part, felt stagnant and she came into my life like a fresh breeze.

You know when you meet someone for the first time, that feeling you get when you want to be around the person again and again? That feeling that can't quite be placed in words, yet it is so pleasurable that you want to experience it over and over? That's what it felt like with Giggles. That feeling not only helped me feel better, but it made me want to hang onto this feeling of... wellness I began to experience. And that is what her friendship in my experience felt like – wellness. It was also at a time when my personal life was falling apart. This new friendship, that felt like an intimate relationship at times, was what helped construct the new world. It sort of fell apart later on too, but only some of it. Just the parts of the foundation that needed to be worked on.

Giggles brought with her an intensely alive energy field, and she drew me into that energy field, which helped to shape this path, this connection within – to the life force. I pulled her into an energy field too; it was unavoidable. But that is not the perspective we are sharing here. Giggles brought with her fresh concepts and new knowledge, and once she realized that I was all ears, she shared her perspectives and thought processes comfortably.

I needed it.

The day she took a leap of faith and asked me if I was willing to try a Deepak Chopra guided (healing) meditation with her over the phone, it forever changed my life. And, mind you, our lives can be changed again and again. It isn't always just *one* thing that changes it. It isn't static. It isn't set into one mold at a time.

Life is fluid.

The day she asked if I was willing to try out a meditation... was in 2015, I think. Today it is 3 February 2020, and I am writing this as part of the revisions and editing process. I wonder if my editor will let these thoughts and dates stay in, or if he'll think such comments will impede the thought flow for you, the reader.

Blame the ADHD.

The feeling I experienced, however, I will never forget. How can you when it resonates within your being? I knew it had resonated somewhere very deep, but I didn't understand it at the time. The feeling I experienced, made everything else disappear. Everything. The nonsense noise and jumbled up garble of... waste.

The harmonious music, the way Deepak Chopra led you into the meditation, the method he used to guide the listener through the stages of... let's call it... tuning in; and then the eye-openers. Or, actually, soul-openers. I felt I connected with the soul for the first time, and that was indescribable.

I was, in a sense, sidestepping all that was in the way of experiencing the *buzz of the soul*, but... I wouldn't realize that till later. Ever felt this sort of thing? The awareness of the buzzing of the soul? What about a feeling like you're touching the stars and mingling with those infinite lights up above?

Yes, sober, obviously.

Before Giggles had played the meditation, she had suggested that there was nothing wrong with me. That there is rarely anything "wrong" with anybody; all there is, is the *thought* of there being something wrong. Yes, the body can be experiencing something irregular, but most times it is something we are mentally and physically playing a part in. Playing a part in with unhealthy habits (like I had), harbouring self-destructiveness (like I was), and spiritually disconnected (like I was). She said that, because I *thought* there was something wrong with me, the body was going to *believe* that something was wrong with me, as it cannot differentiate between thought and reality; it can only respond to the thought that is anticipating the next state of new cells replacing dead ones.

Huh?

OK, let me explain further. Because you *think* there could be something wrong with you, this means that there *will* be something wrong with you. If you *think* you are in need of medication, this means that you *do* need medication. Because you *think* your health is in a deteriorating state, it surely *will be*. So, on the contrary, if you change your thinking to: I am moving towards perfect health, then you surely will, Jujhar.

Oh.

It made sense. I didn't fully understand what she was saying, but something inside told me she was right. Not only right, but this here, this is something *big* that I had been missing. Then she played the meditation. Her words were the perfect primer. The healing meditation knocked my senses into a different dimension. Or the vibrational frequency present within the meditation is what knocked awareness around onto a different plane. And just like that: I was up.

Bingo.

Her words made sense. The words I had soaked up in the 20 minutes of meditation made sense. For the first time, I became aware of the heart of the machine which keeps it running. Literally, the beating heart. I became aware of the way it was beating and the fact that, if it wasn't for this organ, one cannot experience the physical world. How precious it is, how fragile it is, and I went all these years without even realizing that it was there. What a Kool (Yup, capital K) body part.

And.

Now. It had begun to make sense. If your heart is full of pain... you will be full of pain. If your heart is full of anger... your body will carry it. If your heart is full of hate and rage... your body will be, too. On the other hand, if your heart is full of love... well, it will emanate outwards, throughout the body and beyond. I also realized in that meditation, more than ever, that whatever was in my mind would make its way into my heart. Somehow and someway, it was all connected at such a deep level that I couldn't ignore it. I mean, I *had*, all these years. Sure, I had read quotes and little sayings, but I had only related to them superficially. But now I didn't want to relate to them superficially. Not anymore. I wanted to understand, I wanted to experience it all – the feeling of being connected to something... higher... these feelings of... connectedness, again and again.

So began the healing.

Oh. The blood test before the meditation showed a CRP (C-reactive protein) count of around 100 (an increased count signals inflammation in the body). Normal ranges are between 3-5, I think. Yup. My intestines weren't just inflamed, they were on fire. And the immune system was trying to eat them alive. The next blood test showed a decrease by 10 points. As I sat there with the new results, I remember feeling an increased sense of security, that what I had just stumbled upon was exactly what I needed. As time progressed and the meditations continued, the CRP count continued to decrease. I remember a test result which showed it was in the 50s, and with it, I felt a sense of... gracious love for Giggles.

Giggles made an effort to meditate with me every week for months. On blessed weeks she played healing meditations multiple times, and even kirtan in the a.m. For someone who wasn't given to committing to much, she sure committed herself to being a part of my healing journey. And that is something I will always be grateful for. She also made more than just an effort once or twice to come visit me. She visited regularly. The visiting experience was an adventure of its own, an adventure into a world we both disappeared into, for the duration of the through-the-screen shared rendezvous.

Having Giggles in my experience helped me realize that there is such a thing as being connected. I got to experience the feeling of being connected again and again. It helped me understand that, when you're disconnected or always on the brink of disconnect, you are essentially isolated from your inner essence. If you're isolated from your inner essence – in thought anyway (as it is actually impossible to be isolated from the only aspect of us that *is* us) – you are in a vacuum. The vacuum creates separation and also drains vital energy. The distance and drain, in turn, creates feelings, emotions; all of which are forms of energy, and they trickle their way down into the body. If that energy is left there long enough, it will cause serious damage to the body and start to rot the insides away. It will start to suck away the beauty which not only holds together the physical aspect of us, but which keeps the body functioning the way it is meant to.

That is what happened to me.

My guts were literally disintegrating, and the major cause was – who or what I thought was, was falling apart fast. I felt like a big part of me died when Amar and Happy passed on in May and June of 2013. I believed the best parts of me were dying; I felt dead inside when I let my thoughts roll until they became like an avalanche... and my body started to shut down to meet that vibration; a negative and toxic vibration. I felt like there was nothing much left to live for, and so I let anger, rage and hate keep me going. It eventually started to erode me from the inside out. I felt nothing but shame and guilt for leaving my parents and family hanging year after year, and it only lent weight to more feelings of unworthiness which, in turn, kept adding to the pressure within that was nearing breaking point.

I was self-destructing.

I judged myself and the way I looked (colostomy bag, deformed and weird-looking stomach) and used that as a reason, in my head, why Bubu would eventually leave me – which she did, but it wasn't because of weird-looking stomach. I put enough energy into *believing* she would leave me, that she eventually did. I fostered insecurity so much that it helped pull away the bricks that were holding me together inside. I put out an accumulation of negative vibrations, and the Universe's response system – responded.

Law of attraction.

The doctor was shocked that I had developed the condition in such a short time, and out of nowhere. I had displayed no warning signs. He couldn't make sense of it. Once the healing journey had begun and realizations began to surface... it made sense to me. He said I had a "disease". Years later I realized the role I had played in bringing about the specific condition the body was experiencing. But. It was more like *dis*-ease.

Woah.

Woah was my reaction when I realized what I had just stumbled across – "*dis*-ease" – it made sense that (all it was) was that I wasn't *at ease*. So, I got to figuring out how to experience harmony. So simple the answer. Easy though? Dunno. Maybe. Maybe not. It was... definitely an enjoyable journey.

Or.

I only remember it now as enjoyable. Perhaps it is how I choose to remember it, but it doesn't matter. The body is healthy. The sun is always shining, and the Universe continues to reveal cool pieces of knowledge along with awareness-jolting moments.

Each new day is welcome.

The moment I am out of balance and not feeling harmonious, the body responds instantly. It doesn't give me breathing room. So, in a sense, it doesn't take much for me to recognize when I know I need to breathe a little deeper, relax a little, stop taking myself too seriously, and take in the beauty around me. It reminds me to be mindful of what I put in the body (nourishment). It reminds me to drink more water (which contains life energy). It reminds me to be mindful of what I listen to (music) and what types of conversations I engage in. It reminds me to be mindful of the words I use and what thoughts I entertain in the field of mind. It reminds me to sit on the grass on a cool clear night and close my eyes to the swirling energy about. It reminds me to sit there and enjoy it even on the days it rains. And you know what?

It feels pretty good.

CHAPTER 21

EOFI

SIS — THIS TOO SHALL PASS

You will continue to suffer if you have an emotional reaction to everything that is said to you. True power is sitting back and observing everything with logic. If words control you that means everyone else can control you. Breathe and allow things to pass.

—Bruce Lee

Everything is temporary. Nothing stays the same. I was once told to remember the words "this too shall pass" – an older friend, who is more of a sister than a friend, dropped Eckhart Tolle knowledge on me at a time and phase of my life when I couldn't really hear or see anything.[1] Blind and deaf for the most part. She gave me valuable advice at a time when I was rarely conscious. We were hanging out at their home (spring 2011) when she said, no matter what happens, just remember – *this too shall pass.*

Years later, a copy of *The Power of Now* ended up in my hands and, in remembering the author's name, it reminded me of her. It reminded me of what she had told me about him. I remembered her saying that this specific piece of writing was also available on audio – she used to listen to it in her car. I smiled at the memory. I then came across the section "This too shall pass," and remembered her advice. I remember calling her in my excitement, and re-hashing the experience from the moment the book made it into my hands, the memories leading up to the phone call, the realizations triggered so far and then, finally, coming across the section which triggered me into action (making the phone call). She was as excited to hear about it as I was about conveying it.

This phrase has continued to come into my experience in synchronistic ways again and again; a little reminder from the Universe when needed. So has the book itself. A couple of weeks before sentencing it popped up again in a most unexpected way. A friend of mine, a different loved one but also like a sister, someone I call Sis by choice, said it to me.

Pause.

Love you Sis. Always.

Un-pause.

Jujhar... just remember, *this too shall pass.*

She was reading *A New Earth*, also written by Eckhart Tolle, and it was from there that she repeated the phrase. I heard it, smiled, a really big smile, and then relaxed into the chair I was sitting on while she spoke. Humbled once again because, when that phrase hit home all over again, the inner frenzy I felt – all inner resistance just whooshed away. It disappeared, and in that moment – all was well again.

When it hit home all over again, it felt peaceful.

That is what a "not-so-easy" moment can be turned into. *Peace*. Once you accept it, whatever it is, you surrender the resistance. Woohoo! How's that for understanding the lesson in your words, Monsieur Tolle?

Pretty well absorbed I'd say.

In accepting whatever it is, in choosing peace, you give up the opposing force you are putting forth that is resisting the experience. The experience of peace. Once you stop fighting the moment and accept it as it is, unconditionally accept the circumstances or situation, sit with it and just observe your internal reaction. Take a few breaths and you'll feel the peace arise on its own. From acceptance to peace; and from peace you can move to gratitude.

Why not?

So much to be grateful about. By giving thanks and being grateful you can appreciate what you do have, or what *is* in your experience, without wishing things were different. From appreciation – being thankful for all the good and the colour in your experience – you can move to a smile. Once you're smiling… you're *free*.

There goes the not-so-easy moment.

Resistance is rigid. It impedes the free flow of energy not only in the body; it blocks you off from the Power Source. It restricts the flow of the exchange of energy taking place. It cuts you off from the rhythmic, harmonically rhythmic, flow of the Universe, and it isolates energy. It puts up barriers between the manifestation of your dreams and the attraction of circumstances or situations aligned with your innermost dreams, desires and highest visions.

Impermanence is a characteristic of every condition.

—The Buddha

Everything changes.

Nothing is permanent. That includes the not-so-easy moment. So, if you feel frantic, uneasy, or weighted down... breathe... deeply... and remember the advice given to me by my sisters. *This too shall pass.*

And pass it most certainly will.

---

1. She was Dip's significant other at the time she said it. That is, *the* Dip. For those of you who don't know him, he was, is, and always will be, a dear friend and brother.

CHAPTER 22

EOFI

UNEXPECTED WARMTH FROM NURSE

Each relationship has appeared for a reason and will last for as long as that purpose is still operating.

—Carol A. Adrienne

U nexpected warmth is... refreshing. It is refreshing for the spirit. For the soul. For the entire physical organism and the mind. The energy exchanged is profound. It can be life-altering. Genuine, warm exchanges of energy laced with love, care, thoughtfulness, *do* make a difference. It matters not how unexpected acts of kindness are even received on the spot, because on gloomy sorts of days it seems like they won't just pop up – not usually anyway. Experiencing one can be so shocking that it can throw you off. But.

That's the point.

We can do that. And more importantly, *you can.*

It is the warmth in the exchange of energy that might throw you off. *Especially* when it is unexpected. I got to experience what that warmth feels like.

In spring 2016, while in the health care unit at the Surrey Pre-trial Services Center, a nurse *almost* gave me a hug. I had to take my shirt off for an exam, and as I did she yelped – she was the same nurse that had attended me on my first visit, in 2013, and was surprised at the change in me. She was so excited that she responded by putting both hands on my back, and then it went to one, this half-a-pat, slash awkward-ish sideways embrace. All this time later I remember it; and wish I'd asked for a proper hug.

But.

It startled me. Soft warm delicate hands on my bare back after, like, 3 years of no human touching. She was so upbeat and genuinely happy to see me in the physical state I was in, because she had seen what I had looked like, in 2013 when I had to wheel myself into the clinic, weighing about 110-112 lbs. I had been improperly discharged from the hospital (politics) and had wounds that needed daily flushing and bandage changes. I had a colostomy (poo-bag) sticking out the side of my stomach, along with a protruding belly (graft to close abdomen, which left the intestines pushing against the graft due to no abdominal wall). All in all, I didn't look well. Hair frizzled and frayed look-ing, 2 months without showering, barely able to stand without assistance – let alone walk.

Her affection added a warm jolt of joy into my experience when I was expecting it least. It is something I've reflected on many, many times and no matter what, even as I write these words today, it feels good remembering it. A moment I am grateful for, a memory I appreciate and most certainly a reason to smile. That's what that unexpected exchange of energy can do. It affected me more in the moments to come than it did in the moment itself. Still does. That's what happens sometimes.

So, release into the Universe warm energy with a humble and sincere intent and let the law of attraction do the rest.

Let the Universe work out the details.

—Deepak Chopra

Or.

Let go and let God.

Because unexpected warmth is much needed. A lady from United Way, an organization making a difference in the lives of others (in Toronto ON, Canada) was speaking to the host of a TV show called *Let The Quran Speak*, which airs on Saturdays on Joy TV, at 11a.m. Pacific time. She said, there is no way to measure the impact kindness has on the lives of those that need it. Acts of care and acts of kindness extended to those living on the street certainly make a difference, and they are much needed.

But.

More than that is the need of these people to be noticed. What is needed is for someone to take a moment out of their life to share in, perhaps, a conversation, or to sit along the wall they're sitting against and look out at the world from their perspective. What must it feel like to have people walk by you and disregard you like you don't exist?

That's how I interpreted what she said.

What I heard her say was that they, the homeless, don't expect those walking by to notice them. That those walking by don't even regard them as something... worth noticing.

Being seen as *someone* is miles away.

I know of a man who has lived with the homeless. He has slept on the same mattresses those living on the streets sometimes get to enjoy. He has showered in the same bathtubs some get the blessings to wash off in, and has spent a little over 10 years walking up and down the very streets the homeless live on.

He never regarded them as nothing.

He regarded them as someone worth bringing food to. Someone worth taking the time to help, to guide, because they may be self-destructing fast. He earned a living – it is true – by selling a product (drugs) that provided many with temporary escape from the realities before them. But he followed his own moral code in this, always taking extra care to make sure no one was getting something that might result in an OD. He also earned respect in these struggling communities by helping those who were trying to get clean with support and motivation. Who is in a position to judge such actions? It was suggested that he had an angel on his shoulder.

Probably.

It felt like *he* was the angel on the shoulders of others. After bonding with him, it felt like that to me. Being blessed with warmth from someone who doesn't know you or owe you; from someone who takes the time to sit back, reflect and then recognize how he could affect your experience, is the physical expression of having angels walking around you.

It reminded me of how easy it is to become the warmth in the experience of others, especially when the environment around you leaves you feeling... cold. That is what it felt like being in prison – cordoned off and isolated. Cold. The nurse's hands on my back weren't the source of the jolt and feeling of warmth.

It was her heart.

To that nurse – *thank you.*

CHAPTER 23

EOFI

BUBU AND KYLIE 'THE TREND SETTER' JENNER

Do something wonderful, people may imitate it.

—Albert Schweitzer

A re you focused on "keeping up with the latest", "fitting in" or "following" trends? Have you thought about setting your own? Creating... building... sharing... that's Kool. I used to judge the Kardashians way back when I felt threatened by the influence they had on the psyche of my then-girlfriend. I would get into a fight with Bubu when she was talking about something one of the Ks did, something they liked or were promoting.

As I began to change and realize how small-minded I had become, I began a journey of growth that I now accept is continuous and ever-evolving. Somewhere along that journey, I began to let go of judging others. Once I started to let go, it allowed space for understanding to emerge. Every now and then, I smile remembering the lessons that have influenced the very journey that's led me here to this point, pen in hand sharing thoughts with each and every one of you.

Kylie Jenner (google her) – the girl who can 'like' (or not) something on social media and drive stocks up or down with a tap on her phone – may very well have lots of fashion tips and style choices that influence trends and behaviours all over the world; but she also has something much more, much more than that.

She has a voice.

She has a platform from which she can launch or support a product, a movement, or a cause she puts her attention towards. She could, today, say – hey everyone, let's take extra care of our planet and push for governments all over the world to further the voices of those who are cautioning us about climate change; let's do something about the imbalance between the wealthiest and the poorest. She could say – hey, everyone contribute in some way to help the homeless, the hungry, or let's help get the basic living necessities to our family members in Sudan or Iraq – and the world would respond. Not only would the world respond, but those who look up to her and follow her wholeheartedly would put forward their own voices, which in turn could create an avalanche effect – in a good way, obviously. She could say – hey everyone, let's do this today. Not tomorrow, next week or next month, or when I have time to fit it in – but right now.

And just like that… new trends will begin.

Her own journey has had its own unique steps, driven by ambition, dreams, intentions. Those very steps led her to make a difference in the lives of many children and families, by helping put roofs over their heads. It was indeed humbling to learn of this as I watched it on TV. I remember blue-coloured roofs, single and double bunks in brand new rooms. Dirt roads and not much infrastructure, but… much hope. Saw the hope in the smiles and reactions of those who benefited. It was humbling because I had judged her, and in that moment, it just… left me. No more judgement. Who was I to judge? I used to do it a lot.

We tend to do it a lot.

We think something, then we believe we know about someone or something, when we really don't. How about we focus on our own experiences and worry less about others, their blunders, whispering petty gossip to fill spaces with negativity?

Let's fill it with something else entirely. Let's fill it with an attitude that invites possibilities and opportunities. Let's focus our energy in a purposeful way and meaningful manner that sets trends of our own. We can influence those around us with what we say, how we say it, with what we do, and why we do it. It makes a difference.

It is that simple.

Build your own followings for your own reasons. Carve a path that inspires someone else to take steps. I use to judge Kylie Jenner because of insecurities I harbored while I was dating a Spanish Hurricane.[1] I best capitalize it (sweating face turbaned emoji). She (the Spanish Hurricane) will end up reading these words, too. *Waheguru.* Better to just give her credit where it is due.

Empower others.

Self-empowerment and self-love only go so far. Many start a self-empowering journey and then become so identified with it, that they acquire a belligerence that becomes a self-centered ignorance; and in doing so they develop another type of hindrance that keeps them from breaking free. Self-love is important, but it is not the be all or end all. It is just the start.

Only a stepping stone.

Loving others. Caring for others. Sharing that love with others, looking to help them up in some way, making a difference in someone's experience – *that's* where it's at. And oh boy will that energy return to you, tenfold. It is the collective responsibility of humanity to spread love around; it affects our entire collective journey for the better. So be the one that makes the effort and takes steps in recognition of that.

The individual efforts you make will attract more of what you seek. Whatever good you wish upon the world, whatever you wish to spread will find a way to touch the lives of those in need of love, of a little care, and those steps will lay down an irresistible path for you which brings with it the colour of Joy, the sounds of Happiness and the warmth of Love. Yes, I capitalized Joy, Happiness and Love. They are that significant. The Universe will find a way to return the energy to you.

Always does.

Set a trend. You might just enjoy it.

---

1. Spanish Hurricane – Bubu. (Sweating face turbaned emoji.)

CHAPTER 24
SUKHVIR'S CARE

Wish I may
Wish I might
Have you here…
To hug all night.

A nd.

While we are here, at this point in the journey, I would like to say thank you. Thank you for reading up until this point. You are making a difference by just reading these words. By having purchased this book. As briefly mentioned in the preface, we, the Magic Mind Squad, want to use 50 per cent of the profits from this book to make a difference in the lives of our family – humanity. We are closer today to bringing to fruition a promise made 11 ½ years ago than ever.

It is a humbling feeling.

After Sukhvir passed on from this physical realm, we (her loved ones) dreamt of naming a care center in her given name that would service the community, and that one day, there would be "Sukhvir's Care" centers all over this Earth. A care center that has within it, housing, and would offer specialized teaching for those learning in their own unique ways, and at their own pace.

This is a big thing, hey?

There is a real need for teachers who are trained in specialized teaching techniques, to help those with unique methods of absorbing knowledge and learning. I have a family member who learns in her own way, who hasn't really had the opportunity to flourish in an environment that unlocks her potential, which helps tap into her hidden genius. She has still not been given the help she needs; the method has yet to be uncovered. I wish I could have played a bigger role in her learning journey, and not made choices that led to me being locked up for close to a decade. It is something that stands as a reminder of neglected responsibilities. One day soon though, she will get the opportunity to tap into her inner genius.

We – Sukhvir's loved ones – began with the idea of creating a care center that would assist with medical needs, and would serve free food at all hours; like at a gurdwara (the Sikh place of worship, and spiritual congregation). Since then, the dream has evolved into creating a spiritually balanced environment. Meaning, those who are helping bring out the inner geniuses, those who are assisting in inner healing, have themselves harvested a deeper understanding, and so are experienced in healing, inspiring, and teaching in ways that raise the vibrational alignments of their students.

Does that make sense to you?

We are all aligned at a certain vibration. Meaning, we are vibrating at a certain frequency. Meaning, we all give off an energy level. It can even be measured, now. There is mind boggling technology available that can read the energy coming off of you. I do not think all the emanations can be captured by the technology, but some can be, certainly.

It is so capital K Kool.

But yes ADD, back to vibrational alignments. So, each being vibrates at a certain frequency. Those who feel an immense amount of joy, love, happiness, bliss, excitement, those who enjoy the moment before them and experience peace again and again – they align with high vibrations. Those who feel low, sad, grumpy, lonely, unhappy, or even, angry, hateful, spiteful, *judgemental*, well – their alignment is with low vibrations. Ok, alignment out of the way.

We want Sukhvir's Care to be able to adopt children from all over the world, exposing them to an environment which encourages creating, learning, and growing in ways that triggers an exchange of higher vibrations to mingle and enhance everyone in these heightened awareness energy fields.

Sukhvir wanted to adopt children from Africa. I thought I heard her say to me that she wanted to have African babies – how can you have African babies with me, I said? Imagine that conversation, and her laughing hysterically. Oh. She could laugh, that one. And when she did, you filled up with a little more light, with a little more colour. Now, all I want to do is go set up shop in Africa. If any of you are going to come look for me when I'm released, that's where I will be. For a little while, anyway. With a team on the ground – believe that.

This is where Dip and I shared a strong connection – both of us wanted to be part of something that brings hope and colour into this world. *This* is how we became friends and brothers overnight. We would park on the side of the road where Sukhvir sustained injuries, and spend moments in each other's company; we would light candles and stand around, staring deep into the flames; some nights our conversations went just as deep. Other times, we would light candles and stand around in silence, enjoying the light that danced all around us. Sometimes we would light candles, hop back in the ride, and just sit there with the music on low and the sidewalk lit up beside us.

After Dip learned about the dream to create Sukhvir's Care, he shared his own inner dream of wanting to build a youth center, open to all and free of charge, one in Surrey BC first, and then in Toronto ON. He wanted it to have sick basketball courts, indoor soccer fields, and recording studios for the homies back east from the 6.[1] He wanted a floor or two dedicated to music, where young talent could gain access to instruments and connect with coaches and tutors. He wanted a floor or two dedicated to music, where young talent could access instruments and connect with coaches and tutors. He wanted another floor or two for programs designed to bring out the artistic gifts and talents of young ones. A colourful place where kids could come and further their dreams, their ideas, and get away from whatever they were trying to get away from. He wanted to create an environment where the gentle lights of the world could come and grow together, learn together, create together, where they could bond and share – where they could *evolve* together.

He wanted it to be a place that had a built-in community support network open to anyone that was stuck in addiction, psychological troubles, or for anyone feeling lost or confused. A place where boys, girls, women, men, could come to in matters of abuse of any kind – because not everyone wants to go to, well, you know who.

He wanted there to be a place where one could go for mental, emotional, and physical support. A place where children, youngsters would learn to connect with one another in ways that created opportunities, created good, created solutions. He wanted to recreate what certain hood stars from the South (USA) have done for the hood and make a difference in the North (Canada) like Drake be doing ("God's Plan" and all).[2]

His vision is alive, still. The intention. It will be a few years (maybe a little more) before it assembles itself in physical form, but in the meantime it is collecting the necessary nuts and bolts. It is closer to happening now than ever before because of the energy that was just lent towards it as you read, absorbed and some of you – envisioned the vision. That's how it works. This energy. Intention. Attraction.

The manifestation thing.

I met Dip towards the end of his journey in the form he was physically walking around in. His qualities are worth emulating and, personally, I never experienced him as anything short of a stand-up man. His past didn't define him, doesn't define him. Who he was in the moment – his truest inner essence – shone forth, spoke more of his nature than any decision made from a state of low awareness (low vibrational alignment).

If anyone reading these words was present the day he was gunned down inside the Wall Center (hotel in downtown Vancouver) – and many were, including a sports team from the US of A – they would have seen that what happened that day was a karmic cycle running its course. Energies balancing themselves out.

Time up.

But, while it was the end of one cycle of expression, others began. It led to the unique expression of these words, and to their being momentarily directed towards you. Maybe we're meant to do something wonderful, something beautiful for this world, together. Maybe we're meant to bring light into this world in some way, meant to do something that adds colour to this world in, not exactly his memory, but in remembrance of the exchange of energies that took place in order for us to come into each other's experience, because no matter which way you look at it, we've just exchanged energy of our own.

That's just how it works.

Energies brought Dip and I together, too. It matters not how he left this world, this physical realm we see and touch with our physical senses, because he was able to express to the whole, in his own way, what part of his life-purpose was. We just did that here. We just lent energy towards whatever he envisioned – and then some. Told you, we're making a difference already. See how easy it is.

Setting trends we be mmhmmm – Yoda tone.

As I said 50 per cent of the profits from this book are going into a fund named Sukhvir's Care. The intention is to sell a million-plus copies of *Trenches 2 Freedom*, knowing the Universe will do the rest. The intention is to spread the energy of that currency, with love, all over the world. That exchange of energy, of "current" – currency of Love – will start new cycles, new waves – and, so, on and on it goes. Perhaps Sukhvir's Care will get the opportunity to invest into Dip's dreams for a youth center.

It just might.

---

1. The 6 – a nick name for Toronto, ON. I think it may have been Drake that dubbed it that. 604 is an original area code for The Lower Mainland, so this reference is up for debate. My roommate is willing to (friendly) spar Drake over it. He's a Ninja. Ps: Raptors got it done!
2. Drake – Canadian artist, rapper, creator, philanthropist and more. He released a track titled "God's Plan" and was given a million-dollar budget by the producers for the music video. He turned around and spread the million dollars around, recording the footage, which in-turn became the music video. Kool.

CHAPTER 25

A LESSON IN JUDGMENT

Meditate, meditate, meditate in remembrance of God, and find peace.
Worry and anguish shall be dispelled from your body.

Simar, Simar, Simar sukh pavoh.
Kal kalesh tan mahay matavoh.

—Guru Granth Sahib Ji
Sukhmani Sahib – First Astapadee
Composed by Guru Arjun Dev Ji

Guru Arjun Dev Ji, 5th Guru of the Sikh Faith, was responsible for the construction and completion of the Harmandir Sahib, located in Amritsar, Punjab, which is also now referred to as the Golden Temple.

One day, the Guru gave his disciple and friend, Baba Gurdass Ji, a specific task. He told him that langar sewa – service in the kitchens of a gurdwara, where food is freely given to all visitors – was his responsibility for the day. He was tasked with ensuring that no one went hungry, emphasizing that *everyone* should be looked after. Baba Gurdass Ji accepted the task with delight, and all day and evening he attended to his service in his usual humble and sincere manner.

At the end of the evening, after the sangat (the congregation) left, Baba Gurdass Ji was again by Guru Arjun Dev Ji's side. Guru Arjun Dev Ji asked his friend and disciple how the day went, and Baba Gurdass Ji told him it went well. He told the Guru Ji that everyone ate and no one went hungry. Everyone? asked Guru Arjun Dev Ji. Baba Gurdass Ji told him, yes, everyone Guru Ji. Guru Arjun Dev Ji asked again, are you sure no one went hungry today, my dear friend Baba Gurdass Ji? You didn't forget anyone? Or, perhaps, miss someone? And in that moment, Baba Gurdass Ji knew he had failed. He knew he had made an error in judgement and missed the point of the test, realizing that Guru Arjun Dev Ji had specifically put him on to something, already knowing what needed to be seen. Baba Gurdass Ji said one individual had gone hungry. He wasn't serviced because he had recently been accused of committing an indecent act towards the body of a dead woman.

Guru Arjun Dev Ji said to him, yesterday, this man was accused of something, but today he walked into the perimeter of a gurdwara, as a lost and hungry human being. Your task wasn't to judge, it was to serve and ensure no one went hungry.

Oh, I thought, as my father was speaking.

When he shared this piece of history, it was in synchronization with a non-judgment phase I was experiencing. It was right around the time I had seen Kylie Jenner on TV with those children who now had a roof over their heads, thanks to her help. Before my father could say it, I had realized it... *Oh*... yup, it wasn't Baba Gurdass Ji's place to judge, regardless of how he might have felt or what he might have thought.

Regardless of how it made me feel too (that the man should have been overlooked).

I can always tell when my father is smiling through the phone, especially when he knows that the lesson in his words has hit home. He is fond of saying, take care of the dust and dirt at your own door before you comment on someone else's front steps. He is fond of saying, first tend to the blemishes on the face you see in the mirror, before you start commenting on another's.

I used to judge others a lot.

When my father shared the langar sewa story with me, I was at OCC (Okanagan Correctional Center). It had become a... ritual to cook curry and rice on Saturdays while I was there. Actually, it had been a ritual to cook curry on Saturdays for many years, because there are cultural and religious programs aired all day on Vision and Joy TV (as I mentioned in an earlier chapter). The Gurbani Kirtan and cultural music (Punjabi and Hindi) sets the mood, and helps provide this feeling of... comfort. The smell of cooking spices, the serene feeling while listening to kirtan, and the upbeat feeling trending music carries (sometimes it's sad) transforms the jail experience into something else entirely. At the OCC it felt much more like home, or like sitting in a gurdwara, on those days. If anyone on the unit was hungry, all they needed was a bowl and to stand in line once it was ready – usually around 9-9:30 p.m.

My father went from telling me about Baba Gurdass to comments about Maharaja Ranjit Singh (last Sikh Singh king to rule in Punjab) and how he used to carry burlap sacks of grain on his shoulders to those who needed food. My father said, if a king can practise such humility, why can't the likes of us put aside ideas of who or what we think we are, and use his example as inspiration to continue the pledge and tradition established by Guru Nanak?[1]

It helped me realize, more than ever, that one does not need to be in a gurdwara to practise langar sewa or to follow the traditions established by Guru Nanak.

It can be done anywhere.

Langar sewa is being practised wholeheartedly all over the world today. In India, after recent violence flared up (February 2020), triggered by a government policy discriminating against Muslims, langar has been relied upon by many families for nourishment, and gurdwaras for shelter.

Right now (Spring 2020) the COVID-19 pandemic that is pushing humanity back into their homes (physical dwellings) is also providing us with the opportunity to take our practice one step further, and to go within (inner dwelling). The pandemic has also brought to light the vulnerabilities of economic and social structures created for the… comfort of this world. It has provided the opportunity for gurdwaras to prepare langar for communities. This is what it was created for in the first place. For empty stomachs. Who knew the ways gurdwaras would become like a shoulder for communities—? Guru Nanak did. Langar and congregation for everyone alike. Eating from the same bowls and plates, sitting on the same surface as the person next to them.[2]

Pangat.

Before the conversation with my father, the Saturday cooks at the OCC were more of a personal meditation. After, though, it became the practise of langar sewa. I felt like I was in a langar hall of a gurdwara, which made everything I participated in that much more enjoyable. It didn't matter how much had to be done; eat once everyone has eaten. It reminded me that this is the manner in which we are supposed to move. There are countless hungry beings everywhere all over the world. It is our responsibility to do something about it.

I still have much learning to do. There are many times that I go to bed with a full stomach, only to realize that I didn't give thanks for the food in advance, and failed to remain alert while eating, giving thanks again and again. And if I was alert, I wouldn't have over-filled my stomach.

The practise of mindfulness.

I am not saying, I am so mindful that I am judgement free. But, I am learning. I am learning to focus on the strengths and positive attributes of others, instead of getting caught up on the things I don't like. Maybe someone else likes them. Maybe they don't. What does it matter anyway? Why do I have to judge? Why can't I just let it be? I have my own journey to tweak so it adjusts to a setting that aligns to a higher vibration and deeper spiritual understanding.

We judge people.

We judge and create opinions, points of view, spreading them around like germs. Why? Is it to look down on others? What purpose does it serve? Talking about people. Judging them. Sitting down for an elegant dinner or special occasion only to share thoughts and opinions of others in a distasteful manner. Where is the flavour in that? In judging another we aren't really defining anyone, yet we are defining ourselves; as people who think we can judge people and things we don't fully understand. I find myself contemplating this and reflecting on it from the point of fact that worldwide restaurants are shut down and spaces for social gatherings and personal leisure, are off limits. Meeting and eating together, then, is… a privilege? One we do not have right now. I myself am even further removed from the privilege because of the choices that landed me in prison. For as long as "physical distancing" – this is what it should be labelled, not "social distancing" – is encouraged, let's use this time for reflection, and help remove the chains of indifference and judgment which create mental, emotional, and spiritual prisons for so many of us.

And instead.

Let's mimic the goodness we see in others, and work tirelessly to iron out the wrinkles in our character. Let's spread the good we see projected on social media and turn it into an uplifting vibe for someone else. Just as those you follow online leave a footprint, we too can leave a trail behind for others to pick up, and then, in turn... use for some good of their own.

You'll be a part of it too, hey?

Maybe in the form of inspiration and motivation. If someone goes and does something triggered by what you did or said, well then – the energy you put out will be part of it too. There is no way to separate it. And you do leave a trail, no matter what you do. That is just how it works. You always leave behind a trace of some sort.

So, why not the good kind?

Let's use others actions, words, and mindsets, as guiders for this journey. Let's soak up the lessons, then turn around and put out uplifting energy – this adds something of value to our experience and to the world, so why not?

#Whynot indeed.

I switch between writing points of view, don't I? 1st person, 2nd person, 3rd person. I don't indent paragraphs or follow certain writing rules, do I? It is all good. All those rules and standards are just one more kind of judgement, trying to show us who can write and who can't, or who gets to speak-write and who doesn't. A little too unKool I'd say. Because. I write. I am speaking. And... muhahaha to that.

---

1. Guru Nanak established the traditions of Sangat and Pangat. Pangat is the sharing of food from the same plate while sitting next to a man or woman as equals. This tradition shattered the norm of caste divisions by superiority and inferiority. It is still practised at all gurdwaras and takes place before the congregation – the sangat – comes together for worship.
2. We (the editor and I) are sure that gurdwaras are practising all the physical distancing and safeguarding guidelines at the same time!

CHAPTER 26

SHARING/GIVING

Nourishment of the body is food,
while nourishment of the soul is feeding others.

—Imam Ali S.

Whenyou share, when you give, the energy returns to you. It returns to you in ways you couldn't even imagine. Well, you could imagine it, actually, but what I mean is that, if you do it with a quality of sincerity... the return of that energy will blow your expectations away.

That's just the way it works.

I heard someone say that thinking of one's actions as "giving" is to imply that there is a giver, and taking on that role for oneself is to, well, take a superior stance in the exchange. So, to say that one is "sharing", that is viewing one's action in a more humble and polite way. I see the argument.

But.

How about giving with a quality of sharing which has in it the humility of service? The seeds of love, compassion, and most importantly... without expectations. Give to share, not expecting what you have given returned to you, because that would be lending, no? And don't get smart, I know I just said energy returns to you when you share, but that is very different – it *always* returns, the only question is *how* it will return, filled with energy that will lift your vibrations up or take them down a notch. It's up to you, but only genuine intentions will lift you up, when all's said and done.

Giving with the expectation that this will come back to me in some form, removes the element of service. Because it isn't service at that point, but a transaction. It is like a person who commits horrendous acts against others, then goes on a cleansing pilgrimage, with the thought "all will be cleansed from my slate", and then afterwards continues committing atrocities.

This will probably have a reverse effect.

So, don't give from the point of view of ego. Give from the selfless Self. Give to help others, not yourself. When you genuinely help others, it will come back to you anyway (that's just the way it... you know the mantra by now). Give, to enjoy the flavour it brings.

Oh it certainly does bring a flavour of joy, one that tastes like... um... oh, I know what it tastes like. Mangos. Yum. It tastes like mangos (*Mas Preguntas*, remember?). And yes that is plural with an o and an s; not mangoes. Who spells it like that? Man goes. Two words. ADD has definitely kicked in. Focus. Mangos, it's an experience.

Try it.

Giving with the humble energy of sharing. Just give it away. You're not actually giving anything away, only exchanging energy. And that boomerang effect is adjusting itself to your energy output. You are bringing energy to you. You are inviting colour into your experience. So just give. Share. And let it go. Don't give with the thought, I just gave away 10 dollars and I will get 100 back. That's not what I meant by tenfold. *How* the Universe returns it is up to the Universe.

Just give it away. Like Penelope Cruz says in *Spanglish*, "just try it on", because she not only knows it is going to fit, but knows it is going to bring joy.

So.

Trust it, I say. We are building trust with each other, remember? Ask the ones that already do it, they'll tell you. Many of you that do are reading these words right now with a little smile. Feels good, right? Yup, it does. If you don't know the movie *Spanglish* – excellent. Keep your eyes off Penelope Cruz. Because she is married.

Duh.

Share a meal. Share your material wealth. Share your heart. Share your "time". Share your insight. Share your experience. Share your skills. Share your brain power. Share your music. Share your gifts.

Or.

Give them away. Give them to those that need it more than you. Give it to those who need balls of sunshine in their experience. Give it to those who really need the warmth, the care and the love.

However you come to identify with it, do it with humility, with a quality of service that sends out into the Universe *energy*, which will not only be on supersonic mode, but super-Saiyan too.[1] It will return to you, it certainly will, mmhmm – Um, yes. Yoda tone.

---

1. *Dragon Ball Z* anime (DBZ) – Gohan what.

CHAPTER 27
BEING

Trapped people have to do what they want to do.
Free people want to do what they know they have to do.

—Richard Rohr

Are you *being* at the same time as *doing*? Are you enjoying what you do, having fun, or are you "working", puttering away while wishing you were doing something else?

Where *do* you spend your moments, anyway?

Could I have asked "where do you work"? No. And why does it have to be called "work"? Often, work is compared to a chore – what is this dysfunctional thinking that has settled itself deep into the psyche of society?[1]

If the word applies to work that is gruelling, something you do not enjoy, that takes a little something from you... then it is something that is certainly detrimental to one's over all well-being.

If the place you spend your moments on a day-to-day basis is a place that sucks a little colour out of you, sucks a little good out of you, or fails to add goodness to your day, then how will you spread goodness and colour in that environment? What if someone's life path is immensely affected by the energy you project?

For example: within this federal institutional environment, there are some employees of Correctional Services of Canada (CSC) who wear in their outward expressions the pressure(s) of internal conflict, of unease and imbalance. And their emanated vibration certainly seeps into whatever their energy is put towards. Whether that energy comes in the form of reports written to paint an unpleasant picture of some-one, or whether it comes in the form of conversations exchanged with the clients in their care – it shows. It is there. It exists. Like a live toxic substance. And it is live. It is energy. Force-based energy.

The energy we project onto others... matters.

Especially in a "correctional services" environment, where beings are employed to care for, look after and take into account the suffering and plight of fellow beings. How will that exchange of energy turn into an uplifting or inspiring exchange? Becoming aware of the feelings we harbour, and then project at work; becoming aware of how we relate towards what we consider "work", and how we identify with the term, would be a good start. This contemplation could help us expand our field of awareness and experience a shift; a shift which helps assemble a healthier perception.

While I was at the Regional Reception Assessment Center (RRAC) awaiting classification and placement into a federal institution, I was "emergency transferred" out, because I was deemed no longer manageable in that security setting. Paperwork was submitted to override my initial assessment as medium security, and to have me reclassified as a maximum-security inmate. I received the paperwork while I was in segregation, and with time to take it all in and reflect on the previous few weeks, things again made a little more sense.

When an inmate is emergency transferred, a request is made to increase the inmate's security status. A hearing takes place to determine whether or not the request will be supported or denied. This hearing process is called a rebuttal. A lawyer is usually relied upon to do that for you, but you also have the opportunity to write a rebuttal yourself.

So I did.

One of the institution's reports was written by a correctional officer with whom I had had a brief conversation. She pulled me aside because she had been on the receiving end of multiple remarks, one of which came from me. Why are you yelling? I asked. Because I am sick of it, is one of the things she said. We were talking (sort of) privately and so, with no one else around, it was easy to give her my undivided attention. With that came the opportunity to look into her eyes. I saw emotions being displaced with a tiredness that is the source of dysfunctional behaviour and the physical proof of the concept of "work". Have you ever thought about doing something else? I asked.

She took offence.

Don't preach to me, I have been doing this for a long time, she said. I politely said to her, look, no one else is around, it is just us. I am not trying to insult your intelligence nor am I trying to talk down to you in any way. You were just yelling at the top of your lungs with a red face telling people to lock up when you could easily take a different approach. Maybe it is time to do something else, I said, adding that, if what you do isn't fun for you, then what is the point? We didn't end that exchange on a bad note; we actually ended it smiling. Yet what came of it was an onslaught of furious writing which ended up in the report.

Another of the reports arguing for my reclassification suggested that, because of my considerable influence over others, and the affect it can have on the prison environment, the only remedy is to manage me in a high security setting with constant surveillance. The report suggested that others were trying to gain my favor by not following rules: wearing their socks, and crossing the painted lines that separate the ranges.[2] Because of grandstanding, I was allegedly reinforcing my position within the social hierarchy and this was a serious security concern.

I had to write that I didn't gain any status or retain my position in the social hierarchy by getting into an irritating (at most irritating) back-and-forth with a correctional officer. Maybe in high school if I was still in Mrs. Holmes' English class, bent on being the class clown, maybe then it may have an impact.[3]

I also wrote; how does one not see that, not only is everyone getting along, but everyone is friendlier, everyone is kinder, and that everyone is sharing more with one another?[4] Why do you not see it? Because one isn't looking for it.

I wrote that it comes down to *perception*. What is perceived by the correctional officer from the desk he or she is typing from, is a judgment that does not come from an awareness-based observation, but an opinion formed to support pre-existing beliefs, reinforcing conditioned thoughts. It isn't accurate and it doesn't tell the whole story.

It is incomplete.

I was re-supported for medium security and was eventually sent on my way to Mountain Institution. These words were typed here at Mountain. It is a lot of fun. *Being* here.

Typing too.

Perhaps what I have said above is vague, but an aspect of "not being" can be described by such actions. Typing a report from a place of judgment, to support a belief, meant to cause harm, and devoid of an awareness-based observation. It is a common occurrence, this behaviour, which at times is a mixture of ignorance and (almost) indifference.

A friend of mine (Zolaal – whose poem is featured at the back of this book) was put under extreme pressure and was repeatedly road-blocked in his pursuit to not only better himself, but to help others in the process. Obstacles were put in his way, from cutting him off from support within the administration to assist in a post-secondary pursuit (university classes), to the writing of false reports to limit and, even, disqualify him from employment options. He knew, as much as those conspiring knew, each negative report becomes a great hindrance to not only cascading down to a minimum security environment (where there is much more freedom and feeling of moving towards a "normal" life), but acquiring parole; especially for someone serving a life sentence – like he is.

So he decided to do something about it.

He wrote some powerful words, repeated below, to the Honourable Kim Pate (the Senate Standing Committee Chair on Human Rights) in spring 2019, in response to the pressure he was being put under. After this, the dialogue finally began which is helping bring renewed change to environments like these.[5]

> We are all human beings and everyone makes errors in judgement, and at times just simple mistakes, whether caused by a lapse in understanding or by poor judgement. The problems arise when

obstacles are intentionally put forth, a sophisticated design of stumbling blocks, in the path of vulnerable people who are barely coping with the conditions they are forced to endure. In a movie, you would picture an evil villain for the part of those behind these schemes, yet in reality they are camouflaged as productive and effective members of our society.

Those who throw down stumbling blocks display dysfunctional thinking, behaviour and actions. And within this federal environment, where success or failure, a good report or a bad report, comes at the whim of someone's keyboard or pen, it certainly creates a snowball effect where traces of negativity leave stains on an inmate's file that aren't easy to remove. At times, the case management team (CMT) will conspire as one to stain an inmate's file. If that isn't as malicious as it gets, what is?

However.

Within this federal environment, change is already here. There is much change that has come in the last year, and it has a lot to do with the new approaches the administration is taking. Some of it can be attributed to my friend who wrote those powerful words to the Honourable Kim Pate. Misunderstanding, outdated approaches, and attitudes of indifference *can* be affected with a little "amor".[6] With new mindsets, with a little understanding, and with a little compassion – going both ways.

Indeed, a two-way road.

If the colour of joy finds its way into the experience of those left in trust to serve – well, then it will surely start to filter its way into what they do, say, and see. If we understand that our basic obligation is to serve in a way that is for the betterment of humanity, then we can continuously self-check and self-tune our ways, and move in a manner that keeps in sight basic moral and ethical values. Moving in this way, we can surely move from the aspect of doing to a continuous experience of *being*.

So.

Ask yourself, are you doing or are you being? Are you part of the dysfunction, or do you add colour to the environment as you spend your moments *being*?

If.

If you aren't helping others. If you are giving people hate. If you are knowingly intruding on the well-being of others. If you are spiteful within and send it outwards. If you are conniving and scheming to maliciously do someone wrong, if you are looking to inflict pain by playing on someone's emotions. If you are furthering a message of disconnection in the media and fueling waves of energy that revolve around separation, and if and the energy you put out creates further discord, either by your action or inaction: you are part of the problem, you are part of the dysfunction. If you are a news anchor and your only obligation is to read what is written out for you, and you justify it by thinking that you're under no obligation to gauge whether what you say adds harmony, and promotes balance in the world; then you too are not part of the answer. If the only thing that concerns you is ratings... if the content only matters because it influences stats and popularity, then how is that serving the betterment of humanity?

It isn't.

If you are writing biased and tainted reports from a place of indifference, and those reports are filled with ignorance and malice; if you are looking for ways to paint someone in a bad light; you are leading with your ego. If you are bringing the stains of your personal life into the environment where you spend your moments, if you are not leading with love, with compassion, and with kindness: you are adding energy to the dysfunction. You are not part of the solution; you are part of the problem. You might as well lock yourself in a room and give yourself the time schedule imposed on a person inside a prison, until you are forced to re-think, re-evaluate and perhaps re-create yourself. Maybe bring a correction to the errors you are impressing upon the world and collective consciousness. Maybe it will cause you to think about why you are part of the problem, and how you could go about being part of the solution.

Isolation will do that.

If you are truly unaware of your actions and what those actions trigger, when it comes to energy, then expose yourself to awareness-jolting beings: Deepak Chopra; Eckhart Tolle; Wayne W. Dyer; Luis Hayes; Abraham Hicks; the team that made the movie, *The Secret*. There is no push to bind yourself to any religion, only to invite in the light of love, compassion and kindness. Exposing yourself to high energy beings will raise your vibration. Once your vibration is raised, it will affect your awareness level and *that* is when shifts happen. When shifts happen, perception changes. The healthier and higher shift of perception is what lays the foundation for deeper understanding to emerge.

If you continue that pursuit (higher and higher awareness), every religious scripture left behind as a guide (for those that gravitate towards religion) will start to make sense. The simplicity of it all will bring a smile to your lips.

A smile from your being.

You'll realize it is all the same. The drive for division is the ego that wants to claim something for itself – or to claim as itself. There is nothing to claim, as nothing is yours. Everything belongs to the Creator, the Supreme Being of creation.[7] We are but particles of that creation. We are but offspring of that Well. And what a delight that Well is.[8]

Delight indeed.

A Buddhist Sage said, "The finger pointing to the moon – isn't the moon." Get it? Anthony de Mello comments on this quote in his book, *Awareness*:

How mad have human animals gotten, the finger pointing to the moon isn't the moon, but there are those that are trying to take that finger and gouge out each other's eyes with it.

Imagine that.

An instrument of love. A teacher of life principles. Of life ethics. Of ways of being, used as a tool to inflict hardship. Pain. Heartache. Abuse. Twisted, right? Ignorance. But ignorance can no longer be an excuse. Unconscious participation and unawareness is no excuse. What is your excuse? Do you have one?

So... *are* you part of the solution?

How do you relate to where you spend your moments, is it a place of "work"? Or is it say, your place of passion? Or an environment in which you express passion, uniqueness, talent or skill? Do you consider your work environment a place of serenity or meditation? Maybe it is a place that gives you immense joy to be in.

You *are* enjoying your moments, right? If you are – wooohoo! If you're not enjoying what you do, if you aren't experiencing that underlying feeling of... harmony and joy in *being*, if it leaves you feeling lousy, then ask yourself, why am I doing it? Is it temporary? Have you been at it for too long? What is the purpose behind what you do? *Is* there a purpose? Is there a goal in sight? An end number for your hustle?

Bubu's was $99 million dollars.[9]

I drop Bubu in here a lot, hey? Maybe you're thinking there are some unresolved feelings or maybe something left unattended. I assure you that is not the case. She brings joy with her wherever she goes, and she has certainly brought the colour of her enriching spirit into the journey of these words, hasn't she?

Kinda neat how that works.

How the memory of someone's presence continues to influence energy to move around us – well, me anyway. I sure hope I had some sort of influence on her. Although, if I succeeded in rubbing off on her in any way, it was probably my paranoid approach to certain things.

No, wait.

She is naturally a little … different. She is, actually, a commando girl. She found me in the most highly restricted wing of a hospital, through a door that was swipe card access only, past double sets of emergency response team members strewn about, and that was *after* ruling out neighbouring hospitals.[10]

Imagine that.

All that security and it did nothing to keep the atomic brunette at bay. She laid eyes on the room I was in, got this inner feeling of "he is there, safe and breathing" – then she left to figure out how to get in there.[11]

She was in there within a fortnight.

Yes, I need something to counter the ADHD, something to help the focus and keep me on track (sort of). We will get there one day. For now let's get back to the topic.

If what you're doing on a day-to-day basis isn't exciting, or fun, isn't a source of happiness… then maybe it is time to ask *why*. Why am I not doing that which brings me joy, happiness and feel-good vibes? Maybe it is time for a change. Maybe it is time to do that which speaks to me from within, something that I have been putting off, perhaps. If there is something speaking from within, and you have that feeling in your stomach – well, that isn't coincidental. High energy beings will tell you that there is no such thing as a "co-incident". It is all connected. That which is dubbed "co-incidental" is a moment of synchronicity. You are reading these words not by chance, or accident, but because of attraction.

The law of attraction.

You attracted these words into your experience. The vibrations you emitted have within them something that connects you, somewhere in their entirety, to these words. Your mere curiosity might be why you think you went and bought this book, to see what this fool of a boy has to say – but that is just surface layer stuff, the real deal of it is deep. Deeper than deep. Something in this book was written *just for you*, and that is just the way it works.

And perhaps.

It is time to align with that which truly speaks to you from within, maybe something that you have put off, tucked away, or forgotten. Maybe a dream, overlooked or dismissed as childish and unrealistic.

Anything is possible.

If a monk sitting in a cave, in one of the most enriching areas of the world, can grow back a set of teeth in the span of 5 years, all with intention... you can do soooooooo much.[12] Anything is possible. Anything. Bhutan is the area by the way.

Your dreams matter. Your vision matters. Your contributions matter. The difference you're meant to make, matters. It matters so much. Your spiritual energy matters. Your vibrational alignment matters.

You matter in every sense.

It doesn't matter who says what, or who might try to diminish the importance of your existence, to lessen or take away some of the light radiating from you – the life essence surging through the body you're housed in. You matter, and no words anyone ever says to you or about you could ever encapsulate your worth. Your uniqueness is a spark of *life*. That which is you – is an extension and expression of the Infinite. It really is. So remember that.

And while you're remembering...

Be now. To be is to be free. So be, and make a difference; it will set others around you free, too. When you're free, you will affect all those that come into your experience with your energy – whether you're aware of it or not.

There is a new Institutional Parole Officer (IPO) working at Mountain Institution. I heard of her over and over when I came back from Kent Institution, after my 3-week mini vacation (April 2019). The things being said were, the IPO is nice, kind, helpful, and is unaffected by the poison that eventually wears others down who work here. The IPO is not looking to screw you over – is actually willing to help. Wow, I thought, what if all of the IPOs could be like that? Be genuinely kind?

And then guess what?

Others began saying that their IPOs were being... *different* (there are about a dozen IPOs at Mountain Institution, for a little over 300 inmates). They were being... kinder? More... helpful, and more understanding. They seemed like they were more caring, actually trying to be nice. No way, I thought, is this energy source really having this effect on those around her? I also found myself thinking, isn't this what one signs up for, when one chooses the service sector of employment?

It has to be.

Who would choose the service sector to cause further disruption, further chaos?

I saw her after hearing of her for three weeks, while she was attempting to assist another being. She reminded me of the woman superhero. You can *all* be sort of superhero-ish, all of you who are left in responsible positions of care – you can swoop in to affect everyone around you (if you aren't already) for the better. Humanity is in need of it.

And why not make a difference?

Making a difference in someone's life could be just the thing that sets you *free*. When energy is flowing freely, when you are vibrating harmoniously, you naturally emit it to those around you, maybe like the IPO has been doing in this environment. Freedom and power – true power, true strength – flows from *within*.

And.

Up until about a year ago, if someone had asked me, how does one harness it? I would have said simple, go within. *Tune in*. Meditate.

But.

In early January 2018, perhaps for the first time ever, I felt something that loved ones have described feeling. I called a friend, who put me on speaker, and then the other friend he was hanging out with started speaking. She spoke in Urdu, which threw me right off and left me scrambling for responses.[13] She then recited poetry – in Urdu – and added a personal piece of hers at the end in Punjabi, which left me in a daze.

We laughed. A lot. I really enjoyed it.

We shared this genuine, warm, and joyful moment. It was a comforting experience. My friend said, I just felt your energy change, and though I had begun to realize I was feeling better, his pointing it out magnified it. I paused for a moment and told him I would need to reflect on this a little to make sense of what just happened. "You do that Mr Khun Khun," he said, trying hard to mimic the "Mr Anderson" tone – you know, from *The Matrix*?

Focus, Jujhar.

Upon reflection, following the conversation, during the night, and during meditation in the AM, I realized what had happened. The exchange of energy "lifted my spirits", healed something I wasn't aware needed healing. Not in the moment anyway, nor leading up to that conversation. I acknowledged to my friend (on a phone call the next day) that whatever frequency I had been vibrating at ceased to be almost instantly during the exchange of energy last night.[14] I told him I didn't know how to explain it, but I went from feeling heavy and weighted down, to lighter, better... happier. That is how easy it is to change our vibrational alignment(s) from unhealthy to healthy. The quick fix is, through ingesting a dose of very valuable cure—

Laughter.

When I told him this he burst out laughing. "Just be," that's what my friend says, he told me. *Just Be*. Every time he said something, she trumped it with simplicity. She naturally *is* what we are trying to be, he said. She's figured it out. My turn to laugh, as I asked him if he knew why.

Why bro? he asked.

Because you and I are still fighting something that isn't even there and she, my manz, is *free*. Woah... that's exactly what it is bro he said; wow that's totally it. She's not attached, bro, she could stop talking to me today and she would just continue loving, continue healing, continue laughing and...

...continue *being*.

My friend's friend, affected me with presence. Presence is all there really is in a moment. Being free costs nothing, takes nothing, but is *everything*. That simplicity she emitted was *awareness*. She was present, unattached... and *free*.

Attachment in any form – whether to people, past, future, feelings, thoughts (mental constructs) – restricts the free flow of life energy. Freedom from these chains allows one to *be*. Just being *is* the freedom. Just being is the foundational aspect of the spiritual sustenance we require. Just being roots us and connects us to strength. It welcomes in and establishes a base, and everything else starts to fit itself into one's life accordingly. Kind of like Tetris blocks.

Rooted in being.

What we build our world with – relationships, things, circumstances, our life experience – then becomes a construct of understanding, of depth, insight, hindsight and foresight. It becomes a life composed of the very fundamentals that are the core ingredients of *happiness.*[15] Of joy. Of strength. Of *love.*

When you're free, love happens. When you're clutching in desperation, you become imprisoned in a way that sucks the energy right out of you. One doesn't have to do anything extraordinary. Just let the dirt, the filth, the muck go. Let things go. Let things be. *Just be.*

What seems like little more than a minute ago – but was, in fact, 2013 – I was self-destructing at a pace I don't exactly know how to illustrate. It was a treacherous unravelling. I wasn't rooted. I relied on a support structure for everything: my sense of self-worth, emotional security; from feeling loved and needed, to feeling appreciated and happy; from the strength I drew from friends to my mental well-being. Thread-by-thread it all came undone.

I fell apart.

I had to lose myself completely, or the idea of 'myself' anyway, to rebuild again. I had to let go of everything I thought I knew and literally learn how to live again. Breathe again.

But.

After all this time, I think I may have just learned how to live, for the first time. I may have just learned how to breathe for the first time. Experiencing Gurbani, listening to kirtan, reading books, listening to guided meditations, all helped me acquire a sense of balance that had been only an idea for me. An idea that balance and harmony existed in the serene manner that it does, free of any external reasons like circumstances and life situations. I had to accept my life as it was, and then let it be. I had to become compassionate towards the very things that were in the way of experiencing happiness – my own shortcomings, attachments and faults; and that is where it begins and ends: with the person appearing to stand in the way. It is both the hardest and the easiest thing in the world to simply step aside.

When you're free *everything* changes. Existing friendships strengthen and flourish. When you start *being*, the idea of what you thought you were starts to fade away. That which is you begins to shine forth; it stands illuminated.

A space opens up.

Once that space opens up, it creates room necessary for realizations. Once you start realizing of your inner essence – getting in touch with who or what that truly is – an irreversible shift begins.

That shift *is* the much sought-after change.

The shift *is* awareness. Awareness is an illumination of an expanded spectrum. A spectrum through which we not only observe, but experience this world anew. Love will come out from within when you're free. It will set you free.

Told you, it is all about *Mohabbat – Love*.

Take it from the man whose Soul's purpose was to sacrifice his entire family and smile his way through it – Khalsa stands tall on the sacrifices of his youngest sons, who were bricked in alive (a piece of history shared earlier). And his sons, they smiled their way through it. How? Love.

They understood how to *be*. Guru Gobind Singh Ji, the father of those two boys, said:

Those who love, will realize God.

So.

Whether God is a destination to be reached, or an eternal essence to be realized... *love* your way through the beautiful maze, the journey, any and all journeys, and you will see how the beauty around you blossoms. Love has made this life experience... amazing.

It is beautiful.

It is bubbling with joy, and the intensity doesn't seem to fade. I have a feeling that it is here to stay. The colour. The vibrancy. For that is the beauty of cause and effect.

Just *Be*.

---

1. I was sitting quietly in the sheriff's holding cell in Kelowna, BC, when I came across Wayne W. Dyer's concept of "identification", and I thought... wow...unacceptable.
2. Separate ranges, but shared yard space. Have to access the yard from the respective entrance/exit designated for each section; once in the yard, you can mingle at will.
3. Best English teacher ever – Mrs. Holmes (if and when you read this), sorry for raising a ruckus :D
4. We (collectively) experienced a higher morale amongst the general population, with the majority interested in getting along, sharing, and respecting one another. It led to unison and harmony within the kitchen work environment, and the day-day-day's on the ranges. Kool experience.
5. Kim Pate – A Canadian senator, known for her research into and advocacy for vulnerable people (particularly women) in Canada's criminal justice system.
6. Amor – Love in the beautiful Español language.
7. One Creator. Names used for the Creator: Waheguru, Allah, God, Yahweh, Rahm (Not the deity – but the One All Prevailing, Omniscient – Omnipresent – Omnipotent).
8. Well – God's Universe.
9. Bubu – a source of unconditional love.
10. Military-looking team.
11. Method – call the police and tell them she is my girlfriend; on the first phone call she was sort of laughed at, nice try they said. When they realized she was serious, they set up a meet and converged on her like she was the one who had done something wrong.
12. A frend's spiritual mentor spent 5 years in Bhutan. She has seen it happen. She is also a healer. Or someone through whom healing energy flows. Her heart is pure. She isn't one to lie. She does not do hallucinogenics.
13. Urdu-Hindi-Punjabi – Much of the bases of these languages is shared. The languages occur in close vicinity to one another, which is a contributing factor to their similarities.
14. Higher alignment, higher frequency. Higher frequency, happier you are. Happier you are, the higher your vibration! Kool, no?
15. Check out *Happiness*, by Matthieu Ricard. Scientist turned monk. I would leave the book laying on my bed, and it was almost like it was emitting a happy vibration into the room.

CHAPTER 28

REALIZATION OF HOME

If I am not for myself,
Who will be for me? If I am for myself, what am I?
And if not now, when?

——————

Eim ayn ani lee, me lee?
U'chsha'ni l'atzmi mah ani?
V'eim loh a'chshar aymatah?

—*The ArtScroll Siddur*
(Courtesy of O'li)

The Canadian junior ice hockey team the Humboldt Broncos were on their way to a game in Saskatchewan when their team bus collided with a semi-truck and trailer. I was in Okanagan Correctional Center when the news aired. Early reports indicated that there were multiple casualties. I stared at the screen in silence while a wave of mixed emotions swirled inside. One part of me said, wow – only God knows of God's plans. The other said, how in the world does this even happen? *Why* does it happen? How is one supposed to cope with it? How do you accept that, in one moment, so many lives are affected in such an unexplainable way?

How does one even begin to make sense of it?

I felt frazzled as I contemplated what had just transpired, and in response to the storm of thoughts and feelings, I sat down to meditate. The noise within me subsided as breathing found its own rhythm. I visualized sending yellow balls of healing energy to the very site where this... life-changing tragedy had just unfolded. After a moment, this warmness radiated from within, accompanied by the feeling that many will survive, and a humbling thought that quietly said, it will be OK. That this event too has its place in the dance of life at a collective level.

When the survivors spoke in the days to come, when friends and family spoke, how they spoke, what they said, added more comfort to that warmness I had felt during meditation. Then, another realization dawned on me as I listened: no one can actually explain the Unknown when things happen. I found myself thinking... what do we actually know? We know nothing really; we hold onto beliefs, ideas and thoughts that we interpret as true; we derive a sense of meaning from these.

What can we say to another about what they may or may not be going through? What comfort can we provide to someone when what we're talking about is a realm that we cannot see with our physical eyes or touch with our physical hands?

However.

We can hone the God-connection within. We can nurture the channels of communication and not only strengthen the inner channels, but heighten our awareness of them. This awareness can allow us to not only interpret happenings, but like a light let us see and experience the subtle realities from a more... intimate level.

As I contemplated these things, and thought about those who had lost their lives so suddenly... I found myself drifting back in time to my own near-death experience.

I've felt it.

The touch of the "other side". I experienced it just a little after midnight on 15 January 2013, after being shot in the back multiple times from a point-blank range. A little taste of it any way. It is amazing. It is a feeling beyond any physical sensation. I do not have words to explain it. Amazing is a feeble articulation of what the feeling is like.

Heaven.

Feels like heaven. More than heaven. I lay there, on the icy ground, face down, bleeding out. I was slipping into eternity. Felt like I was being... gently welcomed. Returning home for real. I experienced a vivid stream of thought. My parents came to mind – I smiled. And then, for some reason: the thought that I was supposed to train Bubu (I had just become her personal trainer) at 6 a.m. strolled through. I lay there melting into heaven and answered the thought with... I know, but baby this feels so good...

And then. WAM.

Whether I thought it or heard it, the word *baby* repeated itself like a bell and something said: GET UP – it jolted me into the present moment, and into a hyper-alert state. The word snapped me back into the reality of time. Because, where I was, reality and the illusion of time had ceased to exist. Reality – this reality we are viewing with our eyes – is not what that feeling of bliss felt like. And.

It wasn't time.

I didn't bleed out. I got up – lifted up, in fact, by helping hands (an Angel's) and those hands stayed gently close till I made it inside the emergency room lobby of Surrey Memorial Hospital. Delivered safely into the gentle hands of a nurse – who lied to me, I would later recall. She told me she would call my mum and let her know where I was, and not to worry because I was going to make it. As I slipped away, I remembered thinking... liar! You never asked me for the phone number.

I didn't crash or lose my way to the hospital (navigating an area I have had difficulty with under normal circumstances). Angels come to your aide (I said that earlier). Does it make it any different, if I tell you that I felt the presence of an Angel right there with me?

Does it change your perception of reality?

What If I told you that, on the evening I decided to step in front of an SUV (9 October 2007), I was knocked unconscious and launched headlong into the air? The back of my head connected with the hood of the SUV, and my back and legs with the grill and bumper. When you're unconscious, you're unresponsive. When you're unresponsive you're unable to use your hands or arms to break your fall. I landed face-first on the ground, and then skidded across the road – what if I told you that, despite all this, I woke up with no marks on my face? The doctor told us it was a miracle. I told loved ones that in the dream state I saw my face shielded with Sukhvir's hands, and that she gave me a kiss on the cheek, and the last thing I remembered was smiling.

A friend of mine was there with me the night I decided to do this. She had actually sensed I was about to do something stupid. We had just finished lighting candles along the sidewalk where Sukhvir had sustained her injuries, just one night earlier (in the early hours of 8

October), and I dragged my heels getting back into the car. I stalled by saying give me a minute, then started talking to her through the open passenger window saying I still needed another minute. She said she saw it in my eyes that I was about to act the fool, right before I ran around the back of the car and walked out in front of the oncoming SUV. She saw me leave the passenger window, caught a glimpse of me through the passenger-side wing mirror, then through the rear-view mirror, and a quick flash through the driver's-side wing mirror as I dashed in and out of view. She heard the crunch of my body connecting with the SUV, the screech of brakes, and the headlong launch through the air.

She saw me skid across the road.

When she ran up to her dumbass friend laying there on 64th avenue – still in the physical world – her internal gut wreck quickly turned to anger, because she almost instinctively reacted by kicking him in the face. What the *** are you laying there smiling about? she said, she told me later. So I told her about Sukhvir's shielding hands and the kiss on the cheek which produced the smile.

Miracle?

> The world is made up of innumerable planes of consciousness and each has its own distinct laws; the laws of one plane do not hold good for another. A miracle is nothing but a sudden descent, a bursting forth of another consciousness and its powers into this plane of matter. There is precipitation upon the material mechanism of a higher plane. The result we call a miracle, because we see a sudden alteration, an abrupt interference with the natural laws of our own ordinary range, but the reason and order of it we do not know or see, because the source of the miracle is in another plane.

> —Mary Baker Eddy, "Conversation with the Mother" – Sri Aurobindo's Ashram.

> Adapted from *BANDGI-NAMA "COMMUNION WITH THE DIVINE"*, RAGHBIR SINGH BIR (Atam Science Trust)

I guess you could call it that.

Sukhvir's presence does that anyway. It makes you smile. Obviously, if she was going to give me a kiss on the cheek I was going to smile. Oh. Um. I guess I kind of owe an apology for doing what I did to the one whose SUV connected with my back. Sorry for causing a disruption to your life.

Truly.

But, I am so happy it was that particular SUV I stepped in front of and not someone else's vehicle, because then things wouldn't have shaped into what they have shaped into. Certainly wouldn't be here today writing these words in this context. By that same token, it couldn't have been any other way, because that is just the way it was supposed to be! For that is the beauty in it.

The unfolding of this dance.

Does your perception of this world change, when I say these things? So much more has happened in and around the life experience of loved ones (friends and family) and myself. Just wait till the movie comes out. Oh, by the way, we just figured out what we're going to call it, so don't go jacking our idea (and if you do, it's all good, we'll still make it – God willing of course). "Nakumay Munday who wanna do good". Not "Beeba Boys", because we're really not.[1]

I was saying, though, that…

It doesn't end here, in this physical realm. Whatever it is that continues afterward is something marvelous. That feeling I had… is indescribable. So whatever comes next, or at least, what happens in the in-between state… is nothing to be worried about. It is something to look forward too. Because that stage completes this cycle of expression.

But.

We have things to do until then. And perhaps it will be that much more marvelous if we do what we need to do here. If we live *now*. Help others live now.

Live and make it count.

That is what I felt in the comfort of the words I heard from the relatives and friends of those who passed on, in that bus crash right outside of Humboldt, Saskatchewan. That is what I felt when the survivors spoke – those who passed on did make it count, and were making it count.

A week or so after the Broncos accident, I was sitting up in bed watching the news ticker when what I read made me jump to my feet. What the ****, are you kidding me? I said out loud. I was reading that a bus had toppled over in India, and a dozen-plus deaths had happened. I stood there getting riled up – stupid driver, stupid roads, and stupid careless idiots. I was going off until I remembered what had just happened with the Broncos; it made me pause. I stood there, now, and remembered the Broncos, remembered the words of the survivors and the families affected, remembered the ones that passed on, and took a deep breath. That breath again connected me to a place of peace inside. A place of peace from where I could once again send loving energy.

It is humbling to know that... life can just change in a moment. It really can. We all experience effects of unexpected change or sudden loss that test every belief or idea we hold dear.

But.

It is part of the experience. It is part of this amazing life journey. It all finds a way to intertwine itself, or we find ways to intertwine it into our lives. In truth, there is nothing to intertwine, as there is nothing to separate.

It is all connected.

We may think we live in individual worlds, but everything is connected. Sure, we may be experiencing a reality only familiar to ourselves, with an individual point of perception... but that's all that is... *perception.*

And, see how things find meaning in one's life? See how things come to take shape in one's experience? See how everything has its place in the world? Things that happen in the world come to take meaning in their own way in our lives, and find a unique place amongst us. Or within us, rather. Like what happened with the Humboldt Broncos hockey team, and the way it found its way into this writing here, which made its way into your hands.

I also felt more, though.

I had felt something more inside of me a week or so earlier, as I contemplated what had happened with the Humboldt tragedy. I realized it was because it was so close to home. Canada is my home, I thought, that is why I felt that. No, wait. Punjab is my home. No, wait. Canada and India are my homes. I then realized my folly, the lesson and the fact that I am indeed a learner learning, with much to learn still.

Earth.

Earth is home. Mine, yours, ours. Temporarily. And not ours as in ownership. "The Earth doesn't belong to us, instead we belong to the Earth," said Rob Stewart. **Who is Rob Stewart?** We're getting there; a few chapters away – super Kool guy. I humbly realized that Earth is our temporary home. We are all just residing on it for a breath of a moment. Every single individual *is* connected, whether one admits it or not. There is no way to separate it. We're all one community and I feel that each of us has a responsibility to recognize that.

Every single one of those that passed on from their physical form in the bus in India, and all those that were affected by the exchange of energy... they matter just as much as those that were affected and continue to be affected today by what took place in Humboldt. Even the driver of that semi-truck and his family; they matter.

Every single child, human being, who is gunned down at an age when their life journey has barely begun to acquire tastes of experience, in any part of the world... matters.

Child soldiers that are brainwashed and programmed, forced to kill, taught to abuse other human beings in cold ways... matter.

Those that are forced into the sex trade, forced into the labour trade, regarded as pieces of property, of any age or any gender... *they* matter.

Young girls and boys forcefully fed drugs to make them substance dependant, who are turned into slaves for sale... matter. Wow... do they ever matter.

Those that are kidnapped, raped, forced to marry or perform sexual acts and even killed... matter.

Those that are working for pennies in a mine that some don't make it out of with their health intact... matter.

Those that are fleeing war-torn regions in search of a better life, in search of a safer environment to raise a family, just to be able to breathe peacefully... matter.

Those that are trying to escape on rafts, in lifeboats that capsize before making it to shore... matter. Children that drown in the open waters or wash up on shores, never completing the journey... *they matter*.

Those in Syria that go to sleep, to wake up four days later from a coma, to learn that a bomb ripped through their home and 3 family members have passed away... they matter.

Those that are oppressed daily, caught in the middle of proxy wars by the world's "superpowers", caught in the middle starving and thirsty... they *matter*. Someone is going to have to get creative to bring about an intense change to the energy pattern of the area. Someone is going to have to step up in a way that is able to bridge the gaps.

Someone is going to have to be the one who can bring everyone together. It can be done. *Where there is a will, there is a way.*

And there is nothing more to it.

Every individual that suffers from a physical illness that has no means of covering basic medical costs... matters.

Every individual that has lost everything they ever owned or maybe even everyone they ever knew, stuck in a "third world" street or alley... matters.

Those that are stuck in so-called "first world" countries or cities without the basic necessities, like shelter and food... they matter.

Those affected by nature and its changes in Peru, in Mexico, in Japan, in Indonesia, in the USA, in India, anywhere in the world... they *matter.*

The fact that an out pouring of help, an overwhelming gift of aid doesn't arrive from the world in these life-or-death situations; the fact that it isn't there – help – from the "free world" in times of peril, in this technologically advanced and financially capable point in history... is something that needs to change right now. Otherwise, what is the point?

What is the point of being so... capable?

Those that are trying to do everything they can to provide a better life for their loved ones, who are willing to suffer, endure hardship, do whatever is possible for them... *matter.*

Every single family or household that is trying to make ends meet, even at the expense of a literal disconnect with the very individuals they're working so hard for... matter.

Every child that doesn't have a pair of shoes or a bed to sleep on or something warm to eat *MATTERS.* Every child, woman, man, *every human being matters.*

Every single individual on a city street that goes to bed hungry in an alley or makeshift home... *matters*. Every individual that you walk by and may have never paid any attention to in any way... *matters*. It is time for us all to stand up and stand *together* and do something about it. It is our *responsibility* to do something about it.

Individually and collectively.

We need to come together to make that difference. You need to. Look around you. Where are you? What do you have? How is your life? How is the life of your loved ones? What does a day-to-day schedule look like for you or your friends? There are those whose day-to-day is to go rummage through garbage cans looking for food and anything that can be salvaged to sell. Not for themselves alone, but entire families – like in Venezuela.

Why not?

Why not make a difference? Time and time again we hear that we are here for a reason, or that everything happens for a reason. Yup. I one hundred per cent agree that it does. Just like this book, it's in your presence for a reason, and the words you are reading, were written just for you! You can make a difference in this world that triggers a chain reaction of differences made in this world – just start somewhere. And remember, a difference made in someone else's experience *can* make the difference that changes our own experience forever.

So... #Whynot...?

Live a little. Give a little or, rather, share a little. Care a little. Love a little. Let go a little. Breathe a little. *Dream* a little. Hope a little. *Smile* a little. OK fine, then, *laugh* a little. Maybe even cry a little. But most certainly let's open our hearts a little. Maybe let go of all the nonsense that serves no purpose in our minds and *make room in our hearts for something new... something more*. Maybe take a moment to re-evaluate what really matters, and why, because most of the clutter isn't going to matter in the end. End of this physical journey, where one will shed this piece of cloth the soul has put on, that is.

Do you know what will matter, though? Your contribution. It will matter, and it matters now. The uplifting affect you have on those around you. The exchange of healing energy... will matter. That exchange of energy will make a difference. It will make a difference in your life experience, in this physical realm, in the non-physical, and it will come back to affect both you and those with whom you share a collective experience.

No separation, remember?

It will come back to affect all energy fields. It will also emit energy, vibration(s) to the whole of humanity and throughout our temporary home – Earth.

---

1. Nakumay Munday – Bad Boys. *Beeba Boys* is a movie (fiction) made to reflect the Indo-Canadian presence on the streets of Vancouver, BC, and the surrounding cities.

CHAPTER 29

SEX

(YUP, WE'RE GOING THERE)

*Where love, romance and the proper understanding of the emotion of sex abide,
there is no disharmony between married people.*

—Napoleon Hill
Think and Grow Rich

S o. Let's just get right into it.

How do you feel about sex? What does it mean to you? *Does* it mean anything to you? Is it just a physical act, or, is it something beyond that? What about dating, what does dating mean to you? If you are in high school, stop here for a moment.

Contemplate it.

What does sex and dating mean to you?

I grew up in a household that didn't talk about sex. It was silently acknowledged as... forbidden. Sin. If there was a scene on television, it was silently understood that I was to look away. Not only look away, but to change the channel. Not only was sex not talked about; it was almost like sex didn't even exist. Not only was it programmed into my head that you had to wait till marriage to have sex, it was also an inappropriate subject and... wrong? Not only wrong, but something I was to... avoid. And thus, I felt that anything related to sex had to be kept in the dark.

Kept a secret.

I think I got the safe sex tutorial thing in grade 6. It gave me anxiety thinking about what was going on in front of me, and what my mind was being exposed to. I could hear my mum's wooden stir-stick breaking on me because I hadn't covered my ears, closed my eyes and run out of the room. I also missed a lot of what was said – the chatter in my head (mum's voice yelling) blocked out the sounds coming my way.

Waheguru.

High school was a big change for me, what about you? The pace at which everything around me changed, blended well with my personality. My social life changed a lot. I was making new friends. I was able to get away from the house a little more to hang out with those new friends (though I had to lie at times to make it happen). All in all, it was a fun and exciting time.

I enjoyed the change. I was a fan (still am) of new beginnings, but a victim of wanting to be accepted (now not so much). I was trying more than ever to fit in and belong. I wanted to be accepted and regarded as a key piece in other's lives. I wanted to look and be cool. I wanted to fit in – but not blend in; something in me made me want to stand out and get noticed (ego). I *was* getting noticed. From the things I said, to the way I behaved, to the social circles I was creating; I attracted attention. Enough attention that when I started dating in grade 8, I caught the attention of the girls who were regarded as "very cool". Even dated a girl who had a friend who decided I needed a kissing tutorial.

(Mum, I did not willingly participate.)

I dated a few girls in a short span, and the duration was short for a reason. I didn't know what dating was. I thought dating was: you like someone, so you ask them out, and if you got a yes, well congratulations – now you're "dating"! Then you do the fun stuff, like holding hands on the low, perhaps. If it got real serious than maybe you would attempt a kiss (like I did and epically failed).

On the cheek, too.

Yes, I heard of others going further, and I may have even chimed in, like yeah, I will do that, while in my head, another voice said, *no you won't*. Nor did I want to. I could see myself burning in hell for one reason (for having engaged in inappropriate behaviour before marriage). I didn't know what to do, that was another.

Tings were innocent, though, in those years, you know? [1] Really, things *were* innocent. Until I started liking this one girl in junior high, age 14 - I think it was, and not just *like*; I was sure I had *fallen in love* with her. The "never will I fall in love with anyone else" type of feeling. I did love her. Or, I really liked something about her, anyway. I didn't quite understand it, but there was something in the way she looked at me that made me want her to look a little more. So I created a buzz (spread the word that I liked her) and it wasn't long before the buzzing came back at me, and guess what?! She liked me too! Yeeeeeeeeoowwwww hot pizza coming through, hot pizza coming through! Hot pizza as in the hot pizza moment in the movie *Blue Streak*. You have seen *Blue Streak*? Right?

If you haven't, friends off for a little!

Obviously she was going to like me. I had word game.[2] And so I asked her out – the natural thing to do I thought. I felt more confident in my dating abilities (though I still had done no literal practise). I was poised enough to compliment the older girls verbally, and some of them thought I was cute, so it was received well, which boosted my morale and drew attention – but it didn't help me with the torment this girl put me through. She said yes! We were dating! Who knew what I was about to get myself into?

I couldn't have imagined it.

So here we are, in the flirting stage, and then one day our MSN talks go… waaaaaaaaay too far. Yup, MSN, whoop whoop![3] Our talks go too far and I bite off more than I can chew. So much for the practised dialogue I had imagined. The verbal confidence I had built up was nowhere to be found.

Oops.

> *Her* – Meet me at the upstairs bathroom, by your locker.
> *Me* – Oh really girl, you can't handle me. Ummm… (*Sweating/sheepish face*) Why do you want to meet me there?
> *Her* – I will show you.
> (*Show me, I thought. Right. Girl pleeeeeeeease!*)
> *Me* – You don't know me like that. (*Or I said something like that.*)
> *Her* – Dw, I will *get* to know you, big boy.
> (*Or bad boy; or whatever the seven hells she said.*)
> (Gulp. Double gulp. Help!)

I avoided the whole building! Screw the locker and all its contents! I think I left my backpack unattended, locker untouched, and hallway unapproached for a week. When I went back for it, the contents of my lunchbox hadn't just spoiled, it stuunnnnnnk and looked... weird.

Straight ew status.

Al talk, I was. All talk. I would go from being completely comfortable in a group setting, flirting and saying "all the right things" to a nervous mute of a wreck one-on-one. Then she went and broke me heart. Probably because we had minimal interaction (I was avoiding her) and I knew nothing about dating (though acted like I did). Yes, I meant to write "me heart". Don't know to this day what it was I would've got myself into had I showed up. I don't want to know. Don't ever want to speak to, or even look at her again. *Ever.*

I don't mean that.

Sex – in any real sense – didn't cross my mind till later, much later. The idea of having sex at prom wasn't familiar to me. I was hoping to go to prom in 2005, but I didn't graduate. I was re-doing grade 12 the next year and had my mind made up that I was going to score high grades in all my classes, stay out of trouble, and make it to prom. I was dating in grade 12, (yes I had figured out how to "date" by then), but sex was still not part of the equation. I never graduated, again, though.

No prom either.

I was respectfully told by the principal (early 2006) that there was no way he could keep me in the school due to recent police attention. From there I made poor choices, and within a few months of being expelled I went to jail for a year on charges of kidnapping and unlawful confinement.

I was dating for about 8 months before I went to prison. I was beginning to understand (a little) the feelings and emotions I was experiencing, and though I was showing my girlfriend and wanted to continue showing her that I loved and cared for her, I knew it was not necessary to show her that with sex.

Perhaps showing her that it wasn't about sex for me is what led to the deep-rooted care, affection and love we shared. Perhaps it is what led to us sharing such an intense inner-being connection with one another.

Nowadays... having sex *before* prom is normal. Won't even wait until then. Is that healthy? What do you think? What are your thoughts on it? Because I think that...

...Sex... isn't "just sex".

It is the most intimate exchange of energy that can occur between two beings.

For a moment, *two* become *one*.

Energy is not only exchanged; it is shared. In a rare occurrence, two energies combine. They mingle. They touch. At a whole new level, they share an energy field. And when those energies meet, they have the power to create life. Isn't that krazy?

Create life?

The power to spark a process which triggers a mind-boggling, awe-inspiring connection with the Unknown. A connection made with the Infinite, and when the Intelligence sees fit – it responds.

That's not "just sex".

That is something so... magical. It is a wow of a wow. Isn't it though? *That's* the miracle – no science can create from scratch. *Life*. Herein resides the power of God.

I feel that sex at a young age can be detrimental to one's emotional and mental development. Little understood feelings coupled with, perhaps, only mildly understood thoughts; these can cause serious psychological damage and not only taint perception of oneself, but hinder the ability to view the world without the mental and emotional clogging a negative lens brings.

What we don't appreciate in our younger years is the fact that there is a huge gap between our personal lives and the trending culture of, say, music and the related music video, tagged with the whole glamorized sex appeal thing that revolves around it. Young girls are encouraged to look up to idols that are marketed for a wide audience, and it is not easy for a younger girl to differentiate between what is meant for her and what is aimed at an older, more sexually mature audience.

The problem is that the music and fashion media sell us only one kind of sexuality through most of its products. These images and ideas program into a young woman's mind the idea of submissiveness, or the strange "freedom" to be submissive and held captive to someone else's wants, usually a more "powerful" man – and – this is not liberating. For many, it will fortify the levels of lower self-esteem, lower nature, and self-defeating expression, which will further trap a young person within cycles of self-destruction.

Harmful.

The boys, who have it programmed into their heads that they have a superior stance over a girl in some way, are also sold stories that are damaging to the psyche. They get imbedded in those that are unable to dis-identify from low awareness concepts – which is what, essentially, is being sold and bought in much of the music and fashion industries.

A dysfunctional concept.

Bought by vulnerability without much heed, and tried on by many unaware of the repetitive damage linked to something disguised as... fitting. It may not be something that leads to an experience of quality or true intimacy, but is sold as fun and "what everyone else is doing" nonetheless. What young minds often don't see is the programming itself. The programming of, the construction, activation, utilization and expression of the lower nature from which force-based power – power with a small p – stems from.

There is no manual.

Selena Gomez, the young American actor and singer, expressed glimpses of an awakening in the words she conveyed during her acceptance speech at an awards show (I think it was the Grammys) in late 2017. She said she was going through some personal things pre, during, and post her recovery period from a health condition. She said that, when she was expressing herself through music, videos, and social media, it wasn't done to see young girls reflect it back through the pictures she was seeing being posted. That was not what she was trying to promote. I just stood there in my assigned room at OCC, glued to the floor. Shocked. Some of the faces of the crowd looked shocked, too. Ariana Grande was up next. Watch her reaction to it.[4]

Observe closely.

The words of Eckhart Tolle rang in my head like a bell. Selena Gomez had looked deeply and seen something. Tolle wrote, in *A New Earth*, that people will have moments of awakening when they are ill; that they will see and hear through and with the "Power of Presence" – free from the grip of ego. He said, the temporary moments of awakening are brought on by the energy needed to repair the physical organism. He said that energy is pulled away from relentless recycling of toxic energy upon which the ego feeds, and from what "pain bodies" draw on to replenish themselves.[5] In those moments, there is a temporary power that comes to the forefront. The process triggers a higher awareness to emerge, and this not only allows a shift in perspective, but enables awareness of that experience from a point of observation, through and with the power of presence (which is awareness observing awareness). For those who are stuck in cycles of self-destruction or for those whom the lower nature expresses itself more freely, the moments are temporary. The awakening comes to pass, and passes away.

That was my interpretation of what he said.

Selena Gomez saw something on a deeper level, and an aspect of that deeper level is the psychological frailty of a young mind, which is easily influenced, especially at a certain phase of its growth. She saw the destruction her energy output had done, was doing and could do. She saw how she was influencing vulnerability. It takes a lot of courage to say what she said. It isn't conventional. It is perhaps why Ariana responded to it in her speech... in the manner that she did. It isn't what the world is... used too.

Awareness is the key.

On a Saturday in May, 2019, I had the TV tuned to Channel 10 (Joy TV) and, without knowing it, a show came on which I really enjoy. It is a show that combines beautiful scenery with classical music by the greats – Beethoven, Bach, Mozart and more (my bad for not remembering them all) – and this is a backdrop for the words of enlightened beings to appear and disappear on the screen. It encourages the watcher's consciousness to temporarily expand and experience another reality. I was stretching, and when this came on I smiled.

Perfect music.

Perfect moment to absorb the words – while breathing deeply. I jotted down a few of the writings and teachings as I stretched, until words from Eckhart Tolle floated onto the screen. His words made me stand absolutely still for a moment. Still still. The words were, "It is the stillness that will save and transform the world".[6] Words I had read before, but now the meaning they took on was something more, something of depth, something that made perfect sense.

That stillness *is* presence.

If we all stood still – as one – and enjoyed that experience, the world would be healed all the way around. For that is the power of the collective. We can do it. We can turn toward one another at a certain time, on a certain day of the year, as one; we can focus our attention at a certain time, on a certain day of the year, as one; we can stop whatever it is we are doing at that time, on that day, and remember the brave, the ones in need, the innocent, even if it is only for a moment. Imagine what we can do when we all start experiencing *stillness*. When we not only sit or stand perfectly still in observation, but with present-moment awareness as the backdrop of our observation(s). There we go.

World transformed.

The words above stand reinforced today, it is now spring 2020. The world has been countering the invisible COVID-19 virus. The world has been practising physical distancing – *together*. The world, realizing the need to distance one another in group gatherings, social outings, and when out and about, to help stem the silent attacker for the preservation of life. Staying away, but standing together – I think I read this slogan somewhere as part of a COVID-19 awareness campaign. Bottom line is, the world is doing what needs to be done because we have no other choice. Once again we have proved that, when we need to come together, when it's life or death, and when it affects each and every one of us, we will do it. There are housing and foods plans being put in place for the homeless. So, stepping up to the plate when there is no other option. Big pollution producing machines were shut down, and Mother Earth has been breathing and relaxing. My father said that there are reports of visibility for up to 200km in India, something many have never ever seen before. He said from Jalandhar (Punjab, India), there are reports of visuals of the Himalayas. Once this COVID-19 is slowed down and the collective energy of the world begins to supress it into submission, "wrestling the assailant to the ground" – words Mr Johnson (United Kingdom's prime minister) used after recovering from falling ill to COVID-19 – all the world needs to do is remember the fact that the world *did* come together, not to ward off an attack from outside of Earth, but one from within it, and that it saved humanity from self-destructing. All the world needs to do is, remember the climate benefits achieved when the machines were put on pause for a moment.

Earlier, with Tolle and Gomez, what I was saying was…

…that we need to recognize not only the "Power" in "Presence", but harness the "Power of Presence". Because in the harnessing of that strength is the ability to look deeply, like Selena Gomez did in a time of recovery and isolation when the opportunity presented itself. Because then Eckhart Tolle's words of stillness come into full effect, and the expression of Selena Gomez' shift in perspective and heightened awareness makes sense.

And, perhaps…

Create your own image of sexy. Sexy doesn't have to be in the form of sex. Or sex too early. Sexy doesn't have to be in the form of putting yourself "out there" to be noticed. Who said you have to have sex before, or on prom night, to be cool?

#BeKool4u. #Besexy4u. How is that for a hashtag thing? Probably already used right? Maybe yes maybe no. But, it's all good. Use it again. *Be sexy for you*, was the response of a father of a 13 year-young – my friend, Dgib – to a question I asked. I asked him, if he could give a single piece of advice to his daughter, who he is not able to talk to, or hug and hold (personal circumstances) – a daughter I heard him talk about many times and misses very much – what would it be? A daughter who is in this tender phase of the high school experience, an age of growth where the absence of a proper father figure's love and influence could manifest itself in destructive forms. A father who would move a mountain to get to her. He doesn't have the arms to do it, though.

Ohhhh… Check out the pun.[7] Get it? MOUNTAIN. He is currently incarcerated at Mountain Institution. Yup, getting better, definitely getting better.

It would really be something if his daughter gets this book, reads these words, and realizes, that is my dad who is being talked about. It certainly is, young one. His single piece of advice for his daughter would be, and is – be sexy for you.

It is also a piece of advice another loving father (a friend of mine who has passed on) would have for his daughters at this age, too. His Princesses. We will capitalize it, because Princesses are royally important. Be sexy for you. Not for someone else and their idea of sexy. The father may have passed on, but the advice will be around forever.

And.

The lack of a father figure doesn't mean the absence has to manifest itself in some self-destructive way. Nope. It can be the influence that keeps self-correction and self-evaluation at the forefront of one's journey.

Hearing my friends talk about their children, the ooooeyy gooey stages of newborns, and then the blooming, crawling, walking and running phases, has me looking forward to sharing in the experience of raising children one day soon.

Looking forward to raising *at least* a few daughters. They will learn martial arts and a form of strict self-defence early – to deter unwanted advances, and boost self-confidence too. Can't wait to meditate in some sublime settings all over the world with them. Can't wait to observe Awareness growing in them. I want to nickname one... Happy. I have this strong feeling that is what being around a baby daughter will feel like – *Happy*.

Take your time.

Don't rush into things.

What is the rush anyway?

#Besexy4u.

---

1. Ting(s) – How "thing(s)" is naturally pronounced in certain areas of the world by fellow beings.
2. Game – A quality combination of swag. ;)
3. Best online chat thing ever made. Ah... the good ol' days.
4. Search "Selena Gomez and Ariana Grande award acceptance speech 2017" (this should bring it up).

5. Pain bodies – Eckhart Tolle describes these as semi-autonomous energy-forms that live within most human beings, entities made up of emotion. They have their own primitive intelligence, not unlike a cunning animal, and this intelligence is directed primarily at survival. See *A New Earth*.
6. Quotation adapted from *Communion With the Divine*. Permission to quote obtained.
7. I had to remove multiple attempts at what I thought was "a pun" because it wasn't (thanks to the editor :@). This was, I believe, the first successful pun. Even got congratulated for it.

CHAPTER 30
TRUST YOUR HEART: INCLUDE

If the heart be impure, all actions will be wrong.

—Sanskrit proverb

No child should be left to feel inferior, unworthy, or undeserving. Ever. Innocence is innocence. So, never. Especially during a critical growth phase like high school teen years. Before then too, but this phase of one's journey – it's like a fresh start.

Elementary school has passed, and one is growing – and growing very fast. These years are critical for physical, mental, and emotional growth. It is a critical time for spiritual growth, too. It is also an opportunity to create, and re-create yourself (your identity) which influences and impacts the most sensitive steps ahead.

If you, the one reading these words, are in high school, I think you are pretty lucky to be going through this experience. I hope you feel optimistically energized to meet each new day with a smile and with lightness. You shouldn't be made to feel like something is weighing you down or be left feeling like an outsider, nor should anyone around you. Not in your classroom, not in your school, not in your neighbouring schools.

Yet.

Many are regarded as outsiders. Or weird. "Off" in some way. At the core of it, the same dysfunctional thinking that creates the illusion of a superior position, or a more popular one, is the same that creates its opposite. Both ideas are a perception, and both lack awareness; lack the strength of love.

Let's smash those small-minded perceptions.

For those of you in the high school phase, who feel at odds with themselves or others, who come from loving, supportive homes are in a real difference making position, and have a duty to support kids who don't. Have you ever considered what it must be like for someone who feels alienated or lousy? What must it be like for someone who doesn't have others in their life that help them feel worthy, emotionally and mentally supported, or engaged?

It puts you in a position to engage fellow students in a way that may make a difference in someone's life. The high school environment you find yourself in, provides you with a prime opportunity to have an uplifting, inspiring, and maybe even healing exchange. An opportunity to project a little (or a lot) of light (care and warmth) in the direction of someone who really needs it, and guess where? Right at ground zero (the frontlines). Have you contemplated just how much of a difference you can make in another's life? Or other's lives? You really can, and you can make that difference in a way that could change the direction of another's thoughts – forever.

It is all in thought.

The worlds we create, the worlds we live in. When you break it all down, that is where it stems from – thoughts. How we feel about those thoughts then helps reinforce the... perception of the world(s) we have created for ourselves. Have you ever thought what the worlds of those who are not included in outings or, say, group gatherings (dubbed as fun) are like? Or better yet, what must it be like for those who are regarded as...

...different?

In early 2018 I was in Okanagan Correctional Center (OCC) when I learned that an on-site deputy failed to respond with courage as a school shooting was unfolding in the USA. The deputy did not utilize his specialized training to the fullest of his skill. The shooting happened on 14 February 2018, in Parkland Florida, USA, at Marjory Stoneman Douglas High School. He neglected to intervene and inter-rupt the shooting. He could have interrupted it by getting to the source of the shots and engaging the shooter with tact, and perhaps things could have been different.

But.

I turn on the news, and... there it is. Another one. *Ouch* I thought. Ow. It hurt. There is no justification for sadness of this magnitude. I said many things out loud. Some in anger. Some in acceptance. Some in dismay.

I also said that it can be avoided.

Some days afterward, while seated in a room designated for programs (various programs offered from first aid to educational) on the unit at OCC, someone said, *Well what do you expect?* We were gathered as a group for a program (around 10-12 inmates plus a couple of facilitators). Another said, *It's not a surprise, it is what it is.* Someone else said, *I heard that his mother* (the young boy who was being held responsible for the shooting) *passed away recently and he didn't have anyone to take him to the funeral* – something inside me shook at the possibility of that being true. It was followed up with, *I don't think his mother would have wanted him there.* But it didn't register. There it was. The answer.

Love...

Love and understanding. Love and compassion. Love and empathy. The comments, in that group setting, were lacking love and understanding. Awareness-based understanding which elicits awareness-filtered responses. Everyone has the right to feel whatever they feel, but it is a personal responsibility to reflect upon the place those responses are coming from. And, maybe even more importantly, why.

How can someone, in such a cold and disheartening way, say something that has touches of cruel judgement, in the face of... tragedy? Because the speaker is speaking from a place of unawareness. Because the comments are stemming not from understanding, but ignorance. I did it myself, something I share in the chapter *Unawareness: DIA*.

In the days to come, many comments were made (on news media) by those that had seen the young boy being held responsible, around school and the neighbourhood, or who knew of him. *It is not a surprise – we thought he was off in some way, or was the type.* No one said, *I knew him.* No one said, *I hung out with him.* No one said, *I walked to school with him once*, or any words that included him in someone's experience in some way.

Not that I heard, anyway.

Knowing this in advance – someone's "off" or "different" nature – and being able to sense… these vibes that we pick up on, it isn't random. Picking up on the strangeness (or uniqueness) of that boy, that isn't just a "hunch". It is much, much more than that.

Within us, everywhere, invisible to the naked eye, is the part of us which is, in essence, the closest thing you will get to that is the core of the "you" or "me". It is formless. The energy that we are, you can't take it and put it in a bottle or a container, yet it is the very thing that is found within this… physical body that surrounds it. What we are is not only formless, but it is the very thing that is spiritual.

What we are, *is* Spiritual.

What we are, is formless. What we are *is* nonphysical. Intuition, and the inner voice, comes from this place where we (energy) not only reside, but from where we also utilize – through and with the power of awareness and intention – this inner energy. This energy does not come from the level of the restless thinking mind, but beyond that. We are an offspring of the Creator, and that also puts "us", beyond the level of "mind".

The mind is just another tool to be utilized. A vital one.

Beyond thought, there is a space, a vastness of stillness and quietude, that when broached… comes alive. Messages and answers reveal themselves. David Hawkins, in *Power vs Force*, says that according to Carl Jung, it is the "collective unconscious". He goes on to say that, "such a database, comprising all of the information ever available to human consciousness, implies stunning inherent capabilities; it is far more than just a giant storehouse of information awaiting a retrieval process". He also says, "it is the fountainhead of genius, the well of inspirations, and the source of 'uncanny' psychic knowledge, including 'foreknowledge'". Meditation is a key to tuning into it. Albert Einstein, Nikolai Tesla, and the likes of Leonardo Da Vinci, all tapped into it.

They expressed it too.

When we break down the... heartbreaking sadness that unfolded from the level of energy and vibrations surrounding the school shooting and the boy who carried it out... there is a connecting parallel. The very environment that the kid was attracted to, when he was doing what he did in that school shooting, attracted him too, all drawn together by a collective energy field of the ones occupying that environment.

By a collective disconnect and unawareness.

I apologize here if what I am suggesting comes off offensively, because I am not saying that the children who were hurt in the shooting are responsible for what happened to them. I am saying, though, that the young boy who did the shooting chose and picked where he was going to do what he did, and as he did there was a drawing element that pulled him in that direction. I am not saying that the boy was a victim of cosmic forces, but that his isolation and... possible mistreatment (thinking of him as different) helped steer the inner pull he had in not only the direction he set his sights upon, but toward the expression of his own inner disconnect, unawareness and... unconsciousness. That is just how it works, this energy thing. He may have wanted to inflict as much pain and chaos in the places he felt the intense negativity coming from, where he felt the disconnection from.

Where he felt left out from.

It doesn't take much to catch onto how some are feeling towards us, does it? We can see from the way others respond to us, the things that are said, and are not said for that matter, too. We can pick up on subtle behavior, on words, actions, and demeanour to gauge where others really stand with us. It is, at times, that much easier to break it all down and understand it when we have alone time to think. It gives us the moments we need to reflect on just why it is that some treat us the way they do.

And.

Just as those in the school felt what they felt at an intuitive level, that boy felt something too. What he actually did, he did unconsciously. From a state of very, very low awareness; from a consciousness level well below the critical mark of 200 on a map of consciousness scale Dr David Hawkins illustrates in *Power vs Force*. He says that all levels below 200 are destructive of life in both the individual and society at large; in contrast, all levels above 200 are constructive expressions of power (truth).

At the lowest level of shame, the consciousness level is logged at 20. In correlation to the level 20 on the map, one's God-view is despising, life view is miserable, emotion(s) at humiliation and the process is elimination. At the consciousness level of 30 it translates to guilt. Here, the God-view is vindictive, life view is bleak, emotion(s) at blame, and the process is destruction.

No good can come to oneself and the world from low levels of consciousness; from low awareness. It is not only destructive in nature to the collective consciousness of humanity, but it drains and depletes the collective energy field.

I do not know the exact set of circumstances revolving around the young boy's personal life. I haven't seen his psyche reports. And don't know his past history, what his interests were, where and how he spent his time—

But.

What if the kid had nothing to live for anymore? What if he saw no reason to go on? What if he had no place where he felt he belonged in this world? Then what, he must have thought, was the purpose of his existence?

What if?

What if all he needed was someone to walk up to him one day and just say, hey – how are you? With a smile. A cheery one. Maybe an

extended hand with the words, haven't had the opportunity to intro-
duce myself or say hi yet, thought I would – pleasure to meet you.

Or.

Hi, how's it going? I just wanted to say hi and maybe ask you to join
me for lunch, I saw that you were eating alone, and I wasn't eating
with anyone, so I thought – why not? #Whynot indeed. The words,
mind if I join you? leaves the ball in the other's court, and it also
introduces the equation of inclusion. What if someone had walked up
to him and said, hey I am trying out this "meet new people in my
school" thing and I share my lunch with them to see how it makes me
feel afterward, mind if I share it with you? Are you hungry? I brought
too much with me. Or. I am trying to step out of my comfort zone, to
share with others and get comfortable talking to everyone I meet – can
you help me out?

Or.

Hey, I am not having a good day – do you mind talking to me? Do you
mind helping me through this hard time? I really don't want to talk to
anyone I know, or already talk to, they think they know me – but they
don't. Everyone around me seems to think they know what's best for
me, they don't even know the first thing about what I think is good
for me.

Or.

Hey, what is your name? Are you new around here? Do you like this
school? What drives you crazy about it? What do you not like about
it? What can be better? Do you like to read? I read something in a
book suggested by some boy, that all we're really doing is just
exchanging energy, and that we go around exchanging energy all day.
Even this conversation we're having, we're exchanging energy. Lots of
it. He wrote that when we go around exchanging exciting, inspiring,
warm energy it affects not only us in the exchange, but everyone. The
entire world. This guy lost his marbles or what? What do you think?

Do we have any appreciation of just how much of an impact this sort of exchange can have on a ravaged state of mind? And how much of an impact it will make on someone experiencing a state of intense suffering? Life-changing. Inspiring.

Healing.

What if someone had walked up to the young boy and asked him if he was OK, and asked him if he needed a hug? Maybe a hug with a smile and warm words of support and comfort saying, I am sorry your mother has passed on. Do you miss her? Do you have other family that is there for you? What if someone had just taken a moment to start a conversation with the young boy? A moment in which all the built-up energy of hate, of vengeance; a moment in which all the negatively-charged energy of wanting to hurt people so they could feel what he felt, disappeared.

Poof.

Just like that. Like it wasn't even there. All that hate, perhaps, he was projecting with the intention of dispersing pain, hatred, anger, isolation, loneliness into the very environment that rejected him, which cordoned him off, leaving him isolated and feeling deprived of love or inclusion. All that hate – gone.

He may have seen the other students mingling, talking, sharing, enjoying – what was his issue? What was wrong with him? He knew how to laugh too. He understood laughter, why didn't anyone want to share it with him?

What if it led to him breaking down, talking about his hurt, his pain, and his loss, triggering him to cry? When you cry, you release energy.

What if someone had just cared enough to talk to the boy, and created an opportunity for some space to open up for him. For some repair to happen, some room for conscious thoughts to emerge which snapped him onto a healthier mindset? What if that opportunity created the space for a little clarity to emerge, so he might realize, maybe I don't have to hurt anyone?

Not anymore.

Someone had cared. Someone had helped him feel better. What if he just opened up about what he had been planning, and how he didn't want to do it anymore?

Now comes an opportunity to make a monumental impact in the life of someone like this boy, where the engager is helping reinforce ideas of self-worth. Everyone wants to feel supported. Feel validated. Feel cared for. Feel looked after.

We all feel a need to belong.

That's all it takes, a little touch of care and warmth. A little touch of love. Even a little love has in it a hint of healing that affects low vibrational thoughts and feelings. A concentrated touch of love can make low-vibration thoughts and feelings just... disappear. Like they were never there.

Engage. *Heal*. Mend.

Take the step. *Set the trend*. It creates new waves.

If you know anyone who feels unworthy, out-of-place, insignificant, or even if *you* ever get left feeling insignificant – show them, read to them, text them, post on their social media, read to yourself, or post this on your own page for yourself and for others:

> Never forget that you are one of kind. Never forget that if there weren't any need for you in all your uniqueness to be on this earth, you wouldn't be here in the first place. And never forget, no matter how overwhelming life's challenges and problems seem to be, that one person can make a difference in the world. In fact, it is always because of one person that all the changes that matter in the world come about.

So be that person.

—R. Buckminster Fuller

Show these words of Mr Fuller's to whom you think may need to hear them, and tell the soul you're engaging with, that this soul who wrote these words understood that some feel the way you feel. It is why he wrote the words in the first place. It is why they have found their way into your experience. Just to remind you, in case you forgot. Or to show you, in case no one ever told you, that you *are* one of a kind and your value to this dance of life, *is* immense, and the difference you're supposed to make – *needed*.

That includes *you*, reader.

It doesn't matter who you are, what you do, who you think you are, what you think you are, who others think you are, what others think you are. Once you peel away the layers, we're all the same. Just energy. And we share something in common.

Life.

We're all here, now, together. We came into this world naked and we shall leave naked. We came from one source. Our physical existence, temporary. The steps we'll have taken in creating and sending forth energy that makes a difference – will forever remain. The steps taken, and where those steps will have made a difference, will forever remain, and will forever be.

So... why not?

Live a little.

Care a little.

Give a little.

Share a little.

Understand one another. Just a little.

Seek out the silent sufferers. Many things trigger a person to experience a state of suffering, let it not be from a lack of love. A lack of care. A lack of empathy. Make a difference in another's experience in some way.

And.

Cultivate your inner spiritual energy. It will have life-changing effects on those around you. It will guide you to act in a way which is for the betterment of humanity. And once you are doing good for others, doing good by serving, by helping – something higher starts to pull you in and guide you. Pull you in because that is what you are now attracting, and you'll see how that energy starts to manifest itself all around you. It will become the energy that is unconditionally flowing from within you.

That's just how it works.

Understand that, where matters of the heart are concerned, the *answers are simple*. The heart – it feels. It doesn't reason.

Let's try this out right now.

To begin, take a few deep breaths to center yourself. Say a few OMs if you want to.

Now, imagine that you and your favourite human being are sitting in front of one another. It could be your best friend, your lover, someone in your family, or perhaps just someone you enjoy talking to. Or you could choose your favourite pet – whoever it is that makes you really happy.

Point to them. Close your eyes, say "you" and sit with that for a moment before you open your eyes again. Feel the warmth. The love. Keep pointing.

Eyes open now?

Close them again, point again and say "you", then point to yourself and say "me". Hold your eyes closed for a moment and then open them again – continue pointing at yourself.

Where are you pointing?

Most of us will not be pointing at the head.

Trust your heart.

Include.

CHAPTER 31

THE STORY IN SHORT PART 3

When you find the way, others will find you.
Passing by on the road, they will be drawn to your door.
The way that cannot be heard, will be echoed in your voice.
The way that cannot be seen, will be reflected in your eyes.

—Words of a sage

The "other guy" began to take shape, I'd say, in grade 7 (age 11-12). The mistakes I had made brought with them consequences, and I was learning of the repercussions I could face for doing certain things. One thing I was trying to hammer into my head was that, if I was going to do something, I couldn't get caught for it. I couldn't let my parents down. I could take the heat from police, but not from my parents. I realized that if I took heat from the cops, then I would take heat from my parents. Then I learned that the police couldn't involve your parents after a certain age, and it left me wanting to grow up as quick as I could.

Stupid kid.

By grade 11, I was hooked on mob flicks. *A Bronx Tale, Hoodlum, The Untouchables, Gotti,* and was pretty fascinated with the Cosa Nostra thing. The whole "this thing of ours" (that doesn't exist, and is only played up by Hollywood as a fantasy because of the media). Still, I was fascinated by Cosa Nostra and *omerta* (code of silence). It definitely influenced my thinking patterns.

I think seeing the lie in those who portrayed themselves as religious made it easier to let the influence of the street run rampant. Truth was preached, a specific lifestyle was preached, but... it wasn't practised. Not wholeheartedly. That hypocrisy certainly had an affect... I realize that now.

So, I started making compromises.

I was young, and one of the things I was learning was how to bend things to the way I wanted them to be or, at least, I attempted to bend things to my favor. I could have exposed the lies I saw, like the group I was performing on stage with, but instead – I wanted to bend things to my advantage. I didn't know whether exposing the lies would change my mum's thinking – I worried that all it would do was restrict my ability to move around. And I could feel my parents beginning to lose trust in me, because of the stealing. This made me work even harder to rebuild trust, and keep it intact. In came the acting, the appearance of being "good" and obedient. As long as my mother saw me doing certain things, she would think I was good, and if she had my corner, then it would be easier to stay in my father's good books too.

I needed the freedom.

I needed to explore the world, to get what I couldn't get at home. I needed to learn what else was out there. I needed to get out of the house as much as I could, and every chance I had, I took it. Something was driving me further and further away from home. I wanted to be anywhere but home. Now, I want to be nowhere but home.

Not really an option though.

Psychologically, I think, the things that made the biggest imprints in my head were the things I was told to avoid. Why? Why was I to avoid hanging out with friends? Why was I not to go to movies and outings that other kids were going to? Why did I have to always ask and ask and perform chores for us to go to a relative's home? What was so wrong with it? Why did I have to lie to get out of the house? How did my mum know everything? Most of the decisions were made by my mother. She ran the household. My father was the... he was the loyal husband and hardworking father.

Honest too.

Played cops and robbers a lot as a kid. Mostly in high school in Grade 8 (13) with friends who had been dubbed "the farmers". We had even lived in the Farmville area for a bit, grade 2-4 (age 7-9ish) I think it was, but not as farmers, just residents in the Farmville area. When I started hanging out with my new friends in grade 8 I was familiar with the area and it felt like home. Aww, I miss them (friends dubbed the farmers). They were very accepting of me. I don't know if they felt sorry for me, because it wasn't hard to tell the... financial gaps between our families, but I felt that they weren't judging me. It felt like they were truly my friends, and I still think of those early times as some of the happiest. Our friendships drifted apart towards the end of high school because I was intense at times, and I was trying hard to become this… other guy.

I always wanted to play the robber. I started out on foot but it wasn't long before I was rolling around on ATVs with them. This got me familiar with… the border line.

Fun times.

Duffle bags of mighty mites and crackling bombs (firecrackers) stashed away, became duffle bags of … well whatever they became. Got chased one time. A border patrol unit rocked the ride I was in from behind and almost sent me onto my side. Chased me right into Canada. I got away. Did the *Mario Kart* sideways skid, pump-the-brake-and-speed-off thing. I got the ride all banged up but didn't get in trouble, though (lost nothing). I actually earned some props for that.

Phew.

I got used from early on, I later realized. It started with the guys I looked up to in high school, who ripped me off over small moves and were willing to use me for whatever they liked. I thought I was earning my way into something really cool, but – nope. All lies. It was a front.

A façade.

A buddy of one of the guys I looked up to would go on to take advantage of a girl who I considered a friend. It added another layer of uncertainty to my head space.[1]

Later on, when I had moved on from jumping firecrackers, one of the guys I was working for decided to rip off someone's load (weed). He got nabbed over the jack move, and then a couple of the other guys decided to involve the cops. I thought we were going to go get "our guy" back and was mentally preparing myself for some wild wild-west cowboy stand-off thing. A different guy we also looked up to piled us all into a vehicle and said "let's go get him back, you guys ready?" Yup

I thought, ready to rock and roll. Imagine my surprise when we ended up in the parking lot of a police station.

Yup.

The "nabbed guy" eventually ended up giving evidence in court, and accused certain other guys in the hood for being responsible for not only nabbing, but torturing him. The guys he testified against got handed some heavy sentences. Can't profit from the... what do we call it, oh, let's call it *the game* – and then be part of putting guys behind bars.

That is just all kinds of wrong.

The experience tore up the idea of "us" – the guys – having a thing – like those mob crews in the movies I loved watching, who respected "the code". It left me at odds with the world I knew, once again. I didn't know how to put it together. But, it was OK, because without a doubt in my head, I knew I was falling in love with a girl who barely said anything to me.

Sukhvir.

Come to think of it, I barely said anything to her either. I met her in a grade 11 and 12 joint marketing class. I was seated at the front at one end of the classroom, and she at the other. A friend of mine – a farmer – caught me looking (maybe I was staring) and then gave me the *what's up?* – using his face, hands and shoulders to ask the question. I used my face, hands and shoulders to say, *I don't know.* That confused him, I think. What I was saying was, *I don't know who that is!* I asked him if he knew who it was; he looked confused and said, *I don't know either.*

Nice.

I got caught looking, by the way. It's like she sensed me. She looked over and before my brain caught up with the fact that she was looking at me – she wasn't glaring FYI – and before I had the chance to think, perhaps I should look away, my heart was hers. I didn't care if she didn't want it. She could ignore me or hate me for all I cared, as long as she knew my heart was hers, life would be more than OK. The teacher caught me staring too. He said – after the class was well underway – you going to be alright with a computer that doesn't work, JR?

Busted. Blasted. What to do? What would *you* have done?

What did I do?

I got up and moved one row closer.

Want to know more? You'll have to wait for the movie: *Destiny Part 1*.

I don't know how many times we sat by the lake, close to our school (Abbotsford Senior – whoop whoop! In Abbotsford BC, Canada – whoop whoop X2!) barely saying more than a few sentences to one another. Hey... Hey... Wanna chill? ... Sure. And then just staring out at the water. I memorized the layout of that lake and surrounding area. If I close my eyes right now, I can see it.

I can see it as I type, too. That is kinda cool – I never realized I could do that till right now. No, it's cooler than cool, it is Kool. I was also memorizing the shape of her fingers and the way her hair flowed perfectly in the air. We might have sat in silence and not spoken any words to one another, but I wasn't silent or still inside. I was busy imagining what a life with her would look like. From the way I felt sitting next to her, it would feel pretty ... well, hard to describe in words.

Extraordinary. Spectacular. Nah, words don't even come close.

One time I skipped class (science 12, I think) to see her. Almost right outside the science class, and after sitting next to one another for only a few moments, her sister saw us. Or – wait – I think we were walking towards our spot when she saw us.

When her sister saw us, she stopped dead in her tracks, glared at us, stomped her foot, turned on her heels and stormed off. I thought...

we're doomed. Sukhvir, however, for a split second, had a... smirk on her face. Rebel. Then she sighed, I will hear about *that* when I get home.

I gulped. Waheguru.

Sukhvir said it to me early on: most of the guys I consider "friends" are not really friends, and most of them won't be around when I need them because the friendships aren't real. What I finally realized she meant was the friendships were conditional. She tried teaching me to recognize greed, envy, and hate disguised in smiles, compliments and fake respect.

One of the kids I hung around with, someone I considered a close friend, turned on me, tried to surround me with a bunch of guys in a parking lot – after the money had run out. If it wasn't for Happy and his intuitiveness for spotting a bad situation at what was supposed to be a meet-and-talk... things could have turned ugly real quick. Someone was walking up from behind to hit me with a bottle, but he caught it, and... well he isn't exactly friendly once provoked. The kid tried saying I was trying to "buy" friendships – after a year's worth of trips to lunch outings. He would, later, be humiliated after a drunken night out. His "real friends" stripped his clothes off, made a degrading video of him, and circulated it around town.

Sukhvir was right.

I was just ignorant.

She and Happy clicked and vibed, and agreed on things I was short-sighted about. Yes, I should have listened more to both of them. In another book I will definitely share more stories of Happy. Stories of how he tried to light something on fire but, instead, managed to burn his beard, eyebrows, and even the hair on the side of his head, right down to the skin on half of his face.

I tried not to laugh.

I had developed my taste for having money around this time in my life (2004-2006). My moral compass had gone out the window, when it came to what I would or wouldn't do for money. I eventually lost all the principles I had created – such as not taking from the innocent – to keep me... safe from karmic repercussions. I began walking blindly and ended up, in a sense, moving in the opposite direction of where I was expected to go.

Sukhvir's energy provided balance. But —

I blatantly disrespected her. She had said, don't put me in a position that would embarrass me or my family, and I did exactly that.

In a botched get-rich-quick scheme involving a truck driver, his truck and a load I was told I could hook up and take – in May 2006 – that contained one million dollars in goods (estimated street value 750K) – I threw away a life that could have been – for both Happy and I. The information we had was unreliable, and in an overall context that one decision led to much destruction. Deep down the guy giving the information thought that I (and whoever else would be with me) wouldn't go through with it and that it was all talk. He was wrong. When the information didn't pan out, desperation mode kicked in and one stupid move after another ensured our arrest in the days to come.

When the serious crime unit from the Royal Canadian Mounted Police (RCMP) Surrey detachment knocked on my door, it was done in a warm way. When I asked the lady and the guy before me if they were here to arrest me, they said yes. May I put on some clothes and say bye to my mum, I asked, and they said yes. On the way to my room I asked if they could cuff me away from my mother's sight, and again they said yes and cuffed me in the van. I was arrested in May 2006, that was when I walked away from my mum and my home in such a manner that... 14 years later here I am, and I still haven't found my way back into the comfort of my mum's dwelling. It wasn't the last time I saw my mum, or the last time I would spend at home, but it was the moment that – perhaps more than any other – put me on an irreversible path to the cell I am sitting in now.

Stupidity.

It has taken the better part of these 14 years to figure out a way to right my wrongs. A book I read in 2017 at the OCC, *Writing my Wrongs* by Shaka Senghor, left me contemplating my many wrongs. It left me inspired to also "write my wrongs", which may help me right the wrongs I did to my mum and so many others. No idea what it feels like to see your son just up and disappear one day from home; I don't have a son. I can only imagine, and I also know that the imagining doesn't come close to experiencing the actual feeling. But imagination and contemplation have helped me get down on paper some unsaid words, which are written at the very back of this book. Because of my ignorance and inaction, and the ignorance of my friends and their inaction, many young lives have become dust and ashes. I don't even know how to begin imagining what a mother and father experience when they hear that their son is no longer alive and in this world.

Hard-learned lessons.

I had been told, in early 2006, that I couldn't attend Abbotsford Senior High anymore, because of recent police attention. That deprived me of a setting which was helping me stay on point; helping me keep in sight what mattered, and why. Sukhvir was in my math 12 class, and as much as I wanted to pass the class with a high mark, I wanted even more to prove to her I was willing to do what it took to stay on track.

I went to jail at age 19, on charges of kidnapping and impersonating a police officer with an imitation firearm – that's where the get-rich scheme got me. I had made a choice that caused a ripple effect that toppled over dreams and hopes, one after another. I would make bail a year after my arrest, in May 2007, and my release brought with it an opportunity to start anew.

To start fresh.

I would go on to work a junk removal job, mainly cleaning out houses on construction sites, homes that were being demolished or newly constructed. It was an attempt to turn my life around. Sukhvir and I were scheduled to be married on 20 October 2007, but in the early hours of 8 October 2007, that all came to an end. Sukhvir sustained injuries (major trauma to the head) and underwent emergency surgery a little after 8 a.m. The surgery was unsuccessful.

She passed on the same day.

I cannot imagine what Sukhvir's parents went through. No way to gauge what her household has gone through over these years, and it doesn't matter how many times I try to right my wrongs – or "write my wrongs" for that matter – nothing can bring that shining light back into the comfort of her parents' household. For years I harboured the thought that, had I just stayed away from her, life would have been different for not only the both of us, but those around us. Our relationship caused static within her family. She persisted. And I wasn't about to walk away if she wasn't. But. Maybe, had we just not rushed into it and taken a little more time, things could have been different.

I spiralled.

On the surface, I held it together for the most part, but I wasn't well inside. I had built-up frustration, anger, regret, and guilt towards myself – about how I had single-handedly affected so many lives for the worst. At times, these feelings would also trigger some pretty stupid and harmful decisions.

Triggers.

I would end up in prison again in late 2009, and I would stay there till September 2010. I did 10 months in segregation – isolation – which left me no choice but to self-reflect and take a deeper look, at not only my life and the choices I had made, but at what I would need to do to correct the accumulated mistakes. The isolation helped me piece myself back together mentally and gain a clearer perspective on where I wanted to be in the future. It also made me evaluate my mental, physical, and spiritual state. I spent as much time as I could reading – a book a day sometimes – and trained for a minimum of five days a week. I made it my daily discipline to recite Gurbani in the a.m., p.m., and before bed. I was eventually acquitted of the charges I was accused of and walked out (literally) to another fresh start.

Life looked promising.

I was full of ambition, and determined to stay positively motivated. A driving force was that I knew I had many mistakes and shortcomings to correct, and if I wanted to make amends with everyone that I had let down, including Sukhvir's family, I would have to keep it together and follow through on the things I had made promises on.

Then my friend was killed.

It changed everything. Seeing him in a coffin – a life that no longer was – triggered me, deep down, to relive Sukhvir's funeral experience. As much as I tried to stay balanced, and to keep in mind my 10 months of isolation, things began to get blurry again. I became short-sighted and narrow minded.

Revenge seemed like the only option.

I emitted a harmful, violent and destructive energy – and when it was well and ready, that is exactly what came back for me. On 16 September 2011, a few seconds after I had finished speaking to my father and had put away my cellphone, four shooters ran up on me, and the vehicle I was in, and let loose. I don't know how many rounds were fired that day. 20. 30 maybe. Perhaps it was as many as 50.

The boomerang effect.

In what I thought were my last moments on this Earth, everything made sense.

And that sense took the form of a list of last wishes to a friend – who was inside the house I was parked outside of. After she came out and opened the door to find me laying there stretched sideways, and now, sort of dangling out the passenger door, I asked her to tell my mum and dad that I was truly sorry, this is not how it was supposed to be and I wish I had more time. I wanted her to tell them that I was sorry for it ending in this manner, and sorry they would have to get the news of what just happened to me. My friend tried ignoring it and said I would be fine and that I wasn't even really injured, *you're only bleeding a little bit Geni... you're going to be fine.* I remember telling her, I am not fine, and to listen, because I don't have many breaths left and I need you to say these things to my parents.

The last thing I remembered saying was... Waheguru, Waheguru, Waheguru.

This is where the nickname Geni comes from. It comes from her.

Though we are not in each other's life experience at this current time, she is someone who cared very dearly for me. To me, she is my sister. She was then, is now, and always will be a sister. To have said what you thought were your last words to a friend doesn't happen every day. She is someone who had my back through the ups and downs – the hardest of which were yet to come – and someone who genuinely had my best intentions at heart.

It wasn't over, though.

I woke up 21 days later at Royal Columbia Hospital (New Westminster BC, Canada). It wasn't time to leave Earth yet. I was grateful for being alive, for being awake and conscious, but in fact I would remain asleep, ignorant and unaware in the most important way – and I would further self-destruct still for some time to come. Ego in me did not fade, in fact strengthened. Friends I considered brothers started dying, one after another. It continued to happen. Something needed to change.

How was it going to change, though?

I spent one month in isolation again (mid-November to mid-December 2012) at an Immigration and Custom Enforcement (ICE) center in Tacoma, Washington, USA.[2] It helped me start seeing things from a clearer perspective. Again, I knew what had to be done to help steer myself and, hopefully, my friends' collective path in a healthier direction. We would have to admit our shortcomings, our weaknesses, and acknowledge what wasn't working, in order to build something new to sort through the mess of a life we had created for ourselves.

The answers – as I reflected more and more – seemed simple.

As time passed in isolation, I began to see a clearer picture. Quietude brought clarity. I also got a welcome hug from a friendship that grew deep in the month I spent there, with the girl named Bubu. There is much mention of Bubu throughout this book, and that is because of the influence she has had on me and this journey that has unfolded. Words cannot capture the gratitude or appreciation I have for her but, with words, perhaps I can share a little of it. The support she provided, and the care she showed, helped remind me just how important friendship – filled with affection, care and loyalty – is. Before I would be released from ICE though, more friends would pass on. I had a conversation with a friend on 25 November 2012, a day before he passed on. The mutual words were along the lines of, everything is going to work out for us bro, love you and see you soon.

Just as my reset in isolation felt like a refresh, my friend sounded like he himself was experiencing a reset too. I was looking forward to being able to get things off my chest, and the more time I spent in that room, the clearer and easier it became to start seeing the answers. I couldn't wait to share them with not only him, but the rest of my friends and bros. That day didn't come. The day after we spoke, he was gunned down along with another friend.

Too little too late.

I never got to attend either funeral. I tried to get the consulate involved to get an expedited voluntary release back to Canada (which is an option for Canadian Citizens held in the United States), but that didn't go anywhere. I had to sit with my thoughts and unsaid words, feeling the pressure, again, of what could have been.

Every action has a reaction, indeed.

These wounds haven't yet healed, nor have they been fully explored. They have been compartmentalized and put to the side for a later time, should the opportunity be blessed enough to arise, of course. Lingering effects of deep cuts, I guess.

When I did make it back to the Canadian side, the Combined Forces Special Enforcement Unit (CFSEU) was waiting for me. They had questions; they were closing in on their homicide investigation. I walked out of jail into freedom, but instead of feeling free, I felt the pressure; there was tension in the air.

The clock was ticking.

I would catch bullets to my back a little after midnight on 15 January 2013. This time, I would wake up from a coma 28 days later, on 13 February 2013. I will go into this experience in detail in another book (which is well underway). On 22 February 2013, a week after waking up, I was charged for 1 count of first-degree murder and 4 counts of conspiracy to commit murder.

And.

Thus began the journey of realizations that has unfolded over the last 7 years or so. I had much self-destructing to do, and many mistakes yet to make. I had many relationships to tear apart and many loved ones to let down and hurt. This downward spiral would hit bottom and, eventually, the pain and suffering became fuel for the fire that would – finally – push me to stand up, straighten up, and reach for something... higher. Many have been in this position before – it isn't anything new – hardship, pain and suffering, leading to the quest for something more, with many realizations along the way. Many go through a journey that leads them to realize the mistakes that need to be rectified and the character flaws that need to be amended; and to the realization that self-reflection will be necessary if genuine correction is to be achieved. But I don't know how many of them have distances the size of planets between themselves and their families, and their communities.

I have many wrongs to right.

---

1. I write about the incident in "Unawareness: DIA".
2. This is the starting point for the timeline at the beginning of this book. I start here because this is the moment that I thought I could start anew, creating a life with Bubu; but this was a fleeting feeling of hope, and life behind bars was just about to begin.

CHAPTER 32

UNAWARENESS
DIA (DUMBASS IN ACTION)

Father, forgive them.
For they know not what they do.

—Jesus

M rs Carlson is to blame for my inability to list the provinces of Canada. Never gave the individual attention I needed. She was too busy sending me to the principal's office. She was my social studies teacher on 11 September—

Yes, 2001.

We are in class chilling; her voice breaks up our chilling as she tells us to quiet down; she clicks on the TV and turns it up. I think we see the second plane hit the untouched tower, live. I do not recall: perhaps she is crying or looks like she is about to cry, but she definitely implies that the world could end today.

We were under attack.

Guess what this genius did? What would any immature, loud, arrogant and obnoxious kid do in this situation? He started laughing. Then he started cracking jokes. He even said things like, ohhhhh snnnaaaap! Yo check it out, it's going down! Yup…

Suspended.

That was not a fun walk to the principal's office. The fun ended the minute I entered the hallway to start the trek. Off comes the class clown mask, replaced by the "oh I am so going to get it" face.[1] It was a terrifying walk. Even worse, I would have to deal with my mum, who was most likely going to be the one I would have to… face. She was most likely the one that was going to come pick me up.

Guess what this dumbass did next?

When we got home, I told my mum that they, the hijackers, were freedom fighters, so *how* is what they did wrong if there is a war going on in the world, and America is trying to kill them too? *Look* Mumma Ji, their leader has a Turban *and* a beard.[2] Guess what this imbecile did next? There's more you say?

Oh. There is more.

I went back to school with a binder that said, in thick lettering made with a white-out pen on the blue cover, "OSAMA BIN LADEN FOR LIFE". Chest out like, yeah, sup – guess who's back. This dipstick thought to one-up everyone with their Tupac and Biggie-for-life logos. Smart.

Didn't make it through the day.

I look back, to that young, naïve, dumb, peace-disturbing kid, and wonder why he would even joke around about something so... heart-wrenchingly tragic. Something no words could ever try to capture, or come close to describing the pain and suffering felt by those whose life experiences it touched directly. I realize that the display he put on was but a reflection of his unawareness. He thought it was funny.

He thought it was cool.

On some level I knew what had happened was wrong, was horrifying, but my awareness-level was low, and I wasn't present enough to recognize the situation for what it was. I wasn't able to see. Limited perception. The aspect of myself that wanted to belong, to stand out, to be accepted, to be known – trumped all other concerns. The aspect that wanted to fit in and become the idea of who and what was "cool". No, that numb-nut wasn't the only one who laughed, but he was the loudest idiot and so he caught the spotlight.

Paid to play, indeed.

Perhaps we can chalk it up to kids being kids, to a kid not knowing any better – but we really can't. If you, reading these words, think that it can be chalked up to, and dismissed as a kid-being-a-kid type of thing, well that ignores the unawareness, or ignorance of it, my friend. And this ignorance is part of unconscious participation. And this comes from what is referred to as the ego.

The expression of the lower self in play.

My ignorant behaviour was in response to an act of tragedy abroad, and to an act of terror. Whether that terror was indeed at the hands of foreign terrorists, or an elaborate collaboration between some within the US government... I do not know. What I do know is that my display reflected unawareness – and unawareness is harmful.

Unawareness is dangerous.

Displays of unawareness linger. Ignorant behaviour may well be taking place right now, maybe even in the very near vicinity. We're about to switch gears to a tragic happening, revolving around a topic that should be a concern to all of us.

Rehtaeh Parsons.

Does the name sound familiar? While at a high school in Nova Scotia, Canada, she was assaulted by 4 teenage boys who would go on to post pictures of the assault and bully her online. She eventually took her own life in 2013. A movement was started in her memory, to bring awareness to what she went through, and what girls and women still go through today. *#Manup* is the name of the movement. I would like to say that in my immediate circle of friends, we, collectively, would not have joked around about something like this, nor sat by and condoned it.

But.

That doesn't mean it wasn't happening somewhere around us. Because it did happen. At the hands of guys who once thought they would claim an older homie title, or have a claim to being an older bro on the streets. That is not what older brothers do.

That isn't what older homies do.

Take advantage of innocence. Manipulate fragile minds to the brink of self-destruction, and then use the leverage to tear apart what remains of innocence. Not when it comes to a boy, not when it comes to a girl. Not for malicious employment of any sort, not for sexual abuse, not for anything of a predatory nature.

I remember a girl who I would cheerily greet, and was always quick to drop a line or two on that I'd picked up from a movie. It resulted in many hugs and spikes to personal confidence, because I thought we were mutually flirting. I was her junior by two years, and the intentions were innocent; all I wanted was to be acknowledged as a friend.

And I was.

Then one day I learned of what had happened to her. Heard it in her own words. She didn't know I was listening. I was just a kid, remember? But I had ears. She was engaged in a conversation with a mutual friend. We were at our friend's place of work – I hung out there a lot around that time. I pretended to be engrossed in a task at the edge of the kiosk when she started talking. If you couldn't see the mutual friend standing there with her, you would have thought she was just having a conversation with herself. She was trying to make sense of why she couldn't remember the night. She said, I remembered that he was such a gentleman, and that he opened the door for me. We went out and then ended up at his place where we were just hanging out. I remember having a good time, and all I remember next is waking up feeling groggy. Feeling gross and out of it. I had burns on my knees, my body ached, my body aches... there are marks on me which I don't understand. Where did they come from?

How did they get there?

And then she answered her own question in tears, just getting the words out to her friend – telling her she thought what happened – before she started crying. I still remember it. Something changed in me that day. It hurt me to hear the hurt in her voice.

Does a man do that?

For those of you in the high school phase of your life experience, you can add your voices to movements like #Manup, or you can start your own. The opportunity and responsibility rests on your shoulders. You are the ones on the front lines, at ground zero. You can set in play new waves, new trends. You can set energy in play that brings about respect for the human being – or spiritual being having a human experience – to inspire those around you to be the best versions of themselves. Interact in a way where creation and building and caring and sharing is the cool thing to do. Where the definition of fun – is actually fun.

Fun at the expense of no one.

Girls and women are Mother Jewels who have the power to *nurture life*. They aren't dispensable. They are not objects that can be used and taken advantage of. They aren't something to be regarded as... unimportant or insignificant.

If.

If you intrude on the well-being of others – especially those who are young and inexperienced – you will pay for it dearly. If you think it is OK to just slip something into a girl's drink and get her so messed up that she doesn't know what she is doing anymore – you will come apart at the seams. Everything around you will chew you up till there is nothing left. The energy you have given out will come back to haunt you in ways you couldn't even imagine. It will come through your experience when it is good and ready, and it will, like a furious hurricane tearing through a straw hut.

It will leave nothing behind.

So ask yourself: *Are* you hurting others? Are you an unconscious participant? Are you aware of what it is you're truly doing? Don't be a DIA, a dumbass in action. Not if it brings someone else pain. Not if it does someone else harm. Not if it exploits someone else's innocence. Not if it torments and bullies a gentle person. The ego can only exert control over those with low awareness, but that is not to say that those with low awareness deserve to be exploited. What all of us reading these words today (and I am reading them too as I go along, out loud, actually) – what all of us can do in the environments we find ourselves in, is to commit to raise our own awareness every chance we get, and never to prey on anyone.

It usually begins with one person.

What does?

Change.

What can we do?

Trigger it.

How?

Awareness.

By contemplating our behaviour and actions. By asking if what we are saying or doing is bringing harm to another, or if it is helping them in some way. By becoming mindful of just how much of an impact making fun of others can have; or even worse, are we a tag-along on a wagon that is driving over others feelings and emotions?

Don't.

Don't be a part of the herd. Don't share revenge porn. Don't encourage others to do it. Don't encourage others to sexually exploit or assault anyone. Don't encourage behaviour that is harmful to the vulnerable and innocent.

Instead.

Let's reach out to those who are being bullied or taken advantage of, online or in person, and see if they're OK. When things are being said about someone in a negative and harmful way, word tends to travel pretty fast, and it usually gets distorted pretty quickly too. Things get added on. The story grows and, then, by the end of it, a small thing has been turned into something so big... that someone is driven to extremes of suffering. Driven to the point where he or she wants to end their life to escape the mental and emotional torment.

That is so sad.

Let's understand that our choices can have some pretty serious implications. Making fun of what happened on 11 September 2001 could have had some serious implications in my social studies classroom. What if someone in the class had a relative or friend that was directly affected? My immaturity and display of unawareness didn't even factor in the possibility that there could have been someone in the class who had family or friends in the Middle East. Because the Middle East has suffered immensely from this event in history, too.

Nobody won.

Making fun of Rehtaeh Parsons, adding fuel to the fire in which she was burning… ended very tragically. The world is missing a light, a light that can never be replaced. That's really sad.

Do.

Weigh your choices. Evaluate your behavior. Understand that it can take time to strengthen an immature mind and that it needs to be mindfully led through the stages of its growth. Once quality growth begins to dominate thoughts and mindsets… shifts in perspective follow. And our negative outputs from past actions cannot always be easily corrected.

Nor forgiven.

Let's remember that as we progress through this life journey, compassion and understanding, empathy and kindness, love and respect, should be at the forefront of what we do and say; let what Rehtaeh Parsons went through be a reference point, which keeps in perspective the need for everyone to stand up and say, no this is wrong; let it also highlight the importance of projecting strong values and ethics.

Be the Kool one.

---

1. How many masks do you wear? One at home? One at work? One at school? One with your significant other? One with your friends? Is it a mask of your own choosing, or is it one that is being thrust upon you by… others?

2. Conventional method of judgement used by many to categorize someone as "good" or "bad" (religiously/culturally) according to personal beliefs. "Turban and beard" is a big thing in the Sikh faith, but not a pre-requisite to follow the teachings of Guru Granth Sahib. It is an entry fee to be put on the Khalsa roster, though; it is part of the physical identity.

CHAPTER 33

NOW I REALIZE

The concept of balance defines our Universe.
The cosmos, our planet, the seasons, water, wind, fire, and earth are all in perfect
balance.
We humans are the only exception.

—Wayne W. Dyer

Now I realize what enlightened teachers mean when they say that humans have lost their way, that they have lost touch with their inner nature, which in turn is disrupting the natural balance of our physical world. Earth. In the search for "more", guided by destructive drives and self-serving interests. Now I realize why it is said that every other form of life in this world has a natural tendency to operate in perfect balance with its environment and its inhabitants.

At the end of the first episode of the American TV series *One Strange Rock*, I learned just how balanced this Earth of ours is. The episode provided an eye-opening, intelligence-gathering insight into how that balance is maintained, and how humans are putting that balance at risk. I learned that the Earth in itself maintains a perfect balance, maintains the necessary oxygen level for life; we can no longer pretend that we are separate from the Earth.

We never were.

Earth nurtures and sustains life, and in order to remain sustainable with the harmonious tune it hears and adheres to, it sheds what it no longer needs or what has become a burden for it in some way. It finds ways to balance itself out when it is experiencing interference, or when something creates a resistance, pulling it out of alignment with what is to come. The Earth is beyond intelligent. It is *aware* too. Imagine that. It is a *living being*. That is why, perhaps, sages, beings, and Avatars have always referred to Earth as *Mother Earth*. Because it brings – life – in and out of form. It nurtures and sustains it. It feeds it and clothes it. It nourishes and protects it. You cannot find anything within us that isn't found within Earth.

That's so capital K Kool.

Every single form of life contributes to the cycle of life and its completion. They all play their part, dancing to a rhythmic tune which is in harmony with the flow of the Universe. Each is inseparable from the balance that their energy maintains within their designated or absorbed purpose. A purpose which is naturally aligned with higher intelligence.[1]

At the end of the first episode of *One Strange Rock*, which is anchored by Will Smith and a team of brilliant scientists and astronauts, a Buddhist Monk said in a *duh*-ish sort of way that the Earth is always in equilibrium. That we too must discover that equilibrium within us and contribute our equilibrium to the whole. An equilibrium aligned with higher intelligence.

But.

Some of us don't understand the importance and profound simplicity of balance. Some of us don't see the connection between what we do, how we do, what we eat, and its connection to climate change. I didn't.

Do now though.

The day I wrote down the rough version of the words above, I had turned on the TV, after 10pm, and started flipping through channels at random, which led me to exactly what I needed to see. Something that was in complete synchronization with not only thoughts of the day which I had started writing down, but thoughts that were formulating for the day to come. I also recognized that what I had just stumbled across was itself intertwined with the higher intelligence responsible for materializing synchronistic events and moments, when and where needed. It was synchronistic because I had just read about synchronicity at the start of the day in words written by Carol Adrienne in a book entitled: *When Life Changes, or You Wish it would*. She wrote that, when we're open, free and trusting, that which we are attracting into our experience – something we might need to learn from, to understand or simply recognize – will be that much easier to acknowledge and pinpoint as relevant; it will appear as something much bigger than the physical world we stare at with our eyes.

That was my interpretation of the words, anyway.

Then I flip to a documentary called *Sharkwater* (2006). What makes me stop and tune in? These words: "Sharks sense energy and they view humans as a threat". I pause, smile, sit down and say, well... here we go. Thank you, Universe.

Enter Rob Stewart.

Told you we would get there. See the good rewards patience can bring?

The film left me stunned. They have survived 5 extinctions.

Sharks. Not us. *Duh.* Bubu is going to be like, yup yup I knew that – sure you did.

Wow. Focus Jujhar. ADHD. We're almost there. Finish strong. Ok, yes. Where were we?

Sharks have survived 5 extinctions. It takes some sharks 25 years to reach sexual maturity, before they can mate and create babies. And, right now, they are endangered because of – guess who? Humans. Endangered by humans who want nothing more than their fins (for shark fin soup). Next I got a surprise. A humbling one. I recognized the face of someone I had seen before. The face belonged to a man named Paul Watson, the captain of a ship called The Sea Shepherd (of the Sea Shepherd Conservation Society). Poetic name? Fitting name. I realized that I had flipped to this very documentary months before while at OCC and had flipped away not having heard a single word, fully well knowing and understanding in the same breath, I wasn't meant to. Not until this moment.

So I grabbed a pen and started taking notes.

5 humans die a year because of sharks. 8 million die of starvation. More than 22,000 from drugs. Google the number of deaths related to prescription drugs and see what turns up, see if it gives you a shiver. 8 *million* because of starvation. Yes, I know I just repeated it. Because of being *hungry*. Really? Wow. No?

OK, back to the topic.

Sharks have been here for 400 million years. That's 150 million years before the dinosaur era. *Before.* Wow. No? Am I the only one that didn't know this? In the time the film had played, 15,000 sharks were estimated to have been killed.

Savage.

I learned that sharks are the ones who keep the underwater environment in balance, sitting at the top of a food chain that has influenced evolution. That they're mere presence is responsible for a cycle which helps sustain life here on Earth. How? By causing a chain reaction to occur throughout the depths, which triggers roles and responsibilities to be fulfilled by life forms, whose individual purpose has become part of a larger purpose. The purpose of sustaining life. The presence of a shark triggers other life forms to carry out their specific roles in eliminating CO_2, the very gas that is responsible for climate change.

Mayday. Mayday. Act now.

A change in climate, even if it is not seen for what it is by all, is putting at risk a quality of gentle living for generations to come. Ignorance, if we don't rectify it, will eventually lead to another extinction sooner or later. I learned that a shark's presence contributes not only to the elimination of CO_2, but *regulation* of the very air we breathe.

Did you know that? I didn't. That is capital K Kool too. No? Why didn't we learn about this in school?!

Oh. Right. Too busy sending some of us to the principal's office. :@

I re-learned that two thirds of our planet is water. That 80 per cent of life is *in* that water. The anchor's words "Sharks live in balance with the ocean, with the water" triggered deep feelings to surface as I marvelled at what I was hearing, at what I was seeing, and at what I was learning. Captain Paul said that humans need to learn how to live harmoniously with nature. He also said simple awareness and initiatives to protect life won't come from governments, but from passionate individuals who come along and ignite a flame which creates change. He simply said that, right now, what is needed are the voices that will save the planet from humans. I watched this film while I was at the Regional Reception Center in May of 2018.

In May of 2019 I flipped on the TV and saw that the same film was on again – or so I thought. I told my friend to watch it as he left my room to get to his in time for the night time count – where a standing body count takes place to make sure that all inmates are accounted for and locked in their assigned rooms for the night. It took me 20 minutes to realize that it was a different film, though it was about sharks again, and just as fascinating. Same anchor: Rob Stewart. Different film. I then realized something else towards the ending of the film, that although Rob Stewart was the anchor and a part of the filming, he may not have got to see it aired.

Rob Stewart went on a dive and never returned.

I would be lying if I said I didn't feel this thing in my chest. Because I did. It was the feeling you get when you lose something special. When you lose someone special. When the world loses someone special.

But.

I quickly realized the world hadn't lost anything. The world had, in truth, gained colour, gained life; the world gained awareness and the world gained hope because of Rob Stewart.

Have you seen the movie *Tomorrow Land*?[2] If you haven't, it is worth watching, I think. Hope. Hope, will, and action preserve life. This movie is a classic example of not taking no for an answer and moving to motivate like-minded beings to think big, dream big, add colour and inspire those around them for the betterment of humanity.

Rob Stewart is one of those beings who adds hope, colour and signifies inspiration of healing, one of those whose purpose in life it was to awaken and inspire others to do the same.

To do more.

From the new film – *Sharkwater Extinction* (2018) – I learned that traces of shark are now finding their way into cosmetics and beauty care products. Traces of shark are appearing in livestock feed and in pet food.

Not cool.

So you see, now it comes down to our own ethical priorities and personal responsibilities. Refuse to buy them. Raise awareness so others don't. Buy something that is healthy for the Whole. If the consumer doesn't buy the product, there is no demand. If there is no demand, there is no need for supply. Every link in the chain matters. If you didn't even know your beauty product could potentially have shark in it, well – awareness. Awareness. Awareness.

Now you do.

I learned that shark populations 450 million years in the making have been decimated by 90 per cent in a period of 30 years. How? Unawareness. Unconscious participation. That is how.

No more.

Rob Stewart said, we kill 100 million sharks and no one notices. Well, we are noticing now. So, thank you Mr Stewart. He said, conservation is preservation of human life on Earth. He said, be a hero. He said, there is still a bright future ahead if we want it. *#Do-it-for-Stewart. #Do-it-for-the-children. #Do-it-for-us* – humanity. *#Do-it-for-your-loved-ones. #Do-it-for-Life*.

Be the flame. Be a trigger.

This film helped me evaluate my priorities and decide to make changes for the better. I realized we all play a part already – is it for worse or better? This is what we need to reflect upon. I realized that the time to act for betterment all around… is *right now*.

We must take collective responsibility.

Our own inner imbalances play just as much of a dysfunctional role in the world as the unconscious actions of other individuals who wreak havoc and threaten the balance of life. Whether it is above ground – on our city streets, in the hood or downtown areas – or whether it is deep beneath the waters of our oceans – it all matters. At the core of it, it is all the same. Lack of awareness. Lack of connection within and functioning from the level of ego. Definitely small e – ego is small.

The one life form that has the ability to learn, grow and feel a wide range of emotions, the one that can make the biggest impact here and now, the one that can make the biggest difference for God knows how long, is the life form that has the ability to become aware of being aware and become conscious of the field of awareness as a field of energy as it grows. That be super cool. Yup. Be. *That* was a long sentence. Oh. Plants are aware too, just ask Jackie, she'll tell you.[3]

Jus sayen.

You are here to do something very specific that contributes to the betterment of this world. Of others. Here to sow and reap love, to care and share that warmth with those that have been waiting for it to arrive in their experience. They need it, you know. You think you need it? What about the ones who aren't able to buy books – or buy anything, for that matter? What about the ones who don't even know what a book looks like? What about those children who have never been exposed to the radiance of colour?[4] The question is, will you be the one to make a difference in their lives in some way?

I say we put away the small opinions. The tissues.[5] The nonsense, and let's stand up and take steps to make things happen. Why it took me so long to realize how simple it all is, I do not know. Oh yes, rounds (bullets) to the headrest – had to wait for those shells to arrive. But. Have you realized how simple it is yet? That *all* we need to do is, again, learn to:

Live.

Care.

Love.

Grow.

Learn and adapt – *together*.

Rob Stewart ended *Sharkwater* by saying, sharks provide the balance to a cycle of life underwater that influences the flow of life. That, under the water, they live together, move together, and complete their expression of life with a purpose.

What is your purpose?

Is it to raise awareness about climate change – like the steps being taken by children, much of it inspired by Greta Thunberg?[6] Children walked out of school in Toronto as a protest and to raise awareness. I wish I had a reason to skip class, especially for a good cause. *Yeah right* you were going to get me to "sit in class" while the clock just ticked away. A boy on a mission I'd be – yup. Because, duty calls, you know. I would somehow rally the class to walk out with me, too. It is for a good cause. Doesn't get any better than the climate emergency. Stand up for what is right. But do it peacefully. There is no need for aggression. "What you resist, persists", says Eckhart Tolle and many others. Why lend energy towards what you do not want, anyway? Imagine if millions of beings started marching and saying, no, act now. *Imagine* the impact. *Imagine* the difference made. Yup. Imaginable

Or.

Is it your purpose to start a blog that posts everyday examples of practical awareness that will give us insight, knowledge and, in turn, provide foresight into becoming part of the change that will sustain this Earth we occupy?

Like adding voices to *#savethesharks*.

Perhaps you live in Asia or have strong ties to Asia, and your purpose is to rally support and add voices to *#savethesharks*, right at ground zero where shark fin is being bought ignorantly all for... the illusion of status. For the idea of luxury. Not even taste. Unawareness willing to throw away life just to say I bought shark fin soup. Will you be the one to make people aware that the flavor of joy is something one's grandchildren may not get to taste if the world continues to create a demand for shark?

Or.

Perhaps your purpose is to raise awareness in neighbourhoods on how plankton is threatened by the actions and inactions of – guess who? How every year the emissions emitted from one drill in the ocean eliminates 1 million years of plankton growth. *1 million.* Yup.

Ruthless. Capital R.

For those of you that knew this already, or know it now, tell everyone! Raise awareness in schools, churches, temples, monasteries, sporting clubs, night clubs, locker rooms, high school assemblies, parent teacher meetings, and even shopping malls. Plankton, which is believed to be the *base* of life, has been dying and leaving nothing behind for marine life to eat. Plankton, in certain areas, can no longer reflect light from the sun, which keeps the temperature of the ocean at a certain level. A temperature which sustains the balance necessary for life to grow, thrive, and *evolve.*

Raise awareness about the fact that disruption of life's balance under-water is just as detrimental to life out of the water. That it is impacting life chemistry, and without the natural functioning of our ecosystem, the ripple effect will be felt while trying to breathe every-where on Earth.

Raise awareness about big-boat fisherman that are fishing (plunder-ing) at 7000 feet with nets that stretch the length of multiple football fields. Whatever they catch, they catch. Or more so, whatever they carve out of the ocean, they carve out, and whatever is dumped in its stead is, well – dumped.

That's sad.

That's not cool.

There is enough plastic in the ocean right now that, statistically speaking, I think it is sort of unavoidable that we are eating it in the fish we consume.[7] Funny, because no matter which way we try to spin it, or try to separate one thing from another – it cannot be done.

Perhaps you'll add voices to 4ocean.com, whose efforts are removing tonnes of plastic waste from oceans. They are definitely setting trends and making history with the impact and difference made thus far. Thank you, we must say again and again to the beings involved.

Will you be the one to add to the effort?

Perhaps one of you will trigger another to act, which will trigger groups of beings to come together to act in their own way with realizations and visions of spreading light, of spreading good, of helping and spreading warmth in every direction. That is just the way it goes. The energy thing. It is real.

Let us realize that...

Just like the Earth sheds what it no longer needs as it continues to nurture life, as it continues to evolve, we too can shrug off old ways, habits, and behaviours that serve no purpose. That hold us back, trapping us and denying us the beauty that is always present. We can shed the false ideas we think make us who we are, and instead – open our eyes to the wonder of life dancing all around us.

Let's recognize that we are a part of that dance too. That we are a part of it in essence and expression. That we have the power of choice to express the melody that sings within. That we have the power to hear that sound. We will continue to shed and evolve as we learn and grow, but while we do that – lets.

Let's balance ourselves, balance our wants and needs in a way that strengthens and harmonizes everything around us. Let's stand up for what we believe in and use that voice to make a difference along the way.

And.

Just as the sharks are endangered by the greed and unawareness of mortals, let's recognize that ego is what threatens the balance of life out of the water, too. Its threat lingers in our schools, our streets, our neighbourhoods, and threatens the natural balance which, at its best, humanity can achieve within itself and between itself and nature.

Eckhart Tolle suggests in *A New Earth* – which strips the ego down in a way that leaves no aspect of it concealed – that once you become aware of the observer, aware of awareness, and when you begin to operate from a field of higher awareness, the transformed state of consciousness will do more for humanity as a whole than any crusades to save the world.

It is why monks, saints and beings with higher consciousness sit where they sit and meditate for the moments that they do. The amount of energy they are emitting, the quality of the vibrations they are sending forth, vibrations of genuine and Unconditional Love (yes, capitals) are nullifying lower ones across the world. Or around the globe, rather. It is to these rare and precious beings we must extend humble gratitude and appreciation, because they have made it their life purpose to seek higher and higher enlightenment, and to extend the transformed states of vibration to the whole of this world and all its life forms.

Yes, each life form may operate within its own field of intelligence, sure. But at a deeper level, we all share that field. The field of intelligence is the one and same that is connected to all. The only difference being in vibrations. And, if we take mindful steps of harmony, of balance, of love – then it will certainly filter into everything. It will then perhaps be the manifestation of what the Buddha said, that every leaf of a plant is destined for enlightenment. Imagine that. Garden of Eden, I would say.

Finally.

------

1. Higher intelligence – a term I got acquainted with after reading books written by Wayne W. Dyer, Deepak Chopra, Carol Adrienne, Ester and Jerry Hicks.
2. George Clooney is in it. Watch it with nieces, nephews and tuyo hijos and hijas!
3. Google "Simon Vitale" or type in "plants are aware." Can no longer look at plants the same anymore. Jackie – who is she? A close friend in a previous life cycle. This much I know. An inspiration in this one.
4. Radiance of colour – say in in the form of bright, brand new soccer balls, footballs, a lush green soccer field. Or new bikes and toys. Or warm food and comfortable shelter. Radiance of colour has many forms – which of it will you help provide?
5. Tissue for your issue – a dear friend and brother's go-to phrase. He has gone through much in life, yet smiles and laughs, always. His motto is *#love-my-life*.
6. The school strikes inspired by Greta Thunberg, and the marches and protests, have become a global movement. She recently visited Vancouver BC, Canada, holding rallies and marches, joined by locals, for the purpose of sounding the bell and highlighting the urgency with which local governments need to respond to avoid irreversible harm.
7. Mum, I don't mean me literally. I do not eat fish – Waheguru. Waheguru. Waheguru.

CHAPTER 34

MAYBE

To spread righteousness and to uproot the state of repression and injustice. To end the evil of hatred for persons of low castes or other faiths and replace it with love for the whole of humanity, a family created by God.
To inculcate self-confidence, to encourage people to live a humble (not weak) life of self-respect (not egotism) and to serve society as its honorable Sant Sipahi (holy soldier).

————————

Dharam chalavan sant obaran. Dhust saban ko mool odharan.
Yahee kaj tharah hum janum. Samuj layho sadhu sub manam.

—**Guru Gobind Singh**
"Mandate to the Khalsa"
Dasam Granth

I do truly believe we are given an opportunity to do something while we are here, and that it is our responsibility, as a community, to spread love, to spread kindness, and to share that warmth with those we are sharing this breath of a moment with. I believe we are given moments to create it, share it, and spread it in the environments we occupy. We can always carry within us a state of loving kindness, joy, and a deeply rooted peace, and we can direct this outwards, with intention, wherever our journey takes us. It will seep out from within – one cannot contain the perfume of a rose by wrapping it in cloth. It matters not how many layers you place around the rose, soon enough it seeps out, the wind carries its aroma, and thus it blends its elegance back into the Universe. Back into Creation itself. So, if you are vibrating at the levels of peace, love, harmony – the kindness, warmth, and joy shall most certainly seep out from within you.

Try it out for yourself.

Wrapping a rose. Its beauty stems from the power of its seeds. And while it's blooming and living its life cycle, it continues to give off that unmistakeable fragrance.

The visit in which I saw Giggles, for the first time in years, I was walking along thinking. Walking, walking, thinking and then I stopped. I thought I smelled roses. I looked, and to my left was a shrub full of them. Pink ones. Indeed, very hard to mistake that smell, it stopped me in my tracks when my focus was anywhere but on roses. That is what your energy filled with beams of loving kindness will do. It will halt low energy patterns and stop destruction in its tracks. It will trigger something else entirely to take its place.

Try it out for yourself.

Spreading loving kindness. The more we give of love, of joy, of kindness, the more it will spread. The more it will be attracted into our experience, the more it will continue to contribute to Humanity as a whole. The more it will continue to change vibrational alignments of those around you in your day-to-day experience – never mind the setting. The more it will affect those that you happen to walk by on our city streets, passing them once, or maybe passing the same beings again and again. It will do so because we're just a collection of vibrations, continuously creating and exchanging vibrations.

Try it.

Smile at someone. Take a deliberate moment to smile and say hi with your eyes, with your lips or your voice. Say, I just wanted to say hi and share a smile with you, and I hope you have a wonderful day. Spread the love and WHAM, just like that, a whole new world emerges.

There you go, difference made.

Maybe it will throw someone "off" so much that the individual awkwardly musters some sort of feeble response, only to realize days later, while ordering a coffee or tea before starting the day, that she or he has been feeling…different.

Maybe this individual will turn around and spread the energy onwards, *#sending-it-forward*, like "paying it forward" from that movie. Do you know what that exchange of energy will do?

Change lives.

Triggered by humility, by kindness, by compassion. It will bring light into the experience of the very ones who, perhaps, need that love, that kindness and compassion in their experience the most. Maybe those smiles will come in the form of warm meals for the ones living in alleys, or maybe it will be in the form of something else, like a heartfelt interaction in which someone may need someone else to listen to them. Maybe *just* listen to them.

Weight is weight. If things stay bottled up; dangerous. Well, dangerous for those stuck in self-destructive cycles. I am no longer stuck in a self-destructive cycle. Yet, there is weight there still.

Wounds.

The third week of April 2019 was a friend's birthday in here. We had the privilege of making restaurant-worthy cuisine, and getting him a magazine-quality cake made. We had the privilege of being able to spend the moments together. We had the privilege of having our pictures taken together. My friend and I also took pictures holding portraits of loved ones who have passed on. Standing there, holding the pictures with him, brought tears quicker than I thought they could still come. And the tears stayed till we were done. At times, the weight gets real heavy. I feel it in my eyes and chest as I speak-write, right now. Even with an unwavering support structure, that weight is still there. I understand that, in its own time and in its own way... it will leave. But in order for that to happen, healing needs to take place. I am, however, not stuck in suffering. That only came about with the injection of light, laughter, empathy, compassion, kindness, isolation (time to reflect) and loving friendships.

What about the ones who don't have a support structure?

I'd say that they need someone just like *you* to come into their experience. Until the world begins healing itself, it will continue to experience heart-wrenching pain and suffering. What happens on one side of the globe has an effect elsewhere. And, healing is needed right now all over this Earth. Maybe the smile you bring into the experience of a hungry person will trigger him or her to snap out of it, step past thoughts of self-harm, and become determined to affect those in her or his immediate vicinity for the better, starting each day with purpose and a renewed urge to enjoy every living, breathing moment.

Maybe there is someone around you in your high school who would give anything to experience a conversation with someone *just like you*. Some laughter with someone *just like you*, because maybe they feel as if no one looks at them twice, perhaps because of the way they think they look or act. A genuine gesture does not hurt anyone. It only helps. A smile with a "Hi" can be just a smile and a "Hi".

Warm intentions... are warm intentions.

Maybe.

Maybe start your own movement or team up with those who share a similar vision, whether it's safer schools in the USA, promoting higher morale for students to regard one another with dignity and respect – irrespective of country or color. Maybe add your voice to *#Kidsplay*. Or maybe you are meant to add fire to the *#Manup* movement, triggering another wave of energy to surge through schools as a reminder of why it is important to stand together. A collection of energies all intending to manifest one vision, or an individual vision that is part of a collective vision, accelerates the process; *supercharges* it. There is real potency in a collective energy field.[1] If your individual vision supports the whole, it will draw those meant to be a part of it into your experience, on its own. That is how it works. Wavelengths.

Trust.[2]

It may seem like there is only one of you in a physical sense, but even without physical bodies around, a vision that supports the whole will attract support from the whole, because the power of God resides in that realm.

Because the flow of abundance stems from that source.

Because there is no cap on the amount of energy that is available from that infinite supply.

Infinite supply that *is* Source Energy.

Word up.

Maybe ask someone to a dance that you normally wouldn't. Maybe make it about the other person, and not you. Or, maybe sit somewhere you wouldn't normally sit. Create a new norm. Setting trends is the new normal. Supporting those new trends is the new normal. Look how diverse the world is getting. Share something wholeheartedly, or give it away, remember?

Making a difference doesn't take much.

Like, giving a warm meal to your "customer" on the street. Like talking to some young boy or girl, that you know is way too young to be putting such vile poison into the body. Yes, you "D boys-and-girls". Maybe you'll be the one that offers naloxone kits to those you think may be at risk of going a little overboard. Maybe you'll be the one to recognize that someone you see often is going through a rougher time than usual. Maybe you'll encourage them to not get high alone.

Maybe you'll encourage them to eat, sleep and stay hydrated. Clarity is clarity, and small amounts of it is still something. Take a moment or two to ask how they are doing, ask them if they need anything. 5 minutes won't render your schedule useless – it may just help put a piece of someone's life back together.

That *is* making a difference.

The smallest thing, the smallest gesture, and the smallest act – could in turn be the very trigger that summons a much larger exchange of energy to occur. Words of Wallace D. Wattles come to mind here.

> You cannot foresee the results of even the most trivial act. You do not know the workings of all the forces that have been set moving on your behalf. Much may be depending on your doing some simple act, and it may be the very thing which is to open the door of opportunity to very great possibilities. You can never know all the combinations which Supreme Intelligence is making for you in the world of things and of human affairs. Your neglect or failure to do some small thing may cause a long delay in getting what you want.
>
> —"Small Acts May Have Big Rewards"
>
> *The Science of Getting Rich*

Doing for others is doing for yourself, too. Just do it humbly. Because then the Universe will return to you a quality of energy which is from a higher reality. The energy of creation is *unstoppable*. It is magic.

Maybe you'll be the one to utilize it.

Maybe you'll be the one to realize, I am in downtown every day. This is where many beings need some of the simplest things. Food. Water. Maybe you're uncomfortable engaging someone verbally and will instead leave a note with an inspiring or uplifting quote, with a pair of socks or gloves next to someone who is trying to disappear into the ground he or she is lying on. Maybe it will be words of Saint Francis of Assisi:[3]

> Lord, make me an instrument of your peace.
> Where there is hatred, let me sow love.
> Where there is injury, pardon.
> Where there is doubt, faith.
> Where there is despair, hope.
> Where there is darkness, light.
> Where there is sadness, joy.
> O Divine Master, grant that I may not so much seek to
>   be consoled as to console.
> To be understood as to understand;
> To be loved as to love.
> For it is in giving that we receive,
> It is in pardoning that we are pardoned.
> And it is in dying that we are born to eternal life.

Maybe it will be the presence of these words that triggers something to change within for the one receiving them, and they will turn around to pay it forward in a way he or she never imagined possible. It is what happens. The effects of unexpected energy, especially energy super-charged with the Fire of Love. Yes yes, capitals for sure.

Like smiling at everyone you encounter. Yes, like you the one reading these words. Like handing out warm blankets to those living on the streets. Yes, you who reside there, are employed there, or travel to and from there every day.

Maybe you'll be the one to make an extra meal and give it to another being. Maybe you'll organize groups of beings to join you to spread love-filled energy on our city streets. Maybe you'll add the energy you bring and combine it with the efforts of those like Fatima Zahra Helping Hand, an organization dedicated to serve the homeless with warm meals; you'll be helping further a vision that has been and is creating waves and waves of unstoppable energy. Energy that is affecting the direction of paths for souls. Energy that is returning to the surrounding environment that is being engaged, energy that is being sent out into the world, the Universe and beyond.

Boomerangs.

Maybe you'll add energy in support of a group called Smiles for Children, who offer surgeries for children born with a cleft lip. It costs nothing. Time and time again I have sat in the room wondering how many children there even are who need the surgery. I was wondering what it would take to double or triple the effort that is being made to reach these children. I was wondering what it would take to organize a continuous cycle of teams of doctors and nurses to attend to the areas of the world where children need this surgery.

Maybe you'll be the one to come up with a solution for it.

Maybe you'll add energy to those who are attending to beings that are struggling with leprosy. I used to receive regular newsletters with pictures from an organization that helps those with leprosy, and honestly – it was hard to look at the pictures. Some had no toes, some had no fingers, some no limbs, yet – those big smiles. Big smiles for the care and affection received from the world, and big smiles for the hope that they would continue to be showered with blessings. It certainly gave me perspective. Maybe you'll be the one who figures out how to get the most basic of necessities to those that don't even have fingers to eat with and toes to balance on while walking.

Maybe you'll affect the lives of young children, in a struggling part of a world, in ways they may have never even imagined possible. Maybe you'll outfit all the boys in a village with a pair of runners. Maybe it will be a pair of Kobes, who knows? Maybe you'll help a young girl into a pair of comfortable slippers or armfuls of clothes she will love. Let's realize that they deserve all the good the world has to offer too, not only material goods, but the good which flows from the energy of love, of empathy, and of care. Because...

One moment.

One act of kindness.

One act of love.

Is all it takes.

Organizations like Union Gospel Mission, with locations in Vancouver and Kelowna, Canada, and Guru Nanak Kitchen in Edmonton, Alberta could always use support, and fresh spirits. Maybe you'll be the one to join their efforts.

Let's understand that genuine care, affection and love carries a vibration. A potent one, and once it comes into contact with a child, a mother, an elder, it doesn't just end there. The energy is welcomed in with gratitude. Then that energy is redirected, not only back to whoever was involved in the exchange – but to the world. To the whole. When one who is suffering comes into contact with genuine love, its effects are irreversible. The suffering transmuted, joy, love and gratitude are radiated back into the Universe.

Boomerangs in motion.

Let's take a moment to notice the beauty around us that maybe goes unnoticed, perhaps because of moments spent lost in thought or judgement, and spread the love. Love is the potion. It is a precious gem that one cannot buy. But it can be shared. Spread. Created. And it is the energy that is affecting the world, this globe we share – for the better. It is what is affecting our collective path in a beautiful way. You don't have to look far. It is all over the online world. Heroines and heroes. There is much to be enjoyed, much to be appreciated in moments we might be looking over in haste because of our narrow-minded approaches, our narrow-minded focuses and our closed-off ways – like I used to do, a lot.

In November 2017 I read a book written by Jen Sincero, entitled, *You Are a Badass*.

Pause—

Rokhee. You absolutely rock. You really do. *Thank you.*

—Unpause.

My friend sent me this book. Yup. Rokhee did. She's pretty Kool. I took one look at the cover, the writing on the back, and had begun to see it a certain way. I actually referred to it as a beginner's guide on the road to transformation. I looked at the title, read a few words on the back and then made a judgement: yup, I know what is written within these pages, and put it aside. A few days later I was standing by the desk and something made me reach for the book and flip it open. The first few words that my eyes caught sat me down (literally) and the impact of what I read humbled me as I sheepishly grinned, acknowledging how I had – literally – judged a book by its cover. What caught my eye was a quote at the beginning of the book that I had read before, and upon reading the first line, I felt humbly quiet again because I instantly recognized it, and felt this feeling inside – again.

I sat there with the first line for a long moment before continuing. Reflecting on the fact that *this* is how we tend to go about life's moments, *thinking* we know something or understand someone, and in the process, deny ourselves an experience. Deny ourselves an experience of another's energy, possibly an inspiring or uplifting and maybe even life-changing exchange. Moments filled with a learning and growing component, which could be exactly what we need for a realization. An awakening that could change everything going on around us. That could trigger change in the *only* environment necessary for change to occur around it – within. When *you* change, *everything* changes.

It is that simple.

> Even after all this time
> The Sun doesn't say to the Earth,
> You owe me.
> Look what happens with a love like that,
> It lights up the whole sky.

> —*Rumi*

This quote sat me down silent. The re-experience of these words written by the Sufi poet brought with it a flood of memories, as I remembered where and when I first read them – 3 and a half years ago. Words that triggered a flood of realizations, which in turn triggered a release of energy which was swirling around inside me, revolving around the fact that... no one really owes anyone anything in this world. Especially when the thought comes from a place of non-love that says "you owe me". Any thoughts I had revolving around failed expectations and disappointments gone again, poof. And just like that, a new phase of learning, growing, and experiencing opened up.

A week or so later I was sitting up in bed reading Jen Sincero's book. She suggests you look around the room and notice everything that is red. Actually. *Let's do this together.* Right now. Wherever you are. Look around you and take note of all the red things you can see. Glance and take note. Close your eyes and then try to recall how many red things you saw.

Open your eyes and look to see if you were right, or close, at least. Close your eyes quickly after you read the next line. How many things were yellow? Keep them closed and try to recall.

Did you notice them before? While looking for red? What about the green or the pink? Or white, even? We "see" what we think we see and maybe even want to see. I enjoyed the lesson. I was sure I could

recall the yellow things in the room, since I spent so much time in it –
I wasn't even close.

I had judged the book by its cover and after experiencing the written
words, suggested it to a loved one (the rebel) who said she felt motivated after reading it. Well good for you, I thought, because so did I.
Isn't this how we tend to go about, though, at times? Seeing what we
want to see, believing we see things clearly without really looking?

We share this collective moment with all of humanity. Let us grasp
that. We share strengths. The ability to persevere, remain resilient,
and thrive. We are blessed with this human experience. We are
blessed with senses. Let us not lose the sense we refer to as *common
sense*.

Let us realize that we all have much in common and that we sort of do
have a responsibility to spread colour. We have the ability to receive
love and spread it, in kind, caring, thoughtful, non-judgmental and
joyful ways. We have the ability to spread colour in ways that include
those around us who really need it.

Because.

If we are all "God's children", offspring of the Creator, the Source of
Power which is Life itself, the Power that laid down an environment
for us to bloom from, an environment that we live in and an environment that lives within us, then...

When will we realize that God is amongst us?

When will we realize God is waiting for us to redirect light from
within, wherever we go and wherever it is needed? When will we
realize God bestowed upon us the power of choice to reside within a
realm we can consciously exert influence over?

Cultures and faiths have deep spiritual roots, and those roots are the
principles, fundamentals, eternal teachings that will never wither
away. They'll stand the test of time. Eternal in essence and in truth.
We are all an *expression* of the Infinite. We cannot be separated from

the Source from which we came. Some have keen awareness, some have rare and precious being-level awareness. Others have come and gone with a field of awareness, a state of consciousness so potently high, that they left entire religions and faiths built around the energy they emitted. Built around the vibrations that flowed through them.

Christians say that Jesus Christ was God made manifest, Muslims say that he was a prophet, others refers to him as a rare and precious being and many are ready to fight over these points of views.

Why?

To prove what, exactly, and to whom? Is the finger that points to the moon being used to gouge out the eye, as Anthony de Mello said, riffing on the words of the sage, "the finger pointing to the moon isn't the moon"? I know I said it before. It was necessary to say again.

And.

Maybe we can help others understand the spiritual roots from which the teachings bloomed. Hindus, Muslims, Christians, Judaists, Buddhists, Sikhs and many more all had expressions of Source manifest at different times in different regions at different phases of humanity's journey, all for the same reason. All for the same purpose.

To assist in the awakening process.

To tip the balance of the collective field of consciousness in favor of – not survival, not defence, not ideologies – but in favor of realizing Supreme Reality. In favor of creating a world full of love, acceptance and open doors. In favor of manifesting the era of living heaven (era of truth).

Simple as that.

Maybe we should all listen to the timeless wisdom in the words of the Lebanese-American stand-up comic Nemr, spoken after everyone is done laughing. After the crowd is relaxed, laid back and feeling a little lighter. What are we going to absorb when we are all rigid? We restrict the inflow, remember? He said some powerful words in his one-hour special "No Bombing in Beirut" (2017). Inspiring words that have so much meaning in them. His delivery method was a perfect for his message. He said, you can walk down a street in the Middle East and see a church, a synagogue, and a mosque in close proximity to one another. This is a symbol. Not of competition or to say "here we are", but as a reminder that *Yo – we all got along*. So, what is your issue? That's as close as I can recall his words.

And think about it.

As children, what if no one were to tell us – that house over there has kids like this, who do that; but we are like *this*, we do *this*, and so you are like this and you must remember that. Remember that they don't like this, and they don't like that. Oh, and that house way over there? They don't like this, and they do that, and we don't like what they do even more than those way down the block over there. They are completely different and they like to do things that we consider bad and we hate them for it—?

But instead—

Those kids down the street, they're children too. Like you. We don't want to tell you what they like or don't like, what religion or culture they follow, but instead we want you to get to know each other and share your own home stories, wisdom and knowledge. Share with each other your interests and likes and find things in common with one another. Most importantly, learn to look at them through the eyes of love. Of understanding. Of empathy. Then the world, young one, will start to make sense on its own—?

And, wouldn't it? What do you think?

#Changethestory, said Bill Phipps, minister of the United Church of Canada and social activist. Embrace the "new story", he said. I agree. As do many more. In his book, *Cause for Hope: Humanity at the Cross-roads* (2007), he writes that the "old story" consists of disconnection from the Earth, ecological destruction, entitlement and

consumerism, the rich getting richer, a culture of fear… he says that awareness of all this is a cause for hope, because *we can consciously choose a new story*. He writes that the new story consists of wonder, gratitude, abundance, partnership, moments of grace; and says that we can *consciously* choose to transform the world. We, as individuals, teaming up with others. So: collectively. Again – it comes down to us, it does.

Maybe.

Maybe it's our turn to help our family members in the Middle East in some way; helping so there aren't those who say, "Nothing to live for".

I listened to an interviewee say matter-of-factly, in a regular normal tone one would use in a friendly dialogue, that day after day, young children, kids, men, women, beings of all ages, will make a stand and if they die… they die. They don't care. They have reached a point where they have nothing to lose.

Nothing to live for.

It was the father of a two-year-old boy. His child was killed on the Palestinian side of the border, in the protests against the US Embassy being moved from Tel Aviv. He said, my light, my life is gone. I am nothing now. I don't care if I live. *Live for what?* What do you think the guy is liable to do? Anything. Anything he sees as justified from the level of awareness he is operating from.

Seeing the state of peril in that region, the hardships and deprivations of basic needs we in the luxurious world are accustomed to, it is easy to see how someone's suffering becomes dangerous, where one will do whatever he or she sees fit from his or her level of awareness.

The same goes for anywhere in the world.

Let's help those that are being affected daily while we sit and enjoy comforts and luxury. Let's combine our efforts and show them that the world cares. Maybe it is our turn to help inspire those who feel like they don't have much to live for any more, so they can inspire those around them.

Let's help rebuild Mosul, the city in Iraq. The infrastructure needs repairs – the after-effects of years of war. It needs high-spirited energy. Maybe you're here to bring Buddhists, Christians, Muslims, Hindus, Judaists, Wiccans, Sikhs, atheists, the non-religious-but-Higher-Power-believing beings together. Together for one purpose. To restore and mend and help heal the wounds left behind by the carnage.

Maybe you will be the one to organize architects, plumbers, electric-engineers, project co-ordinators, project managers, builders, roofers, and those with keen organizing skills to come together and make a difference.

Every effort counts.

Maybe one of you will help the ones coming together to realize, that we are not Vietnamese or Muslim or Canadian, or American, or Iranian or Chinese, not if these identifications separates us; and maybe you will be the one to tell them the same thing that Bruce Lee said: "I am a Human Being.... under the stars, the Heavens, there is but one family".

That be *us*. Humanity.

Maybe you'll be the one to make others realize that those who call Iraq their home are our brothers, sisters, mothers and fathers. That the elders there are also our elders. 10,000 people putting up 100 dollars... adds up. 1 million people putting up 100 dollars adds up. Imagine *100 million* putting up money... look how quick it adds up!

The power of the collective, I'd say.

Imagine what it will do for everyone involved in this giving, sharing, caring, loving, rebuilding, and uplifting experience? It will heal. Green lush soccer fields. Big swimming pools and training grounds. Huge facilities for music, art and theatre. It will set a trend that can be mimicked all over the world. It will bring an immense amount of joy

into the world. It will bring a stark contrast to the conflict and priva-
tions of the past, one full of colour. Monks in caves will smile while
deep in meditation because they'll feel it. They'll feel it, because that
which they have been unconditionally intending, will be manifesting.
Not just monks, but beings who are meditating to uplift Consciousness, sending out surges of healing energy.

Maybe.

Maybe you'll become inspired by the courage of Malala Yousafzai, and
add energy towards all that she stood up for – education for all girls,
for all children – all that she stands for today; maybe you will add
energy towards the intentions she voices. A point-blank bullet to the
face couldn't silence her voice – imagine that.

Maybe, if you're a young Khalsa, you will understand why energy
needs to be lent towards what Malala is doing. Maybe you will derive
your life purpose from an appreciation of at least one of her purposes
– like standing tall against tyranny. Maybe you will bring together
Muslims and Hindus, Christians and Buddhists, with a quality of
charisma the likes of Maharaja Ranjit Singh possessed, all for an
aligned purpose. Purpose of harmony and unity. Maybe those boots
that hit that ground will be the ones that alter history dramatically.

Maybe, if you are a young Khalsa, you will use the memory of 1984 as
fuel for a fire that lays down the ground work for the manifestation of
true Khalistan.[4] Energy always balances itself out, in exact proportion
to that which was projected – but in order to understand it at the level
of energy, dwelling on the shortcomings of others, or on injustices, by
focusing intense energy towards them, whether in music or thought,
only embeds polarized positions. Imagine you were at war and all you
did was reinforce the opposition's bases and strong holds.

Kind of pointless.

For argument's sake let's call the two opposing forces "good" and
"bad". Why would the good support the bad? Why would the good
help the bad? Why would the good reinforce the ideas of the bad?

Makes no sense, right?

There has never been a more prime moment in history for the collective to bind their brain power together to create magic. If hundreds of thousands can get together, again and again, such as happened in Hong Kong, thousands and tens of thousands can easily get together to spread the colour, the energy, and the love of Khalsa on the ground in India.

Roll through like a wave. Literally.

Let's get the water and food where it needs to be, like Sikh Aid. Let's add more energy towards the Canadian Sikh Cancer Society, whose intention is to reach every being in need, no matter the distance, resources, or challenges. Why? Because the leading voice behind the cause has understood the message of Guru Nanak. Maybe Khalsa can dedicate resources and finances towards the Daswand Foundation, which Lashkara TV features, for the world to see just how dire the need for help in India is.[5]

The true message of the Sikhi way of life is *Peace. Harmony. Strength.* It isn't one of aggression. It is one of doing good, and spreading love. For the young ones that want to establish Khalistan, don't look for a name on a map – bring the values, the ethics, the service of Khalsa to the areas of need.

That is how Khalistan will manifest.

The people's voice will make it so. The voice of love. Of understanding. Of sharing in another's grief and, in turn, helping remove burdens. There are those who still suffer from the hardship(s) endured in 1984. Yet, the collective bank of the "Kaum", can it even alleviate the pain and suffering caused by lack of basic necessities in the disputed area, where illusory governance is wanted?[6]

Oh, but yes it can.

Guru Gobind Singh Ji, the Leader of the Kaum (still), played his part in manifesting Khalsa and laid the blueprint, which cannot ever be misconstrued: forgiveness. Even after Aurenghzeb – the Mughal ruler who bricked his youngest boys into a wall alive – he had this to say in the *Zafarnamah* (Epistle of Victory):

> *You have nothing to fear coming down this way*
> *As the Brars of this area are under my sway.*

> *(Na zarah darin rah khatrah turasat,*
> *Hama quame bairar hukme marasat [59])*

> *Come here that we may converse freely, face to face*
> *And interact we mutually with good will and grace.*

> *(Biya ta sukhan khud zabani kunem*
> *Barue shuma meharbani kunem [60])*

Sacrifice. Courage. Will. It was part of his life-cycle's purpose, to put that energy forward for the likes of us to learn from. Sikhi Way, is the way of resilience and compassion. Of kindness and forgiveness. The way of the sword is a last resort, if it is absolutely necessary in defence and to oust the likes of tyrants. Never aggression.

So why promote it?

The Kaum isn't being attacked by violence today.

Why manifest it?

It is 2020. The world is on public display, and you have the power of that display in the palm of your hands. Adapt. The militarized aspect of the Faith is indeed war-ready.

Always war-ready.

That's the point of being a member of Khasla. That is the point of being on point, always. And the meaning of being at war is that one is constantly perfecting oneself; mentally, emotionally, physically, and most importantly – spiritually. That is what a saint/soldier is. To become a solider, said Sant Singh Ji Maskeen, one must first become a saint.[7] One can only become a saint by striving to emulate the humility, compassion, and internal mental strength of a saint. Only then can one become a true soldier. So if it is a saint/soldier that you identify with, female or male, boy or girl, the purpose is already bestowed upon you – Service. Lift up.

Protect. Protect doesn't mean pick up a weapon, in this day and age. It means use your intelligence. It means use your skills to help. To serve. To mend. To heal. To fix.

That *is* protection.

Let's not disrespect Guru Gobind Singh Ji's symbolization of bearing arms and showing Power. Let's show Power in Unity, of virtues, because the virtues he projected were gentle. They were loving. Kind. Caring. Let's protect the principles he instilled by promoting them.

By projecting them.

Maybe we're all just spokes of a wheel, and without the individual support from each spoke, the wheel collapses. Each individual certainly makes up a vital aspect of the whole, and the support we give to every individual, in support of the whole, is then as important as any individual or collective purpose. It *is* the purpose. Martin Luther King Jr had this to say while he was incarcerated in Birmingham Jail:

> We are caught in an inescapable network of mutuality, tied in a single garment of destiny. Whatever affects one directly affects all indirectly. Never again can we afford to live with the narrow, provincial "outsider agitator" idea. Anyone who lives inside the United States can never be considered an outsider.

He wrote these words regarding segregation and injustice as a whole. If I could do so without offending anyone, I would say that *anyone who lives on this Earth can never be an outsider* and that it applies unconditionally to all of us.

How can one be an outsider while living *on* this beautiful Earth?

1. If you ever want to experience one, seek out a 3-5 a.m. NAAM SIMRAN session at a gurdwara. You can feel it in the air (the intensely alive buzzing energy). They are held consistently for healing purposes – physical, emotional, mental – and yes, spiritual.
2. Have we built any yet?
3. Saint Francis of Assisi – called by God to do God's work. The energy that flowed through him was so potently pure and of a high vibration, that many were healed in his presence. When he finally passed, it was attributed to 'ill health'. When asked why he didn't just heal himself, he replied that it was because it wasn't him that did the healing. This healing energy was also present within Guru Harkrishan, 8TH Guru of the path started by Guru Nanak. The 8th Guru came to sit on the Divine Throne, at age 5. Imagine that.
4. In June of 1984, the Indian Government, in a cold and ruthless manner, carried out attacks on Harmindar Sahib (the Golden Temple) – regarded as one of the holiest Sikh sites, and on Akal Thakat Sahib – the seat of temporal authority for gurdwaras. The Sikh central reference library was also targeted and looted. Children and beings of all ages were targeted and girls were raped. Murdered. As were the improperly labelled, so-called "freedom fighters" – they were Khalsa. Indira Ghandi was a tyrant then. Modhi (the prime minister now), if he neglects to take steps toward justice and unity, will be remembered as a tyrant in years to come.
5. The Daswand Foundation helps people who are struggling financially to meet medical and living costs (www.daswand.ca). Lashkara TV usually airs on Saturdays at 8.30 p.m. Pacific time, on Vision TV.
6. Kaum – A reference to the Sikhi Community. Khalsa Community. The family of Khalsa, including its relatives. That be everyone. Matter of perspective it is, again. Perspective. Perspective. Awareness. Awareness.
7. Highly respected preacher and writer of the Sikh faith.

CHAPTER 35

GUESS WHAT?

Never an ending,
Always a new beginning.

—Ninja

O ur journey here is nearing its end.

You have no idea what it took to get this book into print and into your hands! We have access to computers, I mentioned this before; however, word documents can only be saved on floppy discs (remember them? – some of you will be too young to have ever seen one!). There were times when the floppy discs decided they weren't going to work anymore, and so the saved work was... gone. There were many days when the (external) floppy drives would just eat the disc, wipe it and make it useless. Grr...

Then came the printing. At times there was no ink or paper; sometimes the printer wasn't working. Getting the material to the editor – all the way over in the United Kingdom – was another mission. At times I sent the writing out in printed form, so someone else could type it up and send the editor a digital copy. Other times, had to wait weeks to get a floppy disc into the hands of a friend or business associate to convert the saved files to a digital copy, and then e-mail it. And no, they don't make computers with floppy drives anymore!

You can buy a converter, though.

Getting the writing back into my hands after the editor had made comments and edits was yet another challenge. The material had to be meticulously printed (with editor's comments) then mailed to me, and this process had, like, a 6-week turnaround period. But. Where there are challenges, so there is opportunity. We developed a system that worked, and if it weren't for the reliability and consistency on the part of Allegra Printing (Abbotsford BC, Canada) this project would not have come to fruition.

Then there was the challenge of ADHD (attention deficit hyperactivity disorder).

It is real.

ADHD, or ADD (attention deficit disorder), whatever the label – you can put me under both. At times I just struggle to keep my attention on one thing, other times lack of attention moves into extreme forms of hyper-activity and other behaviours, like repeating the same phrase over and over until someone starts laughing – um.... I think I did that a lot in my favourite English teacher's class. She was my favourite because *she*... never told on me. She let me sort out my... nonsense.

I was never diagnosed as a child; I didn't even know I experienced it, but thanks to a doctor in Surrey Pretrial Services Center, it came to light. I think it was only possible because of steady encounters with the same doctor during 2016, which allowed her to make the assessment. One day I was sitting in the chair across from her desk, fidgeting around while waiting for her to finish typing something up before our visit started, when she abruptly asked me (and not very politely) *what are you doing? Why are you doing that?*

I stopped moving.

I felt like a kid who had just been scolded or caught in the act of making a ruckus he shouldn't have been making. Um, sorry, was my response.

She asked me if I had heard of ADHD, and if I had ever been diagnosed with it or had been on medication for it. She then asked me what my behaviour in high school was like, I said I didn't understand the question.

The eyes to the top corner emoji (top-left).

What did your teachers have to say about you, she asked? What did they say about your marks? Oh. Um, they said *if only* he tried harder. *If only* he paid more attention... I saw the light bulb go on in her eyes. She thought I could use some medication to help me focus, but before offering any suggestions, she referred me to a psychiatrist for an assessment.

I got to see the psychiatrist fairly quickly. He asked a few questions about childhood and high school. I told him that I ended up going to jail before graduating. I told him, at the time of arrest I was re-doing grade 12, and had higher grades than the previous year. I told him I was heading for an A in Math 12, but felt a lot of it had to do with the fact that I was consuming small doses of marijuana, which I felt was helping me focus.

The consultation lasted maybe 5 minutes.

When I saw the doctor next, she was excited to see the psychiatrist's report, and what (if any) recommendations had been put forth. After a few clicks she burst out laughing. She was laughing so hard that a nurse from the adjoining room walked in, curious. Are you ready for this? She looked at me, at the nurse and then read what had been written: "Inmate has used marijuana in the past, he is drug seeking". Now the nurse and I started laughing. We were joined in the room by yet another nurse, who also started laughing after hearing what had been written.

When we were all done laughing, I told the doctor, but I didn't ask for anything. I only answered questions. What does this mean? Does this go on my file permanently, that I am drug seeking? I took issue with the fact that someone had the authority to write such an impactful thing in someone's file after barely a 5-minute consultation.

So did the doctor.

So did the nurses.

The nurses went to bat for me, saying I rarely took medication (narcotics) when it was legally prescribed to me – such as Percocet – and not only that, when I did I kept a self-check tab to avoid exceeding the prescribed amount. Besides, I had weaned myself off this medication anyway; personal choice. The doctor entered a new report, and went as far as saying that the psychiatrist's assessment was insufficient, and completed with no knowledge of the history of the patient.

Thank God.

The last thing I needed was my mum to be told I was seeking drugs in jail. I definitely did not want to hear her say... *Like there wasn't anything else left for you to blemish or stain, you had to go to the lowest of places and display the lowest of behaviours – wait till you see what happens to you when you get home!*

Waheguru.

The doctor took it upon herself to help me. She tried a series of medications: non-stimulant... Conserta... Dexidrine. I went from feeling gross, to feeling focused but anxious; jittery; not right – nope, and nope again.

After a pause, she prescribed a low dose of Adderall. I came back with 4 completed Spanish 11 assignments by the end of the week. I'd been trying to finish them for *10 months*. I wanted to do them, something kept me from absorbing the information and getting them done. I would just stare at the assignments, trying to figure out how to get it all done. She asked me how it made me feel, I told her that I felt really calm and focused. Not only calm and focused, but patient.

Bingo.

I completed Spanish 11 & 12, both with an A+. Got my dogwood (equivalent of your grad diploma) too! Had to redo English 12, got an A+ in that too. Finally! It only took 10 extra years after school. More like 12, actually.

My friend – the Ninja – recently said, who says ADD/ADHD is a disorder? Who said it is a negative or a curse? It is a blessing. It is a gift, it should be nurtured. It shouldn't be supressed. It certainly shouldn't be mismanaged or go unrecognized. Until it is recognized though, it *is* a disorder, because you are hindered at performing your best. But once it is recognized, and you find what makes your brain function better and better... then forth pours the creativity. If you don't even know you have it... then I agree, your creativity will be supressed and life can become very disorderly.

And.

That is what happened with me. It went unrecognized and, because nothing was done, it went unmanaged – I was left to cope with it on my own. I just found out that GSP (Canadian MMA fighter) is blessed with the "gift" of ADHD. I found myself wondering, when did he learn of it, how did it hinder his progress through life, and at the same time, were there any ways in which it helped him? Did it help? I remembered words of GSP's from a documentary that had an impact on my mindset. The words were along the lines of, *respect your adversary, for your adversary completes you.*

Deep words.

I wondered how much focus and discipline it took to arrive at that perception. I then remembered important questions by the editor of this very book, a doctor based in the United Kingdom.

One of the questions was, did you struggle in the classroom and were your difficulties ignored? I did struggle in the classroom. I don't think the difficulties were ignored, as much as they were misunderstood. There is a big difference. What if those who are supposed to pick up on your difficulties aren't trained or experienced enough to do so? Then it isn't anyone's fault.

But.

Had my "gift" been recognized, maybe the journey would have been different. Had I had the medication that mixed well with the chemical balances in my brain earlier, I may have been able to focus on assignments and prioritize what truly mattered in life. It would have been easier because I wouldn't have been all over the place, or so... sporadic. I would have organized my thoughts and taken time to categorize them.

I wouldn't have been so hyper and intense.

I stayed on Adderall for 2 years, without the need to increase the dose. I took it in moderation. I found a system that worked real well for me. I read up on the medication and, sometimes, in synchronistic ways, new knowledge would fall on my ears, which helped reinforce my approach to consuming the prescribed focus enhancer mindfully and in moderation. What a neat new way to categorize the "medication"—

A focus enhancer.

I was taken off of Adderall when I arrived at my designated mother institution. BOOOO!!! A prime example of a systemic failure and "what isn't working" within the system known as "Corrections Canada". The only way for an inmate to have a prescription for ADD or ADHD meds in this place is if the person was on the medication before they were incarcerated. In my case I wasn't diagnosed until I came to jail. Why should this matter? It was a respected doctor that diagnosed me, but somehow that doesn't and didn't suffice. And FYI, it is easier for a kid to get a prescription of methadone and Suboxone than it is Tylenol 3; not cool. And not only did the doctor's diagnosis from SPSC not suffice – I was told by a new doctor, upon entering the federal prison system in May 2018, that Adderall had been replaced by Vyvanse. Vyvanse was the go-to choice for college students "these days", he said. Been in prison for quite some time there, young man.

Not true. It just costs Correctional Services Canada too much.

He wasn't only feeding me a line but, I would say, he risked some pretty significant liability issues. Vyvanse messed me right up. It took me a week to start feeling normal again. I was advised to give it another try by the same doctor (it takes time for the brain to adjust, he said), so I did. Felt even worse, maybe because I anticipated the crash and then the depressing recovery period. I even told the doctor that I had already gone through a trial and error process 2 years ago, but that fell on deaf ears. He did suggest he could increase the dose if I liked.

Ya, no thanks, good on that.

How have I coped with ADHD since? No medication has been provided. Any and all attempts at acquiring over-the-counter cognitive function enhancing or memory recall remedy has been denied.

Ummm... so music has been a blessing. The fact that we can have headphones on and listen to music via a CD Walkman is a luxury. Get it, "Walkman"? A device that walks with you while you stroll. Or "walks" with its "man". Hmm... I wonder if there are any "Walkwomans"? Wait, are there?

Interesting.

I keep headphones on a lot of the time – keeps away the ambient noises that my ears pick up, and the mind takes upon itself to decipher, analyse and then send forward a stream of thought related to it. Beats headphones get it done.[1] The type of music in my ears matters immensely. Usually it is kirtan, like right now while I type away. Spanish guitar sounds are another stabilizer. Punjabi music. Sounds with an uplifting, inspiring and healing vibration, do mesh well with the mental imbalances.

Do I self-medicate at times? I don't know. Do I?

Would you blame me if I did? Would you blame me, after I told you that I have been asking for natural remedies which help with cognitive functioning and memory recall, for over 18 months? If I did self-medicate, would you blame me? What if it helped me stay calm, focus, read, write, and be a better version of myself all around, which in turn would affect those around me in a positive way, would you blame me, still? So, do I self-medicate, then?

I don't recall. ADHD can be a blessing, like GSP said – If I do, it is only natural or gentle helpers that I reach for.

I HOPE you've enjoyed reading this as much as I've enjoyed writing it.

How did I do?

It was even more awkward doing research in here; you're not allowed to have content printed off of the internet mailed in. You cannot order books straight from the publisher, nor magazines (like *Nexus*). Only way to get books and reading material in is through the original pack of belongings you are allowed during the first short period of your induction, and that has a monetary cap on it.

So.

We relied on the Universe to deliver whatever it was we (the Magic Mind Squad) needed to complete this writing – yes, it was a... *team* effort ;). And if it seems incomplete – tell it to the Universe! But feel free to let us know what you think, too – I would be happy for this to be beginning of a conversation.

Shall we complete this journey then?

Let's.

---

1. Beats headphones are a brand created by the Dr Dre and Jimmy Iovine. They sold the Beats music subscription service that gave birth to the headphones to Apple for $3 billion.

CHAPTER 36

AND NOW WE'RE LIKE BASICALLY THERE

#LETSMAKEADIFFERENCE

Your journey has molded you for your greater good,
and it was exactly what it needed to be.
Don't think you've lost time. There is no shortcutting in life.
It took each and every situation you encountered to bring you to the now. And
now is right on time.

—Asha Tyson

This human experience is a gift and an opportunity. Within it, we cannot avoid making choices. Every choice we make is based on our understanding, our level of awareness. Our level of awareness determines how unconscious or conscious we are of the choices we make, and the actions they lead to.

Every choice I made, that corresponded with my level of awareness, led me here to this point, pen in hand, filled with the urge to share the thoughts and opinions that really want to be expressed. Oh, and to say... *Hullo world.*

The past contained exactly what was required to make this present moment. The future isn't promised. Any idea about what it will contain – is only an idea. *This moment*, however, is in our grasp. And what matters is... the use we will make of it. I truly believe the journey I took to get here, to share this human experience, is a gift, a treasure, and that my purpose as an individual is to open my eyes, connect with intention, and make use of my experience. As a community our purpose is the same: to share our talents, our strengths, our weaknesses, our love; learning from our mistakes and making a difference in any way we can.

As a kid growing up, when I was asked what it was that I really wanted to do, I would tell those I trusted that what I really wanted to do was help people. Why? Because I want to change the world. *Duh.* A year or so ago, if asked, how? I would have said one person at a time. Now, when I'm asked about what I really want, my response is, *to make a difference and enjoy every living breathing moment.*

Don't you want to change the world?

The world *is* changing. For the better. It is constantly experiencing change. Constantly evolving. All we need to do is become conscious participants and to add something of Pyaar (love), of colour, of a positive influence to this dance of life. All we need to do is – *wake up.*

Each individual who experiences a shift affects the whole; and the power of presence can trigger a shift in even the most unsuspecting of individuals, and so-called "negative" environments. The shift *is* the much sought-after change. As one's awareness grows, as consciousness expands, one realizes that, all this time, we have fallen back upon a "bundle of conditioned behaviors and responses" that are now withering away, which Eckhart Tolle sheds eye-opening light on in *A New Earth*. An eye-opening read, indeed, written to jumpstart or accelerate the process of waking up. And what remains, when this bundle is gone? Nothing but pure awareness, and this moment.

For years (at SPSC and OCC) there was little-to-no interaction with anyone except a handful of individuals, because we were housed in smaller units. We finally got to live in a larger unit 6 months into our stay at Okanagan Correction Center, and it brought with it the opportunity to connect with others in a way that was humbling. It brought with it the moments to see shifts first hand happening around us like a domino effect. It also brought with it the opportunity to better understand the obstacles (ignorance, me-first mentality, will-full blindness of abuse and disrespect in "love" relationships, greed, envy, hate, engaging in harmful behaviour – just a couple of drinks attitude) that become like physical barriers hindering healthy growth, and keep many stuck in repetitive cycles of ignorance. It has helped me better understand my own behaviours, the past, and what is referred to as – the ego. The opportunity to sit down, observe, and listen, has led to a deeper appreciation of words like "ego". Perception. Self. Healing. *Awareness*.

It is now easier to recognize the illusion (ego) that says to those it is strongest in, "I am you". The, "I am your name, your thoughts and your past". The, "I am your behaviours, emotions, and your wants and needs".

I realized that it doesn't matter where you are, what you have, or who loves you or doesn't. If you are not at one within, if you are not at peace within, if you are not harmonized within, then circumstances, situations, people and things will not provide that balance for you. I came to that realization while listening, whether it was on the unit, on the phone with friends and loved ones in the "real world", or observing the noticeable disconnect, at times, and not-so-high vibrational alignments around me. The culprit behind every disconnect? The illusion of ego, whispering in the ear of its victim, telling stories that are not true.

Word up.

It is indeed a critical time in our evolution, with artificial intelligence able to cater to us in many ways; in crafty ways, to facilitate ease. But. In that same outer-world leap, there is an inner-world gap which is critical, is vital, and that requires bridging to ensure we maintain balance in not only our individual worlds, but to ensure that we contribute balanced vibrations to the Universe. Our Universe, which operates in *harmony*. A harmony which maintains the balance necessary for life. It is our individual responsibility to become aware of what it is exactly we are putting into this world, putting into the Universe. It is our responsibility to be aware of the quality of energy we're exchanging with any and all environments we spend our moments in.

Stephen Hawking marvelled at the beauty of the unseen and unexplainable. That is why he devoted his moments to uncovering as much as he could about the "Universe". He said the Universe is infinite. And it is. There are no words to explain the Unexplainable. There are only concepts and limited phrases that do nothing, in a sense, to capture the infinite. He also said that it operates in harmony. I read a book written by Shirley McClain, *Going Within* (1990), where she wrote about Stephen Hawking and her interaction with him. It is a book worth reading.

Mohabbat (love) is the potion. Harmony is the lock-pick (necessary balance) and Awareness the key to unlocking the riddles and colours of this life experience.

Let's set some trends of our own. Let's spread the love and tune in, not only to ourselves, but to one another and a share a moment or two that could be the very thing, the very exchange of energy that sets one *free*.

Free from ego. *Free* from small-mindedness. *Free* from anger. *Free* from hate. *Free* from jealousy. *Free* from small wins and small gains. *Free* from judgement. *Free* from needing to validate oneself by having to prove oneself worthy to another for reasons not fully known. *Free* from low energy vibrations. *Free* from the destruction they manifest.

Let's.

Let's learn to be true to ourselves, and share warmth with others so we can be a part of this everyday joy of life as active participants – as co-creators.

Let's stand together and be individual links in a collective chain that spans the length, height and width of this beautiful blue-green globe of a planet we call Earth. A chain that mends the wounds around us, that helps bridge critical gaps needed for understanding. Bridging those gaps will bring greater balance within the whole, as one cannot truly be separated from another.

The likes of Stephen Hawking said that we originated in a big bang, and that it was one single occurrence from which the Universe came to be. There is no mention of two. There is no mention of something other, or something separate. About 600 years ago, Bhagat Kabir said:[1]

> *God first created light. All men are born of it.*
> *The whole world came of a single spark.*
> *Who is good and who is bad?*

So.

Let's not. Let's not be ignorant. We may have to pay later for that ignorance. Once you're aware – you're aware. No going back.

And instead…

Let us get together to make a difference in a way that triggers new karmic cycles, new karmic waves to flourish, sending forth a wave of light, of energy that washes away the darkness. It's not as if "darkness" really *is* anything – darkness is only the absence of light.

That's all.

Let's put forth light that washes away karma from the past. That brings hope and purpose into the eyes of beings who are on the brink of despair, gasping for air, who are praying for food and water, and perhaps for – a saviour to show up. *You* are that hope. *You* are that light. *You* are that trigger.

Let's.

Let's stand for something else. Let's all stand as one and embrace the concept of unity. It is time to dig deep into our hearts, identify what no longer serves, what keeps us separated from harmony, from love, from understanding one another – and it is time to let go of it all. Let go of the small-minded beliefs, small opinions, small thoughts, small points of view which are nothing but the poison of ego and the prison of an illusion.

Let's be grateful for what we have. We only need to type into Google simple searches on the subject of those suffering from a lack of basic living necessities, things that we're so accustomed to, to realize how fortunate we are.

Let's appreciate all that we have, giving thanks and being grateful for all the things we at times overlook in our search for "more", our search for "something else".

Let's recognize that where we are today, in this moment, there is someone out there who would trade her or his life for our situation; for a loved one, for themselves, for a whole family, even.

Let's recognize suffering when it arises and, instead of offering sympathetic talk, pity, or opinions that shed no light and do no good, let's learn genuine *empathy*. Let's tap into the empathetic field of energy, using it as a bridge to form a connection, not only with someone who may really need it, but – ourselves.

Let's bring compassion into the equation. Compassion allows space for understanding to emerge, which can be used to connect with the worlds of others that are, sometimes, depleted. They may just not have the inner clarity to see the world in its true illumination. With loving kindness, new light and new beginnings become possible.

Love is kind.[2] Caring. Thoughtful. Understanding. Humble. It inspires. It keeps no record of right or wrong. It looks with empathy, not pity. It is light, not spite. Intelligent, not clever. Let's take steps to bridge the gaps of misunderstanding.

Let's connect the dots.

Let's worry less about trivial matters and set our sights upon higher ideals. Let's leave no child's need unattended. Children are the lights of the world. Let's put more energy into taking the initiative to connect with children who are already suffering, who are already hurting and suffering silently – maybe even feeling really alone in this world. Silent. Afraid. Alone. The lights of our world who are suffering from a lack of love. From a lack of meaningful connection. Maybe from a rumbling stomach that keeps them from concentrating. Every aspect matters. Every being matters.

Everyone.

Let's focus on what we want manifesting. The law of attraction can only respond to one's point of focus – remember? It doesn't matter, to the law of attraction, if the very thing you *don't want* is the thing that you are focusing on, because it cannot tell the difference and make that distinction on its own – remember? When you focus, you create a vibration. That vibration locks in on the thing you are focused on, which itself has a corresponding vibration. The correspondence in the two vibrations causes the thing to vibrate its way to you (cool hey?). So, once you start to focus on something, you are already sending out signals into the Universe, and then it goes to collect. On its own time, in its own way, and when it is meant to – it *will* manifest.

Invisible energies come into play the moment your point of focus is directed towards something, and the quality of your focus will continue to attract things, people, or the necessary nuts and bolts for the intention to manifest. If you are doubtful, or contradictory in your focus, it will only scramble the signal. So getting clear, and staying clear, is important.

You do not have to stress about the "how", Deepak Chopra says it simply:

> Let the Universe work out the details.

And, yup, it is true. Focus on the "what", take steps to align yourself with that vision, and do what is in your ability to continue fueling the intent with thoughts that support it.

With actions that support it.

Let's come together and make a difference in the lives of others, each exchange of energy will trigger healing, leave warm, heartfelt wishes in the experience of those you encounter – which could, in turn, create a lasting feeling of purpose, meaning, and belonging. *#Pay-it-forward. #Create. #Sow. #Cultivate-and-Harness.*

Snowball effects.

The steps you take to help another, the good you project into the world, and any form of service you are able to engage in... Snapchat that. Post that on social media. It *will* inspire. It *will* create a flood of energy that *will* go supersonic and be felt like ripples all across this Earth – which we all reside on for a breath of a moment. The energy will add itself to the energy already circulating, sent forth by spiritual beings going about this human experience – like yourselves.

We *can* make a difference, even if it seems small, which contributes towards balance. We can share with each other and the world in a way that spreads love... spreads kindness... and invokes harmony.

Harmony is a natural way of being. If we are in harmony, we are in tune. If we are in tune, we hear, we see, we perceive and do that which reflects balance itself. Making a difference, in the smallest way, puts out a gentle, yet *ferocious* vibration into the world because of the higher energy it summons forth. And once that begins, my friends... *magic* happens.

There starts a whole new level of energy exchange. One that can correct and re-correct karmic courses, for oneself – and for all of humanity.

And.

This too shall pass (this life experience), one day soon, for the all of us, so why not say the things we need to when we get the urge, before it gets too late, or before we find ourselves making up all sorts of reasons not to? It could be just the thing that sets you free. Love will set you free. It will take you out of the trenches and lift you into the realm of freedom.

Trenches 2 Freedom indeed.

Enjoy the freedom.

It's certainly been a pleasure.

Waheguru Ji Ka Khalsa, Waheguru Ji Ki Fateh.

---

1. Bhagat Kabir – A rare and precious, God-realized being. A being whose level of consciousness was so high and refined that it triggered his writings, realizations and experiences to become part of the collection of eternal teachings and wisdom present within Guru Granth Sahib Ji.
2. Wayne W. Dyer presented these words on love in a book I read entitled, *The Power of Intention*. It was while serving a 21-day segregation bit. For the first time I realized how far off my definition of love was.

WORDS FROM THE AUTHOR
AND YES, THIS JOURNEY COMPLETES HERE

The influences, lessons and experiences my mother and father exposed me to early, which were intended to shape me for the better, have been coming back to me recently. I did not forget everything, and what they taught me, I now realize, makes me want to become worthy, once again, of being called their son. Not because I need praise or recognition, but because it might communicate to them (mostly my mother – because we rarely talk) that simple truth – I did not forget everything; and no, I do not want to let this gift of a life go to waste. I will not.

My mother was and has always been the reason I want to prove myself better. If we can't do it for the one who brought us into this world, then who? I failed in the past, but now want nothing more than to give her the respect that she is due.

She is my mother.

However, it is the message in the words of the late Gurmit S. Dhak which helped trigger even deeper realizations of what matters and why. Though much had been contemplated, realized and learned up until August 2017, nothing had hit me as hard as his words did; words he left behind on a video for others to one day reflect upon. I realized, to another degree, just how important our parents are, and just how important family is. The impact of Gurmit S. Dhak's words are immeasurable. Here is someone who was regarded as the dakuu (outlaw) of dakuus, labelled a kingpin by the media. In his video, he laid out what he thought the worth of a dakuu was. Nothing.

No value.

Gurmit S. Dhak redeemed himself from a being a dakuu and alleged kingpin, to being an inspiration for change. An inspiration to those wanting to become something of true value and worthiness. His spirit continues to be a helpful light, reflecting the source of love that he was. Through his words he has helped redeem his younger brother from the same dysfunction that claimed his life. Through his words he is helping redeem others who look up to him still.

He is a friend, older brother, and mentor, who in expression of his transformation and growth, helped inspire much of this writing. Writing that hopefully lands in the hands of high-schoolers all over the world. Into the hands of every high-schooler that rolls through high schools in not only Beautiful British Columbia, but all of Canada.

And.

I get it. The words I wrote are, perhaps, pretty opinionated. They are just forms of thought – a physical expression of what is perceived, felt, and experienced within. Words directed specifically at beings at certain stages of their life experience. Words meant for the inner child. Words for the high school phase – a time I wish I could go back to because Sukhvir would still be around, and so would most of the loved ones who have passed on since. But then we wouldn't have enjoyed this journey, would we? Nope.

Meant to be, it certainly was.

Maybe someone might be saying, OK cool. So what? I'm gonna do this or let's do that. I'm gonna just be this and let's just be that. Who said you knew what you were talking about anyway?

Yup.

Sure.

Maybe.

But.

Thank you.

Thank you for reading, for sharing in these words. If you didn't just skip ahead to this part, then I figure you enjoyed it… at least a little.

With your purchase of this book, you have just contributed to Sukhvir's Care. 50 per cent of the profits will go towards this dream, which will be used to make a difference on this Earth we share and call home, because *every being matters*.

Oh, and we just did that… we made a difference… *together*.

See how simple it is?

Let go of the smallness. Let go of the hate. Let go of the pettiness. While we are here, why not? Why not…? Live a little. Care a little. Give a little. Share a little. Love a little. Give thanks a little. Make a difference… a little.

Just a little.

Let it go. *Be free*. Free from hate. Free from anger. Free from jealousy. Free from greed. Free from envy. Free from small-mindedness. Free from small gain and wins. Be free. *Free as a bird*.

This book here, is dedicated to Gurmit S. Dhak (KMK) – Aladdin lives.

Bet you didn't see that coming.

Keep it real.

ACKNOWLEDGMENTS
AKA THE THANK YOUS: TOLD YOU THERE WAS MORE

I would like to start by saying thank you to those who have supported and helped me over these recent years. There have been many twists and turns along this journey as well as extreme challenges and hardship. If it weren't for the doses of loving kindness, compassion, empathy, patience and understanding... I don't know where I would be today.

Trenches 2 Freedom has become a book worthy of publishing because of the effort, due diligence, and consistent quality of both mindful thought and delicate care injected into this project by our editor, Dr Simon J. Tilbury. He challenged my thoughts and helped them evolve. He brought forth provoking questions and made me contemplate deeper life's most important laws, like the laws of karma. There were times when I meant to say one thing, but in writing it came out saying another. A couple of these instances could have resulted in controversy and in undeveloped awareness, and an almost skewed pereption on universality and the concept of collective inclusion. Thank you for helping bring this project to fruition.

Thank you to Nadine McGregor who was the official ARC reader for this book. It was her referral that connected us with the editor and oh wow – are we ever grateful. Thank you for your insightful and challenging comments, they made us laugh and smile more than once.

Z, someone I consider a sister, was there for me in times of need when no one was. Ever ready to back my play and quick to administer a protective barrier of fire when needed. Some journeys must separate so the Universe may assemble new coordinates in life. I understand that now. Thank you for being a friend, for being a sister.

The Rebel, a little sister, who is more of a living earth angel (and a Pokémon), helped me realize what the cost of misplacing priorities is – and where it gets you. I was lost for years looking for acceptance and belonging and, in that search, I walked away from home and everything that signified home. When that search ran dry and I accepted the present moment, that which I had left behind was waiting for me with outstretched hands to welcome me along this journey. And, what a delight it has been. I hope one day she writes a book on empathy.

When I burn dim, Giggles came around with an irresistible glow, transferring light, helping me heal. She inspired me to be better, less judgmental and more understanding. She encouraged me to turn the gaze inwards and connect with the potency of the spirit. Her innermost desire is to heal others, to mend, to uplift, and she has been doing exactly this, whether she is aware of it or not. I may have been the first to feel the effects of the healing energy and glow that emanates from her. For it was the moments shared, giggles enjoyed, smiles and laughter created that kick-started the healing.

Karen, a friend of mine, whom I feel is a soulmate and guiding light, is perhaps one of the most kindest, thoughtful, humble and empathetic beings I have met – her presence has been a blessing. Thank you for making sure I looked presentable at court, thank you for being an emotional and mental anchor during those times. She was one of the first to learn that I was writing a book and after sharing a little bit of the writing, said it was a must that I continue writing. You have a grand purpose to contribute to this dance of life! Keep at it.

Bubu deserves another thank you (maybe two more) – your presence has been a gift from Heaven. You affect everyone around you for the better, at the core of you is a tenderness that has in it healing energy; keep it around. The only way to keep it there is humility. Stay humble, blessed one. And blessed you are indeed.

Also, M.B. – thank you for adding much more wonder into my life.

I don't know how to thank my friends and brothers who have been there for me through these times with encouragement, motivation and support. It took a lifetime to come to terms with the words "love you bro" – it took all the bumps, bruises and lessons to finally understand and appreciate the weight of these words. Thank you for standing shoulder-to-shoulder. N.S. & M... always remembered.

In the earlier years of this journey, I had many influences who were role models from afar – roadrunner tournament on smash.

Thank you to the city boys/girls and farmers.

In high school I had girls around me who started out as friends and quickly became like sisters. Thank you to all of them – S.B., R.B., R.B., I.K. In the later (or more recent) years, more girls became like sisters who looked out for me in thoughtful and caring ways – K.S., R.S., P.S. – the Rakhris mean a lot and always will thank you for the lessons. And P.S., the build-a-bear has definitely has been like a coat of armour.

Thank you to the nurses, physicians and specialists at Royal Columbia Hospital and Surrey Memorial who helped keep the body together. So, for keeping me alive. Some helped keep me in this world twice. Awww... you are all so kind. Thank you.

Thank you to the nurses and staff at NFPC, SPSC, OCC, and within the Federal CSC system for all that you did, for all that you do. Some of you went above and beyond – like leave at midnight to get necessary medical supplies because there weren't any – the kindness will always be remembered. Thank you to the physicians and healthcare staff, too. (Nurses – living angels – deserve unlimited bank accounts.)

Thank you to the staff who coordinated medical appointments, and a much-awaited surgery with ERT members on the technical and strategic aspects. Yes, the same "rearrange your life permanently detail" as Justin P. J. Trudeau – yes, the prime minister of Canada.

Thank you to the kind staff at RRAC, Matsqui and Kent, you played a role in the unfolding of this journey too. Thank you to the CMT from RRAC who re-supported me for a medium security institution, along with the warden who made the final decision to send me to Mountain. Thank you to those in CSC at Mountain, who helped with research for this book, and took moments to help compile relevant and useful material. Thank you for letting me use the computer. Thank you for spellchecking names and being willing to help. Double-M the coolest shift, tho. Ladies first, always.

Thank you to the chaplains and employees of the Mountain Chapel.

Thank you to M. A., warden of Mountain Institution, and the staff who supported the decision to allow me back into this population. Thank you for helping provide the opportunity to not only bring the journey of these words to fruition, but to continue on.

Thank you to the girl at YULU PR who pointed me in the right direction.

Thank you to the likes of Tarsem Jassar, Kulbir Jhinjer, the Mann brothers, Ranjit Bawa, Rajvir Jawanda, and Gurdaas Mann for creating the type of music that helped me realize how far I had ventured from home; may you be blessed always and may you create the type of music which awakens beings from slumber and inspires them to move in ways that reflect a higher standard. That speaks of higher ideals. To all artists and writers that create uplifting and inspiring music, thank you.

Thank you to Lashkara TV, Sandli Para, Sanjha Punjab, Sardari TV, Pyaar Hi Pyaar, Gaunda Punjab, Jagriti TV, Waqt 4 U, *The Harpeet Singh Show*, Aikam TV for airing cultural and meaningful programs which helped me realize what matters and why. May you always inspire and trigger realizations with your shows.

Thank you Wayne W. Dyer (*The Power of Intention*), Eckhart Tolle (*A New Earth*), Deepak Chopra (*Becoming MetaHuman*), Louise Hay (*You Can Heal Your Life*), Abraham Hicks (*Ask and It Is Given*), Shirley MacLaine (*Going Within*), Charles Haanel (*The Master Key System*), Rhonda Byrne and *The Secret* team, Jen Sincero (*You Are a Badass*), Emily Esfahani Smith (*The Power of Meaning*), Anthony De Mello (*Awareness*), Ragbir Singh Bir (*Bandgi-nama: Communion With The Divine*), Humble the Poet... for writing, inspiring and teaching.

Thank you to those who published the writings of these authors, the energy is changing lives.

In high school, one afternoon, I was backed into a corner and with my back up against the wall, it was Sunny H. who stood right there with me. Home runs all day. Learning curves my friend. Thank you for being there for me and standing with me. I wish things could have been different and I am truly sorry.

Thank you to a rare friend from elementary school years, Eddie S. to whom I owe many thanks. You have helped guide, heal and inspire. Intentions have certainly manifested, haven't they?

Roopi, Karen, Sonia – thank you for being there and knowing in your heart what the earlier years of our lives were like. I am sorry for neglecting responsibilities... can't wait to have my arms full of rakharees.

To my friend Angel Be – I have observed a girl become a woman. Your trials and tribulations will have a ready due for the difference you have already begun to make. Thank you for injecting much light, color, love and inspiration into my experience, and for those around me. You are indeed a healer, a helper and a guide.

I have a bestie! Aww – thank you, thank you, and thank you. Magic Mind Squad's journey has certainly begun. Our journeys have indeed been intertwined for many life cycle expressions. Let's enjoy the rest of this one!

Do you have a homie who has had your back through everything? Like a "no matter what I've got your back" type of homie? I have been blessed enough to have a presence of this sort in my experience. I called her homie. And to her I say you're a G-girl. Thank you for helping me see my faults for what they were, and helping me realize what a true friend really is. Loved ones never walk away indeed, they all walk with us still (SKG).

Thank you to Chaplain Joanne – our journeys shall certainly share a path again. Until then, continue having the effect that you have on whomever ventures into your energy field. Continue being because you are here to enable the divine purpose of the Universe to unfold. That is how important you are! Loss and change of circumstances are part of this experience.

Thank you Mumma... Dad... happy Mum's Day and happy Father's Day: today, tomorrow, every day. Thank you for teaching me, guiding me, and um, hopefully, one day I'll be allowed to visit you... despite the number of times I said the S word. (Sweating-face-turban-boy-stamped-with-red-slap-marks emoji – if it doesn't exist, make one! Going to need it soon. Make sure the emoji has the biggest grin too!)

To LHW... to a young woman whose world was crudely and uninvitingly intruded upon... someone who perhaps has every right to be full of anger and hate but is full of kindness, empathy... compassion. A mere thank you doesn't even begin to encapsulate the impact nor appreciation for showing the smallest of us just how big one person can be and that one person not only has the power to change another's life but that one person has the energy within them to manifest Heaven on earth – thank you and may your big heart continue to change people's lives.

How to thank those who have helped and are helping further the Magic Mind Squad mission and vision? How to thank the team who believes in the intangible and dreamy intentions of Sukhvir's Care initiatives?

Let's give it a go:

The loved ones who I consider family. You know who you are. Within prison and outside, thank you. And, psycho sis, thank you for Evolution to be part of my life experience. Waheguru (sweating face emoji).

To the ones who have joined this journey for the launch, thank you for believing and wanting to be a part of bringing *Trenches 2 Freedom* to the world. It means so much when someone is willing to devote and share their time with another. Thank you.

To support, here is an example of a true soldier. Ethical and morally sound, you understand the words "family" and "responsibility". Pretty sure we were brother and sister in a past life and, yes, I was a boy in that life too. I have always been a boy :@ The birds-eye-view is indeed a unique and delicate observation post, and I thank you for allowing us to share this journey together. Here comes...the Magic Mind clothing line.

P². .. is someone who has always been an encouraging, motivating, and uplifting energy source. From the first set of the most Koolest taco ever made – Annie – to an unforgettable Xmas dinner. From city alleys to the top of Vancouver. Through and through the trials and tribulations... the heavens indeed had something wonderful planned! Look out for you like a sister and look up to you like an older homie, thank you. May your life – and the newest additions to it – be full of hope, promise, light and Love.

Tonan – yes, I just spelled it like that. You matter. Be bold. Set a trend. Because you can. Thank you for bringing on board the team's Digital Master (Os...) see how paths cross and come together to do something wonderful? And, that is what (I believe) we have done here and hopefully get to continue doing – something wonderful.

Dejin – what you give off is potently vibrant. Maybe it was hanging out with children and the "rocks and sand" they love to play in that rubbed off on you. Or, maybe, the natural innocence you harbour is just the youest you! Stay vibrant, full of hope and optimism – the rest will sort itself out. Thank you for spearheading and carrying the wave to the world.

L – for not judging. For being blunt and for speaking both your heart and mind. For adding creative – "modern" – touches to the covers, and for applying your skillset to elevate the profile of the project. Thank you for allowing this project to mean something to you.

Amarpreet & Amy – keep reaching for your dreams. Both of you have the power to make a difference in this world. Thank you for believing. May both of you be blessed with love, happiness and a life full of joy. I hope we get to connect on another project.

And, last – but – most definitely, not the least.

A special thanks to a woman who, at her core, is full of an innocence that not only wishes everyone well... but just wants to make an impact – who truly desires to make a difference. A light who wants to help others, who stands for what is good, and wishes others would truly mean what they say, and say what they mean. Lethal connections mixed with a blend of honourable mentality... that is certainly someone whom one should respect and get to know. I am humbled for the thought, care, and loving kindness you have shared. Everything does happen for a reason. I so look forward to touching down locally and internationally – and yes, with presidential-like style – buhleee dat.

Thank you for putting money second.

Thank you for being you.

Thank you for being my mentor.

Mentor?

Yup. Who? :s (confused emoji with a question mark on head).

I'll never tell! Muahaha.

Control tower to launch team...

The Magic Mind Initiative is a green.

UNSAID WORDS

There's this thing that I want to say, and I want to say it to Mumma. But I can't. It is 13 May 2018, and I am locked up for the evening. Even if I wasn't, I couldn't. Having newly arrived at the RRAC, this means restrictions and a procedural process that operates on its own schedule. Cannot make a call until the number is approved, added to the list, and funds to pay for the call are transferred into the appropriate account.

A song was just played on Lashkara TV. The singer's words first sat me down into a chair, and then broke past the barriers of a tranquil mind – the state of mind that accepts happy just as easily as it accepts sad, and lets it rest with peace. Then the singer's words made me reach for a pen. What words? "When your mother walks off this Earth…"

What *can* you say to your mother when she walks away? Walks off this Earth in the physical?

It is Mother's Day tomorrow.

How many mother's will go without hearing the words I love you or Happy Mother's Day?

I know of a few.

Many, because it is no longer an option for them to hear it from their children. Mine because, here I sit. Here I sit in the city I was born and raised – Abby. With a view of Huntington Road, a road I travelled daily with my mum in earlier years. The Punjabi school I went to is a stone's throw away from here, too. So is the place of work where my dad worked away at all hours of the day... evening... night.

I want to say: I miss you Mum. I miss you and can't wait to see you smile – or frown, for that matter. I remember that you sat up long hours into the night waiting for me to show up. I am aware that some nights you never really slept, catching a minute here and a minute there, while you stayed seated upright in the corner of the couch, eyes on the street, waiting. Yes I do recall that there were days you didn't even hear from me for days. Only now do I realize how unimaginable that feeling, that weight must have felt like inside you. Who can feel what a mum feels?

No one.

But your son remembers. He remembers the love you gave. He remembers the values you taught. He remembers all the favorite dishes you would make to keep him close to home. He remembers all the times you cooked a meal despite the stress, the heartache and sick-to-the-stomach feelings he triggered, the sounds of a siren or screeching tires in the distance. He is also well aware that mere thoughts about your feelings don't come close to one iota of the real experience.

If I were in front of you now, I guess I would hug you and probably not let go for a bit, maybe even hang on until the last 12 years of suffering heals itself. I guess I wouldn't really say much, judging from the way typing these words is going. What I would do for any lunch prepared by your hands! Every meal in the world couldn't replace the warm feeling of biting into a butter, jam and cheese sandwich made by you.

Today I heard a song on TV and something inside me slowed right down. I know that tomorrow – Mother's Day – there will be no card, no phone call, and no one to say the words to you, from me. The ones who would say it on my behalf, need someone to say it to their mothers now. The singer sang, "When your mother walks off this Earth... they don't return..."

It sat me down.

"When your mom walks off this Earth, you will not be able to find a place on this Earth to walk away yourself..."

It made me reach for a pen.

Our time isn't guaranteed. The next moment, or even a breath; it isn't promised. The things we have to say, that we might put off, are left unsaid at great cost. Words. Feelings. Thoughts. If they stay bottled up and tucked away, there is no chance for healing to begin.

To the mothers (and sisters), whose sons (and brothers) considered me a friend and brother: words cannot bring your sons or brothers back. They never wanted to hurt you, no one wanted to hurt anyone they loved; but we did cause hurt. They thought they had more time is all. We all did. I am so sorry for the pain and heartache you have experienced. I wish we could turn back the hands of time... wish indeed.

How many of you are holding onto heavy words inside of you? How many of you are holding onto grudges, regrets or resentments? Do you have a full appreciation of what you are holding onto? What does it even matter? Will it matter in the end? In your final moments on this Earth? How many of you have been trying to say something that really means something to you, but just haven't been able to find the voice to do so?

Our loved ones are in our experience not by accident or chance. An Intelligence system, an unfathomable Intelligence system operating in a harmonious, karmic and miraculous way, has orchestrated a highly complex, beautiful, creative dance. That which became manifest, that which made up the physical world around us, within which we dance our individual and shared times together, did so because it was meant to.

Till next time.

O Boy

In a shattered mirror I see
The powerful thoughts from dreams
The swans tend to fly higher
The sky is not beyond the reach.
Absorbing the fragrance of Life
Mesmerized by the power of shadows
Over there under the great old vine
Right along some beautiful meadows.
There is this treasure I have hid
Deep inside the forest of dreams
Wind will take you there, you see
Deep inside an imaginary mind
A maze, amazed you will be.
At the sight of an illuminating light
Pass, o pass from the scene
Just like the early glow after a night
Mysteries keep me up at times
They seem to power up these beams
Darkness I no longer feel
Over the borders, free…? Oh but I am free.
Raising the voice of will.
Rising to meet my mission.
Regardless of the melody of night…
This lad's journey has begun.
O my, it is a dream within vision,
O boy… I can sense your ambition.

(Poem written by Zolaal)

Keep an eye out for Zolaal's first book in English: *Surfing… a New Wave*. There will be updates on IG account: @jujharskhunkhun.

And yes, it will be a Magic Mind Squad Production. Forshizzlez.

Made in the USA
Monee, IL
24 May 2021